MW00817915

Communicators-in-Chief

To Bill,

Thanks for a
great evening of
Conversation at my
daughter Kelsey's book
event at The Loft.

Julie :)

Communicators-in-Chief

*Lessons in Persuasion from
Five Eloquent American Presidents*

Julie Oseid

CAROLINA ACADEMIC PRESS

Durham, North Carolina

Copyright © 2017
Julie Oseid
All Rights Reserved

Library of Congress Cataloging-in-Publication Data

Names: Oseid, Julie A., author.
Title: Communicators-in-chief : lessons in persuasion from five eloquent
  American presidents / Julie Oseid.
Description: Durham, North Carolina : Carolina Academic Press, LLC, 2017. |
  Includes bibliographical references and index.
Identifiers: LCCN 2016058567 | ISBN 9781531003883 (alk. paper)
Subjects: LCSH: Legal composition. | Persuasion (Rhetoric) | Jefferson,
  Thomas, 1743-1826--Writing skill. | Madison, James, 1751-1836--Writing
  skill. | Lincoln, Abraham, 1809-1865--Writing skill. | Grant, Ulysses S.
  (Ulysses Simpson), 1822-1885--Writing skill. | Roosevelt, Theodore,
  1858-1919--Writing skill.
Classification: LCC KF250 .O837 2017 | DDC 808.06/634--dc23
LC record available at https://lccn.loc.gov/2016058567

e-ISBN 978-1-53100-395-1

CAROLINA ACADEMIC PRESS, LLC
700 Kent Street
Durham, North Carolina 27701
Telephone (919) 489-7486
Fax (919) 493-5668
www.cap-press.com

Printed in the United States of America

To my family

Contents

Preface

As I tell my law students, it is impossible to look ahead and know which people and experiences will shape your life, so it is best to assume that each person and every experience might play a role. Some of those people and experiences will be the surprises that enrich our lives. It is immensely fun to look back and take note of those surprises.

But it was actually neither a person nor, strictly speaking, an experience, but a thing—a shoelace worn by a very small person—that started me on the road to writing this book. After several years practicing law, I spent 13 years at home raising my family. I knew I was ready for something new when I was volunteering for playground duty at my children's school and a kindergartener asked me to tie his shoe. I wanted to, but of course didn't, reply, "Tie it yourself."

My reaction to that perfectly reasonable, but nonetheless surprisingly frustrating, request for help with a shoelace inspired me to pursue something I had long been interested in—an academic career. After joining the faculty at the University of St. Thomas School of Law in Minneapolis, Minnesota, I spent my first few years researching and writing about a variety of topics including professionalism, state constitutional law, and legal writing. A few unexpected surprises were about to combine to give me a focus for my work on the presidents and persuasive writing.

Eight years ago I was in the Milwaukee airport on my way home from a conference in Indiana. Abraham Lincoln was on my mind because Indiana (along with many other states) proudly claims him as its own. Just three weeks earlier, my brother sent me his old Smithsonian magazines, and I was immediately captivated by the April 2002 issue covering Ronald C. White Jr.'s book *Lincoln's Greatest Speech: The Second Inaugural.* A cancelled flight led to a seven-hour layover in the Milwaukee airport and a magical time spent in the Renaissance Books bookstore browsing through the Lincoln books. Two weeks later, I was waiting for a child at the dentist's office while I paged through a *National Geographic* article about Lincoln's writing. Like countless authors before me, I was unable to resist the call of Lincoln, so I wrote an article about his use of brevity to persuade his audiences.

That could have been both the beginning and the end of my foray into presidential eloquence, but a peer reviewer for my Lincoln article noted, "It would be interesting to read a series of articles about persuasive writers." I thought, "What a fabulous idea. I'd like to try that with other eloquent presidents." So I spent the next several years researching and writing my series about eloquent American presidents.

Five American presidents make up my presidential writing dream team: Thomas Jefferson, James Madison, Abraham Lincoln, Ulysses S. Grant, and Teddy Roosevelt.

Modern presidents have not made the list, not because there have not been some very effective communicators among them (as clearly there have been), but because only with some distance can we fairly evaluate the strong qualities of any person, including writing qualities. Also, as presidential staffs have grown in both size and influence, it has become increasingly difficult to determine what a president wrote on his own and what speechwriters wrote for him. That was true as far back as George Washington whose First Inaugural Address was ghostwritten by James Madison. But it is even more difficult in our modern era, when it has become common for presidents to hire several professional writers in fulltime positions. In the end, I chose these five presidents because they wrote with the qualities that modern legal writers still use to persuade.

My family recently spent long hours together in a car. We started talking about the three people, living or dead, we would each invite to dinner. That game usually proves too hard for us, so we have to further refine the rules to provide a category such as relatives, social activists, artists, naturalists, athletes, or teachers. My middle child said, "Mom, if it was three eloquent presidents you would pick Jefferson, Madison, and Lincoln, wouldn't you?" I hesitated a minute and responded, "No, I would have to beg for a further modification of the rules so that I could invite five guests because I would want Roosevelt and Grant at the table. I think five guests would be just right for my dinner."

My list may be shorter, or longer, or otherwise different from your list of a presidential writing dream team. And I am okay with that. Sometimes it is enough to start the discussion.

This book is the result of many generous hours of work by many people. I am indebted to the editors at *Legal Communication & Rhetoric: J. ALWD* who published earlier versions of my articles on Jefferson, Madison, Lincoln, Grant, and Roosevelt. My peer reviewers were generous in accepting the articles, and one made the comment about a series which prompted my work for the next eight years. All were anonymous, so I can't thank them by name, but I am sincerely grateful for their contributions to what has become a major portion of my scholarly life's work. The editors at every level were outstanding, and this book is far better than it would have been without their input. A very heartfelt thanks to Melody R. Daily, Joan Ames Magat, Suzianne D. Painter-Thorne, Ruth Anne Robbins, and Melissa Weresh who worked on several of my articles. Thanks also to Sara R. Benson, Linda Berger, Timothy D. Blevins, Jessica Clark, Ian Gallacher, and Sara Gordon. They set their own scholarship aside to help me with my work. That is the biggest sacrifice one can make in the world of academia, so I will forever be grateful.

I am also indebted to my co-authors on the Madison chapter—Professor Thomas C. Berg, James J. Oberstar Professor of Law and Public Policy, and Joseph A. Orrino. Professor Berg is a Madison expert, so if that chapter seems particularly thoughtful it is all because of him.

Other members of the faculty supported my work, including Ben Carpenter (thanks for friendship), Jenny Cornell (thanks for listening), Mitchell Gordon (thanks for the title and for editing), Rob Kahn (thanks for great advice), Tom Mengler (thanks for the encouragement), Mike Paulsen (thanks for recommending Grant), Chuck Reid (thanks for telling me about Renaissance Books), and Rob Vischer (thanks for the sabbatical).

I also thank many others from the St. Thomas community. Henry Bishop is a fabulous administrative assistant. The St. Thomas law librarians are intelligent, creative, persistent, and dedicated. Thanks to Dean Ann Bateson, Megan McNevin, Molly Butler, and John Giesen for proofreading this book. I also thank Valerie Aggerbeck, Nick Farris, Megan McNevin (again), and Mary Wells for finding sources and for providing endless research assistance. Thanks to Paddy Satzer for creating the index. My former students Subia Beg, Al Heavens, Mark Spooner, Franz Vancura, Jeff Wald, and Christopher White provided additional research assistance, plus their enthusiasm was invaluable. Ed Edmonds, our former Library Director, and Rick Goheen, our former research librarian, encouraged me throughout this project.

Thank you Chief Justice Lawton Nuss and Justice Carol Beier of the Kansas Supreme Court. Both took an interest in my work and gave me opportunities to speak at the Kansas Judicial Conference and at the National Judicial College. Thanks also to Linda Lacy; the day I learned that Carolina Academic Press would publish the book was a very happy day for me. I also thank Ryland Bowman, Scott Sipe, TJ Smithers, and the rest of the wonderful team at Carolina Academic Press.

My family played a significant role in the creation of this book. My brother, Professor Stephen D. Easton at the University of Wyoming College of Law, started it all when he shared his Smithsonian magazines. I'm lucky that he has helped guide me through teaching and book writing. My mother Zonie Easton took over many of my home duties during the early years of this project. My children, Kelsey Oseid Wojciak, Danny Oseid, and Olivia Oseid, were teenagers when this project started and they are now independent adults. We added Nick Wojciak as a son-in-law along the way. All encouraged me at every step, and they even claim that they will read the finished product. Finally, thanks to my husband Jeff Oseid for his support, encouragement, loyalty, and wry smile. We have been together for 40 years. Yes, that means we started dating when we were 15. We sure couldn't have predicted all of it. But one thing is certain — this family is the very best surprise in my life.

Introduction

Add presidential style to your legal briefs by using the writing qualities perfected by five eloquent American presidents. These five presidents each mastered one persuasive writing quality that is still critical for persuasion today. Thomas Jefferson used metaphor so effectively that his famous metaphor of the "wall of separation between Church and State" has replaced the literal language of the First Amendment in the minds of most Americans. James Madison wrote with rigor that, to our good fortune, helped him develop some of the most significant political theories—and practical proposals—shaping our government. Abraham Lincoln's brevity in his speeches persuaded his audiences, and it continues to persuade and inspire us. Ulysses S. Grant's clarity made him an astonishingly effective writer and military leader. Teddy Roosevelt combined his energy with his conviction to write with zeal that moved his audience. These five presidents should be our writing heroes.

This book examines why each president, at his very best, was so persuasive. Although parts of the presidents' stories will be familiar, I hope that my focus on one writing quality—and the habits the presidents used to achieve that quality—will bring new insight to the stories. The book also provides examples of each president writing with his signature quality, lists each president's favorite books, and shows how the presidents influenced each other's writing styles. Each featured president had some natural writing talent, but each also worked hard to hone his writing. The real stories are not as glamorous as the myths that the presidents dashed off perfect writing without any effort. But the real stories offer us hope that we, too, can become more persuasive writers by adopting the character traits and writing habits of our eloquent presidents.

Chapter 1 examines why each of these writing qualities is important today for those who want to increase their persuasiveness. It won't come as a surprise that the use of metaphor, rigor, brevity, clarity, and zeal are the writing qualities emphasized. These have long been the hallmarks of great persuasive writing.

Chapters 2–6 each focus on one of the presidents and his signature writing quality. I focus on the influences in the president's life that shaped his writing style. Jefferson's use of metaphor was rooted in his classical education. Madison's rigor resulted in large part from his shy personality and his hesitation to speak extemporaneously. Lincoln's brevity emerged from his experience practicing law for 25 years. Grant's clarity was honed during his years as a military commander. Roosevelt's zeal was simply who he was as a passionate and enthusiastic person.

In each of these five chapters, I also include the habits that helped each president develop his particular writing skill. I want this collection to offer hope. If the five featured presidents had strong writing wired into their DNA, then we could not believe that we, too, could develop a skill that would make us more effective. It is encouraging to learn that someone as inspiring as Lincoln had to work very hard for his eloquence.

Several examples of the president using his signature writing quality are also included in each chapter. The presidents' own words demonstrate the quality more than my paraphrasing or analysis. It is enriching to read these examples of the use of metaphor, rigor, brevity, clarity, and zeal at work.

I feature only one writing quality for each president to highlight how the president mastered that particular, essential quality. Of course all the presidents in this collection wrote with more than just one quality. Abraham Lincoln has often been called our most eloquent president. I write about his use of brevity, but he was also a master at metaphor, alliteration, and the measured antithesis. Thomas Jefferson used many metaphors effectively, but he also used elegant and vivid language. James Madison's rigor alone would not likely be enough to make his writing memorable, but in combination with his organization, logic, and direct style his writing becomes superb. Grant's clarity is remarkable, but his use of the active voice and short words also made his writing sparkle. Roosevelt's zeal jumps from the page, but he could also capture a concept in pithy and memorable phrases. My focus is on the one quality I have selected for each president, but I also point out the other effective features of each president's writing.

Chapter 7 analyzes the reading habits and preferences of all five presidents. Reading influences writing, so the presidents' reading habits offer some insight into their writing styles. The chapter includes a list of the authors and books preferred by each president. It then provides a combined list of the authors and books read by multiple presidents. These reading lists can provide some inspiration for our own reading.

Chapter 8 analyzes how the five presidents influenced each other's writing. The thirty-year collaboration and friendship between Jefferson and Madison was a political partnership that influenced how many early American political issues were decided, and their influence on those issues remains today. Their extensive letter writing to each other also affected their writing styles, including word choice and tone. Lincoln and Grant respected and admired each other. Their relationship would have become one of the great friendships in our American history, had John Wilkes Booth not been in Ford's Theater on the most fateful Good Friday in American history. Still, even in the short time that they knew each other, each was impressed and influenced by the writing style of the other. Lincoln's brevity and Grant's clarity are complementary writing qualities; each also wrote with the quality I analyze in the other. And the presidents continued to influence other presidents even after their deaths. Lincoln was influenced by Jefferson's writing. Roosevelt, who believed Jefferson was overrated, admired both Lincoln and Grant, and adopted some of their writing habits to increase his persuasiveness.

Chapter 9 reviews the character traits and writing habits of all five presidents. The presidents were hardworking, determined, confident, realistic, and creative. These character traits helped them persuade, and they would help us as well. All of the five presidents shared several writing habits, including starting writing projects early, visualizing audiences, editing ruthlessly, and asking others for editing help. By adding these habits to our own writing practice, we will be able to write more persuasively.

Theodore C. Sorenson, former special counsel to President John F. Kennedy, studied all previous 20th century inaugural addresses to help Kennedy prepare his inaugural speech. Sorenson noted, "Lincoln was a superb writer. Like Jefferson and Teddy Roosevelt, but few if any other presidents, he could have been a successful writer wholly apart from his political career."[1] He is right, but Madison and Grant should be on the list, too.

Not all five presidents would acknowledge that they had a particular writing skill. It would not be false modesty that prevented them from thinking they should not make the list, but simply that they did not think of themselves as particularly gifted writers. Lincoln's personal secretaries John G. Nicolay and John Hay remarked, "Nothing would have amazed him [more] while he lived than to hear himself called a man of letters."[2] We know better—Lincoln was a brilliant writer. So were Jefferson, Madison, Grant, and Roosevelt. This book celebrates them.

---

1. Theodore C. Sorenson, *A Man of His Words*, Smithsonian, Oct. 2008 at 96, 98.
2. Douglas L. Wilson, *Lincoln's Sword: The Presidency and the Power of Words* 9 (2006) (citing 10 John G. Nicolay and John Hay, *Abraham Lincoln: A History* 351 (1904)).

Communicators-in-Chief

Chapter 1

Five Qualities of Persuasive Legal Writing: Using Metaphor, Rigor, Brevity, Clarity, and Zeal

We lawyers are professional writers.[1] And we aren't just any professional writers—we must persuade through our writing. For much of our work, "[p]ersuasion is the only test that counts."[2]

I ask my new law students every year why they decided to come to law school. Never, not one time, in my twelve years of teaching, has a student replied that it was because the student wanted to write for a living. They are surprised that they will most likely spend more time writing than doing anything else. That is the reality for most lawyers, no matter what their area of specialty, whether they are litigators or transactional lawyers, or whether they practice in the public or private sector. Those lawyers who do not spend the majority of their time writing are still communicating; all the lessons of good writing transfer to other forms of communication.[3] The persuading part of lawyering is what drew most of the students to the profession. The most common answer to my question about my students' motivation to attend law school

---

1. Linda H. Edwards, *Legal Writing: Process, Analysis, and Organization* 1 (6th ed. 2014).
2. Ruggero J. Aldisert, *Winning on Appeal* 135 (2d ed. 2003) [hereinafter Aldisert, *Winning on Appeal*] (referencing brief writing).
3. In fact, classical rhetoric was first designed for speaking. Michael H. Frost points out that most classical rhetoricians gave guidelines for oral advocacy, but that "their advice regarding how advocates can enhance their credibility applies just as much to written as to oral arguments." Michael H. Frost, *With Amici Like These: Cicero, Quintilian and the Importance of Stylistic Demeanor*, 6 J. ALWD 5, 13 (2006) [hereinafter *With Amici Like These*].

is that at some time in the student's life an adult suggested that the student was "great at arguing," so the student decided to become a lawyer.

But it is the combination of persuading through writing that lawyers need to master. For inspiration and guidance in this quest, we should look to our persuasive, eloquent presidents. Each president is included in this book for his skill and elegance in writing with one particular persuasive quality. Each of these qualities continues to be critical for effective persuasion today. The five qualities featured are the use of metaphor (Thomas Jefferson), rigor (James Madison), brevity (Abraham Lincoln), clarity (Ulysses S. Grant), and zeal (Teddy Roosevelt).

Of course, the presidents used not just one, but many, qualities in their persuasive writing and speaking. Many of their techniques, like their use of alliteration, allusion, and repetition, are not analyzed in this book. Even limiting the analysis to the five featured qualities, all the presidents frequently wrote with more than one of the five. Jefferson's use of metaphor stemmed from his zeal. Madison's rigor resulted in clarity. Lincoln used both brevity and clarity in a delicate, intertwined balance. So did Grant. Roosevelt persuaded with his zeal, but also with his rigor.

Further, I do not suggest that the presidents were single-minded in prioritizing the quality I assigned to their writing over all others. One example is telling. Lincoln was famously brief in his most persuasive speeches, but the Gettysburg Address begins with "Four score and seven years ago" instead of the much shorter "Eighty-seven years ago." His outstanding awareness of rhythm and sound resulted in the longer opening.[4] The protracted opening also reflected the solemnity and sacredness of the event. I assigned one quality to each president so that we can focus on and learn from how the presidents used that particular quality so effectively.

Admittedly, this is not a complete list of all the important legal writing features. As any lawyer knows, the use of metaphor, rigor, brevity, clarity, and zeal are not the only qualities that persuade. In persuasive legal writing, strong organization is absolutely essential, but I assign it an undeservedly minor role as one component of rigor. Using transitions is also indispensable, but I don't focus on that quality. Instead, I chose the use of metaphor, rigor, brevity, clarity, and zeal because the presidents persuaded by using those writing qualities and those qualities remain key components of persuasion.

Lawyers and presidents share a professional goal—we all strive to make sure our audience understands the issue we are addressing. And then we hope that

---

4. Theodore C. Sorenson, *A Man of His Words*, Smithsonian, Oct. 2008, at 96, 103.

the audience will agree with our view about that issue. These five presidents were our Communicators-in-Chief, and by following their lead we will be better communicators and persuaders, too.

Metaphor — Thomas Jefferson

A metaphor is defined as "the application of a word or phrase to an object or concept it does not literally denote, suggesting comparison to that object or concept."[5] The Greek etymology of metaphor is "carrying over" or "to stand for."[6] Metaphors permeate our language. Metaphors are not simply rhetorical devices but are fundamental to the way we think.[7] George Lakoff and Mark Johnson note, "[W]e define our reality in terms of metaphors and then proceed to act on the basis of the metaphors."[8] Our human language itself is a set of metaphors, and we understand with the help of that language.[9] Cognitive theory describes metaphor as "a way of thinking and knowing, the method by which we structure and reason, and it is fundamental, not ornamental."[10]

Metaphor is critical to all humans to facilitate understanding and to help build understanding, but it is particularly important to lawyers. The law is dependent on words. Legal metaphors are "indispensable pieces of the legal culture, not merely tolerated, but needed."[11]

To Jefferson, "a metaphor stood for something it did not state, carrying over the meaning of one word or phrase to the meaning of something else."[12] A metaphor can only help someone understand an abstract concept if it is explained in concrete and accessible words.[13] Jefferson described the First Amendment religion clause as "building a wall of separation between Church &

---

5. *Webster's American Dictionary* 504 (2d College ed. 2000).

6. Charles A. Miller, *Ship of State: The Nautical Metaphors of Thomas Jefferson* 4 (2003).

7. *See* Michael R. Smith, *Levels of Metaphor in Persuasive Legal Writing*, 58 Mercer L. Rev. 919, 921 (2007) [hereinafter Smith, *Levels of Metaphor*].

8. George Lakoff & Mark Johnson, *Metaphors We Live By* 158 (1980).

9. James E. Murray, *Understanding Law as Metaphor*, 34 J. Legal Educ. 714, 718 (1984) (citing Owen Barfield, *Poetic Diction: A Study in Meaning* 140–41 (1964)).

10. Linda L. Berger, *What is the Sound of a Corporation Speaking? How the Cognitive Theory of Metaphor Can Help Lawyers Shape the Law*, 2 J. ALWD 169, 170 (2004).

11. Thomas Ross, *Metaphor and Paradox*, 23 Ga. L. Rev. 1053, 1076–77 (1989).

12. Miller, *supra* note 6, at 4.

13. *See* Haig Bosmajian, *Metaphor and Reason in Judicial Opinions* 45–46 (1992) (citing David Rumelhart, *Some Problems with the Notion of Literal Meanings*, in *Metaphor and Thought* 69 (Andrew Ortony ed., 1979)).

State."[14] The "wall of separation" metaphor follows the normal metaphoric comparison between something concrete and a more abstract idea.[15]

The role of metaphor in the law frequently has been a topic of legal scholarship in recent years, but "many of these works seem to talk past one another."[16] Michael Smith, a contemporary law and rhetoric scholar, attributes this disconnect to a failure on the part of scholars to acknowledge or recognize that they are often talking about different types of metaphor.[17] The problem also likely stems from our changing understanding about the appropriate use of metaphor. Miller points out, "Until a century or so ago ... and certainly in Jefferson's mind, metaphor was strictly a rhetorical device, a 'mere' figure of speech."[18] Smith suggests that currently there are four basic types of metaphor which correspond to the four basic components of any legal argument: (1) doctrinal metaphors (the legal principles governing an issue);[19] (2) legal method metaphors (the tools of analysis applied to the governing principles);[20] (3) stylistic metaphors (the writing style of an advocate who is presenting the legal argument);[21] and (4) inherent metaphors (the inherent language itself).[22] Doctrinal and stylistic metaphors are relevant to a discussion of the "wall of separation" metaphor.

A doctrinal metaphor is a metaphor that expresses doctrinal law, the rules and principles governing a legal issue, in the form of a metaphor.[23] Doctrinal metaphors are the most powerful but also the most dangerous.[24] When a doctrinal metaphor is present, substantive legal rights are described not in literal terms, but in metaphoric terms.[25] Metaphor is attractive and useful because, in Aristotle's words, it "give[s] names to nameless things."[26] We use metaphors because our other ways of understanding are not sufficient.[27] Yet the danger of

---

14. Letter from Thomas Jefferson, Pres. of the U.S. to the Danbury Baptist Assn. (Jan. 1, 1802), *in* Daniel L. Dreisbach, *Thomas Jefferson and the Wall of Separation Between Church and State* 142–43 (2002).

15. Miller, *supra* note 6, at 4.

16. Smith, *Levels of Metaphor*, *supra* note 7, at 944.

17. *Id.*

18. Miller, *supra* note 6, at 4.

19. Smith, *Levels of Metaphor*, *supra* note 7, at 920–21.

20. *Id.* at 920, 928–29.

21. *Id.* at 920, 932.

22. *Id.* at 920, 942.

23. *Id.* at 921.

24. *Id.* at 923.

25. *Id.*

26. Aristotle, *The Rhetoric of Aristotle* 188 (Lane Cooper trans., Appleton-Century-Crofts, Inc. 1932).

27. Ross, *supra* note 11, at 1073.

metaphor is that "[o]nce the particular reality is seen through the metaphor, nothing is quite the same ... [W]e have seen a particular and new reality ... We are in this sense changed."[28]

Benjamin Cardozo cautioned, in his often-quoted warning about doctrinal metaphors, "Metaphors in law are to be narrowly watched, for starting as devices to liberate thought, they end often by enslaving it."[29] The potential problem with doctrinal metaphors is that they can reduce a complex concept like church-state relations to a metaphor, and metaphor is not capable of capturing all the nuances, complexities, and dimensions of the original concept.[30] This is one common criticism about the "wall of separation" metaphor.[31] The United States Supreme Court admitted, "Candor compels acknowledgment, moreover, that we can only dimly perceive the lines of demarcation in this extraordinarily sensitive area of constitutional law."[32]

Jefferson studied the classics; he used metaphor in a controlled, classical sense. Classical rhetoric was the first study of persuasion, and it still influences our modern understanding of effective persuasion.[33] Rhetoric, as understood by the classical teachers, meant "the use of language for persuasive purposes."[34] Scholars note:

> Classical rhetoric was associated primarily with persuasive discourse. Its end was to convince or persuade an audience to think in a certain way or to act in a certain way. Later, the principles of rhetoric were extended to apply to informative or expository modes of discourse, but in the beginning, they were applied almost exclusively to the persuasive modes of discourse.[35]

---

28. *Id.*

29. *Berkey v. Third Ave. Ry. Co.*, 155 N.E. 58, 61 (N.Y. 1926) (referring specifically to "the mists of metaphor" surrounding the relationships between parent and subsidiary corporations).

30. Michael R. Smith, *Advanced Legal Writing: Theories and Strategies in Persuasive Writing* 206 (3d ed. 2013) [hereinafter Smith, *Advanced Legal Writing*].

31. *See e.g. Wallace v. Jaffree*, 472 U.S. 38, 107 (1985) (Rehnquist, J., dissenting) ("[The] 'wall' has proved all but useless as a guide to sound constitutional adjudication.").

32. *Lemon v. Kurtzman*, 403 U.S. 602, 612 (1971).

33. Smith, *Advanced Legal Writing*, *supra* note 30, at 11 ("[M]uch of the contemporary literature on persuasion is based on principles first explored by classical rhetoricians some 2500 years ago.")

34. Edward P.J. Corbett & Robert J. Connors, *Classical Rhetoric for the Modern Student* 15 (4th ed.1999).

35. Corbett and Connors further explain,
> Classical rhetoric was associated primarily with persuasive discourse. Its end was to convince or persuade an audience to think in a certain way or to act in a cer-

Classical rhetoric was essential in the Greco-Roman culture because individual citizens advocated for themselves in the courts, marketplace, forum, and church.[36] Classical rhetoricians emphasized the importance of three types of arguments: *ethos* (arguments based on the author or speaker's credibility), *pathos* (arguments based on emotion), and *logos* (arguments based on logic) in persuasion.[37] All three types of argument are important and intertwined.[38]

In contrast to a doctrinal metaphor, which addresses what is said, the stylistic metaphor relates to how it is said.[39] But stylistic metaphors should not be dismissed as mere ornamentation without legitimate rhetorical power.[40] Instead, stylistic metaphors serve several rhetorical functions and can be powerful.[41] The following rhetorical functions of "stylistic metaphors" are essential:

(1) The *logos* function of providing an analogy that helps communicate the substance of the writer's point,

(2) The *ethos* function of establishing the writer as a credible and intelligent source of information,

(3) The *pathos* function of evoking favorable emotions, and

---

tain way. Later, the principles of rhetoric were extended to apply to informative or expository modes of discourse, but in the beginning, they were applied almost exclusively to the persuasive modes of discourse.

Id. at 16.

36. Smith, *Advanced Legal Writing*, *supra* note 30, at 12. This lasted from the fifth century B.C. to the fall of the Roman Empire in 410 A.D. During that 1000-year period, the most influential scholars and authors of the treatises on rhetoric were Aristotle (Greek, 384–322 B.C.), Cicero (Roman, 109–43 B.C.), and Quintilian (Roman, 35–395 A.D.). Michael H. Frost, *Introduction to Classical Legal Rhetoric: A Lost Heritage* 2–3 (2005) [hereinafter Frost, *Introduction to Classical Legal Rhetoric*]. Michael Frost further elaborates on this education in rhetoric:

Although all Roman citizens did not complete the full course of study, many completed a substantial part of the ten-to-twelve-year rhetoric course.... Designed for use by all members of the educated classes, the rhetoric course included, among other things, detailed instructions for discovering and presenting legal arguments in almost any context and to almost any audience. A student's rhetorical education prepared him to meet all his public speaking obligations, especially his legal obligations.

Id. at 3.

37. *Id.* at 5.

38. Frost, *With Amici Like These*, *supra* note 3, at 9.

39. Smith, *Advanced Legal Writing*, *supra* note 30, at 214.

40. *Id.*

41. *Id.*

(4) The rhetorical style function of drawing attention and emphasis to the writer's point.[42]

Stylistic metaphors can become doctrinal metaphors.[43] That is precisely what happened with Jefferson's "wall of separation" metaphor. It started as a stylistic metaphor, but it became a doctrinal metaphor. Jefferson would likely recoil from that modern development because his classical training meant that he was wary of metaphor standing in the place of truth. He also could not comprehend that metaphor could be used to completely replace an abstract idea.

In the end, though, both doctrinal and stylistic metaphors help lawyers persuade. An accurate doctrinal metaphor can explain a complex legal concept in a fresh way and ultimately convince a reader. Nor should lawyers overlook the value of stylistic metaphors. An accurate analogy can clarify legal and factual arguments. An astute metaphor will show the reader that you are knowledgeable about every aspect of the case. A creative metaphor may help a reader see the issue through your client's eyes. An inventive metaphor will underscore your point.

Rigor — James Madison

The word "rigor" is used here to capture the qualities of thoroughness, preparation, and diligence. Admittedly, it is a lot to ask of one five-letter word, and hopefully Madison, who was well aware of the importance of word choice,[44] would agree with the selection. The word "rigor" seems able to handle the challenge. Based on the Latin word meaning stiff,[45] "rigor" means

---

42. Smith, *Levels of Metaphor, supra* note 7, at 940.

43. *Id.* at 941.

44. Madison himself knew the importance of word choice when he noted, "Perspicuity therefore requires not only that the ideas should be distinctly formed, but that they should be expressed by words distinctly and exclusively appropriated to them." *The Federalist*, No. 37 (James Madison) (reprinted in *James Madison, Writings* 194, 198 (Jack N. Rakove ed., 1999) [hereinafter *James Madison, Writings*]). All references to *The Federalist* are to this edition.

45. *The Pocket Oxford Latin Dictionary (Latin-English)* (2005), *available at* http://www.oxfordreference.com/view/10.1093/acref/9780191739583.001.0001/b-la-en-00001-0008891?rskey=cuK22r&result=7. "Rigor mortis" means stiff joints and muscles after death. *Oxford Dictionary of English* (3d ed. 2015), *available at* http://www.oxfordreference.com/view/10.1093/acref/9780199571123.001.0001/m_en_gb0711510?rskey=iJ01ig&result=5.

"scrupulous accuracy" and "precision."[46] When used as an adjective—"rigorous"—the word means severely exact and precise as in "rigorous research."[47] It also means logically valid.[48] Of course, a rigorous approach to work does not always result in a rigorous product. But Madison's rigorous approach did result in several writings that demonstrated that rigor—and could stand on their own as severely exact, precise, logical, and thorough.

Like Jefferson, Madison studied many classical works of rhetoric. He knew the value of *logos*, *ethos*, and *pathos*. Madison was masterful in his use of logical arguments (*logos*);[49] one of his major opponents, Patrick Henry, was masterful in his use of emotional arguments (*pathos*).[50] Henry's opponents were frustrated by his emotional arguments. Historian Joseph Ellis notes,

> Jefferson was especially irritated by Henry's mesmerizing way with the spoken word, which he regarded as a crudely emotional appeal that ought not to defeat his own lyrical and logical prose. But so often it did. Jefferson explained to Madison that Henry's oratorical power was an inexplicable and unpredictable force of nature, like a hurricane, and the only thing to do when confronted by it was to "devoutly pray for his imminent death."[51]

Although they do not describe it in terms of *ethos*, many historians believe that the quality that gave Madison the edge over Henry was *ethos*—Madison's credibility and character as displayed through his intelligence, rigor, and preparation. Garry Wills explains,

> Good as Henry was as an orator and debater, he was not a reflective or studious person, and he was up against a man [Madison] who had

---

46. *Webster's American Dictionary*, *supra* note 5, at 678. Other definitions of "rigor" include rigidity, hardness, inflexibility, and severity. *See The Pocket Oxford Latin Dictionary*, *supra* note 45.

47. *Merriam-Webster Dictionary*, http://www.merriam-webster.com/dictionary/rigor (last visited Aug. 31, 2016).

48. *Webster's American Dictionary*, *supra* note 5, at 678. The antonyms listed for "rigor" are also informative, with "laxness" as the most informative opposite definition for how the word "rigor" is used here. *Merriam-Webster Dictionary*, *supra* note 47.

49. *See* Jack N. Rakove, *Original Meanings: Politics and Ideas in the Making of the Constitution* 56 (1997) (Madison knew that he would need reason, justice, and political savvy to succeed as a lawgiver at the Constitutional Convention).

50. Patrick Henry's reputation as a formidable orator was sealed ten years before American independence when he "hurl[ed] his verbal thunderbolts at George III." Joseph J. Ellis, *American Creation: Triumphs and Tragedies at the Founding of the Republic* 120 (2007).

51. *Id.*

thought and debated and persuaded on this subject [the Constitution] through two years that sharpened all of Madison's analytical power and parliamentary deftness. The tiny David slew the mighty Goliath.[52]

Rigor—that quality of being intelligent, prepared, and thorough—is an important part of the author's *ethos* (credibility and character).[53] Aristotle offered some practical suggestions on how to increase credibility and character: "[T]here are three things that gain our belief, namely, intelligence, character, and good will."[54] Michael Smith has analyzed exactly what intelligence, character, and good will mean in the persuasive legal writing context, and what specific traits help advocates prove they possess each of the qualities. Smith started with character and explained that legal writers "must demonstrate that they are of good moral character or at least that they are not of questionable moral character."[55] Supreme Court Justice Antonin Scalia and Bryan Garner also emphasize "the human proclivity to be more receptive to argument from a person who is both trusted and liked" because of the advocate's good character.[56] Traits proving that an advocate has the required moral character include truthfulness, candor, zeal, respect, and professionalism.[57] Character is an advocate's general moral makeup and personality; good will refers to the advocate's disposition about the specific issue at hand and those involved in the current case.[58] Advocates are advised that good will suffers if an advocate acts with anger or malevolence.[59] The final quality, intelligence, reflects the human tendency to have more trust and confidence in a speaker who "knows what she is talking about."[60] An intelligent persuasive writer is informed, adept at legal research, organized, analytical, deliberate, empathetic toward the reader, practical, articulate, eloquent, detail oriented, and innovative.[61] A rig-

---

52. Gary Wills, *James Madison* 36 (2002) (referring to the Virginia ratification convention of the Constitution).

53. Quintilian believed "the perfect orator is a good man speaking well." Frost, *Introduction to Classical Legal Rhetoric, supra* note 36, at 69 (citing 2 Quintilian, *Institutio Oratoria* 9).

54. Aristotle, *The Rhetoric of Aristotle* 92 (Lane Cooper trans., Prentice-Hall, Inc. 1960).

55. Smith, *Advanced Legal Writing, supra* note 30, at 127.

56. Antonin Scalia & Bryan A. Garner, *Making Your Case: The Art of Persuading Judges* xxiii (2008).

57. Smith, *Advanced Legal Writing, supra* note 30, at 128.

58. *Id.* at 145.

59. *Id.*

60. *Id.* at 149 (quoting Ronald J. Waicukauski, JoAnne Epps & Paul Mark Sandler, *Ethos and the Art of Argument*, 26 Litig. 31, 32 (1999)).

61. *Id.* at 150.

orous approach to persuasive writing, and a resultingly rigorous work product, will improve a lawyer's *ethos*.

Rigor is crucial in modern legal persuasion. Preparation is the key to successful lawyering.[62] Lawyers increase their credibility when they show they are capable and intelligent about the law and the facts.[63]

Judges are busy people who expect, and often rely on, lawyers to do the hard work of thoroughly researching, analyzing, and evaluating the legal issues before the court.[64] Justice Lewis F. Powell Jr.'s beliefs about the necessity of rigor in writing are instructive: "Clear writing, to him, meant clear thinking, and the rigor of writing to a high standard of clarity and simplicity helped ensure the integrity of the writer's analysis."[65] Kristen K. Robbins Tiscione reported the results of a comprehensive survey conducted in 2000 asking federal judges what they thought about lawyers' briefs.[66] Judges want to see more rigor in lawyers' legal analysis.[67] The list of specific comments shows that the judges are looking for someone with Madison's rigor. One judge commented, "The bulk of briefs ... lack thoroughness regarding legal analysis."[68] Another added, "Counsel tends to state what they think is sufficient, but often will not adequately discuss the various implications of the issues."[69] Yet another judge noted, "Most of the briefs ... ignore or gloss over obvious weaknesses in their argument and fail to address the compelling counterpoints of the other side."[70] One frustrated judge even used "rigor" to describe the problem, "We often get

---

62. Nancy L. Schultz & Louis J. Sirico, Jr., *Legal Writing and Other Lawyering Skills* 322 (6th ed. 2014) ("The key to a successful oral argument is preparation."); Stephen D. Easton, *My Last Lecture: Unsolicited Advice for Future and Current Lawyers*, 56 S.C. L. Rev., 229, 251 (2004) ("For a lawyer, the three most important things are preparation, preparation, and preparation.").

63. Smith, *Advanced Legal Writing*, *supra* note 30, at 150–51.

64. Richard K. Neumann Jr. & Kristen Konrad Tiscione note, "Judges are busy people who view any assertion skeptically and who must make many decisions in short periods of time. Thus, they need complete but concise arguments that can be quickly understood." Richard K. Neumann, Jr.& Kristen Konrad Tiscione, *Legal Reasoning and Legal Writing: Structure, Strategy, and Style* 269 (7th ed. 2013).

65. Judge T.S. Ellis, III, *In Memoriam: Lewis F. Powell, Jr.*, 112 Harv. L. Rev. 594, 595 (1999).

66. Kristen K. Robbins, *The Inside Scoop: What Federal Judges Really Think About the Way Lawyers Write*, 8 Leg. Writing 257 (2002) [hereinafter Robbins, *The Inside Scoop*].

67. *Id.* at 269.

68. *Id.*

69. *Id.*

70. *Id.*

the feeling … that the parties are satisfied simply to identify issues and leave the rigorous research and analysis to the court."[71]

This is not to suggest that exercising rigor *when* writing, or demonstrating rigor *in* writing, is easy. Quite the opposite: rigor requires very hard work.[72] Perhaps writing with rigor is the hardest work of all because the task of writing is itself so difficult. Legal writing is challenging because good writing is good thinking.[73] Many who begin writing find that their ideas and arguments are not quite as developed and clear as they suspected before they put their pen to paper or their fingers to the keyboard. Legal writers must approach the task of writing with rigor because the rigor involved in putting ideas into words tests whether the writer's arguments are valid.[74] Yet the hard work will pay off. Good writing may look easy, but "[i]t takes training and work and fair time to compose—all part of the lawyer's craft."[75] Ultimately, writing with rigor will increase the persuasiveness of our writing.

Brevity—Abraham Lincoln

Lincoln gave us a glimpse of his definition of brevity by describing what it was not. Lincoln made the following observation about another lawyer: "He can compress the most words into the smallest ideas of any man I ever met."[76] The opposite of that practice, the quality of expressing much with few words,[77] captures what brevity means. This quality is what judges mean when they plead

---

71. *Id.*

72. *See* Easton, *supra* note 62, at 251 ("Your goal, though not always obtainable, should be to know more about your case than anyone else, especially opposing counsel.... [Y]ou can acquire that superior level of knowledge only through hard work.").

73. *See* Neumann & Tiscione, *supra* note 64, at 49 ("[L]earning to write [like] a lawyer is another way to learn to think [like] a lawyer.") (quoting Terrill Pollman).

74. Dean and former Judge Donald Burnett explained,

Through the discipline of putting an argument into words, we find out whether the argument is worth making.... Each issue is defined by a cluster of facts and governing legal principle. If you cannot articulate this nexus of law and fact, you do not yet have a grasp of the case.

Donald L. Burnett, Jr., *The Discipline of Clear Expression*, 32 Advoc. June 1989, at 8 (quoted in Edwards, *supra* note 1, at xxv).

75. Joseph Kimble, *Plain English: A Charter for Clear Writing*, 9 T.M. Cooley L. Rev. 1, 22 (1992) (noting that "clear writing only *looks* easy").

76. *Lincoln's Own Stories* 36 (Anthony Gross ed., 1912).

77. Webster's Dictionary defines brevity as "the quality of expressing much in few words; terseness; succinctness." *Webster's American Dictionary*, *supra* note 5, at 99.

for brevity. They are beseeching the advocates, "Please, tell me exactly what I need to know to make the right decision, but not one single thing more."

Several other words make multiple appearances in "brevity" definitions such as terse, succinct, few, concise, pithy, and brief.[78] The word "brevity," as opposed to another synonym, suggests the art involved in writing and editing. Lawyers are professional writers who write legal briefs for professional readers.[79] Writing is the craft of our profession, and writing with "brevity" best captures that particular part of our craft.

"Brevity" also encompasses more than simply using the shortest paragraphs, the least number of words, or words with single syllables. The goal of brevity should be clarity. Striving for brevity means the writer is seeking a delicate balance. The legal argument must not be obscured, either by so many words that the heart of the argument is lost or by so few words that the argument omits critical assumptions or connections.[80]

Lincoln scholar Ronald C. White Jr. notes, "The opposite of verbose is not simple. [Abraham] Lincoln was not bent on brevity alone. He was intent on precision. Sometimes precision might mean more."[81]

As lawyers writing briefs we know who our audience is, and those readers have repeatedly told us about their preference for brevity. Brevity is routinely listed by judges as the quality they consider most essential for brief writers.

Scalia and Garner offer compelling advice about the persuasive power of brevity:

> [A] long and flabby brief, far from getting a judge to spend more time with your case, will probably have just the opposite effect.
> Ponder this: Judges often associate the brevity of the brief with the quality of the lawyer. Many judges we've spoken with say that good lawyers often come in far below the page limits—and that bad lawyers almost never do.[82]

---

78. "Succinct" is defined as "expressed in few words; concise; terse; characterized by conciseness or verbal brevity." *Id.* at 786. Terse is defined as "neatly or effectively concise; brief and pithy, as language." *Id.* at 812.

79. Alex Kozinski, *The Wrong Stuff*, 1992 BYU L. Rev. 325, 327 (1992).

80. *See* Ruggero J. Aldisert, Stephen Clowney & Jeremy D. Peterson, *Logic for Law Students: How to Think Like a Lawyer*, 69 U. Pitt. L. Rev. 1, 7 (6th ed. 2000) (citing S. Morris Engel, *With Good Reason: An Introduction to Informal Fallacies* 20).

81. Ronald C. White Jr., *Lincoln's Greatest Speech: The Second Inaugural* 76 (2002).

82. Scalia & Garner, *supra* note 56, at 98; *see also* Ruth Anne Robbins, *Painting with Print: Incorporating Concepts of Typographic and Layout Design into the Text of Legal Writing Documents*, 2 J. ALWD 108, 111 (2004) (arguing that visual effects of a document can influence the writer's credibility).

Judge Ruggero Aldisert lists the criticisms expressed by judges about briefs: "Too long. Too long. Too long."[83] Judge Alex Kozinski expounds, "[W]hen judges see a lot of words they immediately think: LOSER, LOSER. You might as well write it in big bold letters on the cover of your brief."[84]

Federal judges see brevity as absolutely essential to persuasiveness.[85] Judges want "shorter, harder hitting briefs."[86] Judges do not view brevity as optional; instead they list conciseness as "essential" and "very important."[87] A few of the judges' handwritten comments responding to a survey question about what law schools can do to improve persuasive writing are revealing:

- A brief can be brief. Please tell your students that I have a lot to do and little time to do it. Write a brief that I can adopt as my opinion with a straight face and you will please me.
- Brevity, brevity, brevity....
- Remind the students that as they learned in English 101, clarity and brevity are virtues....
- Conciseness! ...
- Excessive length may hurt your case.
- Encourage brevity and precision....
- [A] judge has only a limited amount of time to devote to each case ... [T]he good advocate must be sure that none of that time is wasted. If briefs are too long, the judge's attention will often stray and the good arguments will be lost in the sea of irrelevance.[88]

Today, brevity is just as persuasive, and even more necessary, than it was in Lincoln's time. Lincoln is particularly inspirational for lawyers because he learned the persuasive power of brevity while practicing law. He is also inspirational because, contrary to popular myth, he worked hard for his eloquence.

---

83. Aldisert, *Winning on Appeal, supra* note 2, at 25.
84. Kozinski, *supra* note 79, at 327.
85. The survey of federal judges showed:
    Judges seem most interested in an advocate's ability to be brief. From the judges' perspective, conciseness is not inspirational, it is essential. Seventy-three of the 355 judges who participated volunteered that the best briefs are concise; 70 said that the worst briefs fail to be concise; and 118 said that conciseness should be taught in law school writing courses.
Robbins, *The Inside Scoop, supra* note 66, at 279.
86. *Id.* at 257.
87. *Id.*
88. *Id.* at 281.

Clarity—Ulysses S. Grant

In many ways clarity is the most important quality of all legal writing. The law is complex, changing, and organic. A persuasive writer must work hard to clarify the law for the reader. In fact, the more complicated the law is, the more important it is for the writer to be clear.[89] "Clarity" means easily understood.[90] The word derives from the Latin noun "claritas," which means "clearness" or "vividness"[91] and the Latin verb "claro" meaning "clear" or "explain."[92] Clarity, as a quality of writing, means that the written words accurately reflect the ideas or arguments of the author.[93] Clarity in the written product leaves no trace of doubt in the reader about exactly what the writer means.

Grant best described the goal of his own writing as clarity. Recalling the events of April 9, 1865, at Appomattox Court House, Virginia, when General Robert E. Lee surrendered the Army of Northern Virginia, Grant wrote,

> When I put my pen to the paper I did not know the first word that I should make use of in writing the terms. I only knew what was in my mind, and I wished to express it clearly, so that there could be no mistaking it.[94]

Grant revealed the two essential aspects of clarity in writing: clear thought and clear expression. Clear thinking can precede clear writing.[95] At least at Ap-

---

89. Michael R. Smith noted,
> The substance of legal analysis is complicated enough without adding to the confusion by using unnecessarily complex sentence structures and complicated wording. Thus, a clear, understandable writing style—commonly referred to as "plain English"—is essential to a legal writer's credibility as an intelligent, articulate advocate.

Smith, *Advanced Legal Writing, supra* note 30, at 182.

90. *Webster's American Dictionary, supra* note 5, at 146.

91. *Oxford Latin Dictionary* 332 (P.G.W. Glare ed., 1983).

92. *Id.*

93. Clarity is an elusive and opaque concept. Robbins, *The Inside Scoop, supra* note 66, at 283. Robbins (Tiscione) described the traditional concept that ideas exist separate from the writing about those ideas, but further noted that more-recent theories emphasize the importance of the process of writing and social construct to formulate ideas. *Id.*

94. Ulysses S. Grant, *Personal Memoirs of Ulysses S. Grant* 631 (1992).

95. Elaine A. Grafton Carlson noted,
> Of all the attributes of a good brief, the greatest is clarity. To have clarity of writing there must first be clarity of thought. It is only when the brief writer understands the issues clearly that he or she can write about them in clear terms.

Elaine A. Grafton Carlson, *Elements of Well Written Briefs, Clarity of Meaning*, 6 McDonald & Carlson Tex. Civ. Prac., App. Prac. §20:5 (2d ed. 2010).

pomattox, Grant had no difficulty with clear thought, so his clear thinking came before his clear expression there. Most of us are not as fortunate as Grant at Appomattox in knowing exactly what is in our minds.[96] Before we begin writing we often have a vague sense of the important issues, potential arguments, and best organization. But it is often the process of writing itself that helps us writers formulate, hone, and simplify those thoughts and ideas. This is particularly true of legal writing. The physical and mental act of writing forces the legal writer to develop the legal arguments, face the strengths and weaknesses of the case, and organize those arguments into a comprehensible product.[97] So clear thinking is typically a process, as is the process of clear writing, which often requires multiple edits. Sometimes clear thinking comes first. Sometimes thinking is not clear until after writing. In any case, both the thinking and the writing must be clear in the final product.

Once thinking is clear, whether that happens before or during the writing process, the writer faces the second challenge of conveying those ideas in a direct and simple way. The ultimate goal is for the reader to read the words and come to only one—the intended—understanding of the words.[98] Confucius said, "If language is lucid, that is enough."[99] Clarity eliminates ambiguity and confusion.

The primary goal for any legal writer should be to make things easier for the reader. Clarity "makes reading effortless."[100] Some readers may be willing to work to understand what an author is writing, but most are not. Even a willing reader will tire of the effort required to understand an unintelligible written document. And who should we be visualizing when we think about

---

96. McFeely suggested that Grant's clear thinking did not always precede his clear writing. William S. McFeely, *Grant* 498 (1981). McFeely wryly suggested that Grant may have been more successful as a president if he had governed by writing notes of instruction instead of holding cabinet meetings. *Id.* at 498.

97. *See* Edwards, *supra* note 1, at xxv ("Your working draft is nothing less than 'grasping the case.' It guides, deepens, and tests your analysis in a number of ways, but its most important role is in forming your ideas into the kind of structured, linear reasoning that lawyers must master.").

98. Paul H. Anderson, Associate Justice, Minnesota Supreme Court, A Judicial Perspective on Legal Writing and Oral Argument (U. of St. Thomas Sch. of L., Minneapolis, Minn., Mar. 31, 2011).

99. Confucius, *XV Analects*, ch. 40 (Ltd. Ed. Club 1933).

100. Mayanne Downs, *… And I am Here to Help!*, 85 Fla. B.J., Feb. 2011, at 4, 4 (Downs compliments an appellate lawyer, Kris Davenport, for her "gift for crafting the most complex concepts into easily digested small bites, writing with a clarity that makes reading effortless and the point she's making the only possible conclusion."); *see also* Philip J. Padovano, *Writing Style*, 2 Fla. Prac., App. Prac. §16:19 (2011) ("Clarity in legal writing is best achieved by placing oneself in the position of the reader.").

that reader? We should follow the lead of Bayless Manning who said his target audience was "a reasonably intelligent, English-speaking, fourteen-year-old" because "if he could explain something to her, anyone would understand it."[101]

It is not easy work to write with clarity. Multiple drafts help the writer through the tortuous work of analyzing the problem and laboriously trying to clarify and explain the pertinent facts, issues, and law.[102] But this is exactly the value that lawyers add when writing. It is this hard work of thinking, analyzing, and clarifying that makes a legal brief so much more effective than simply providing a stack of cases for the judge to read.[103] Not surprisingly, clarity in judicial opinions is equally important.[104]

One thing is certain: "[I]t's impossible to separate good writing from clear thinking."[105] Perhaps that is why judges routinely ask for more clarity in legal briefs.[106] For legal writers, "Clarity is mistress of all."[107]

---

101. James J. Hanks Jr., *Legal Capital and the Model Business Corporation Act: An Essay for Bayless Manning*, L. & Contemp. Probs. 211, 212 (2011) (quoting Bayless Manning). Bayless Manning had a successful legal career as a lawyer, professor at Yale Law School, dean at Stanford Law School, and president of the Council on Foreign Relations. *Id.* at 211–12. Hanks reports that Manning, "avoids grand words when simpler ones will do" and "does not need or want to show off in his writing." *Id.* at 212. Hanks concludes, "[a]lthough [Manning] writes with greater elegance than any lawyer I have known, it is the elegance of uncluttered clarity, focus, and brevity—like the writing of another great lawyer, Lincoln." *Id.*

102. *See* Hon. Bruce S. Jenkins, *The Legal Mind in the Digital Age*, 58 Fed. Law. 28, 30–31 (Feb. 2011).

103. *Id.* at 30. Some suggest that lawyers have a professional ethical obligation to improve the legal system by writing with clarity. *See* Robert Rich, Current Development, *The Most Grotesque Structure of All: Reforming Jury Instructions, One Misshapen Stone at a Time*, 24 Geo. J. Legal Ethics 819, 829 (2011) (noting that jury instructions should be written so that they are understandable); *see also* Charles C. Tucker, *The Evolution of Legal Language*, 40 Colo. Law., Jan. 2011, at 91, 91 ("Thus, it seems courts are especially inclined to promote clarity in legal documents [like jury instructions] that are intended to communicate substantive legal principles to nonlawyers.").

104. *See* John D. Feerick, *Judge Denny Chin: A Student of the Law*, 79 Fordham L. Rev. 1491, 1493 (2011) Feerick compliments Judge Denny Chin, United States Court of Appeals for the Second Circuit: "A review of his decisions reveals a person who pays close attention to the facts and applicable law and expresses in his judicial writings a clarity and directness…, leaving little room for guessing at his reasons for deciding a particular matter."

105. Bryan A. Garner, *Legal Writing in Plain English* xiii (2d ed. 2013).

106. Robbins, *The Inside Scoop, supra* note 66, at 284. "Of all the advice offered by judges to improve legal writing…, the need to be concise and clear appeared most often." *Id.* at 264.

107. Joseph R. Nolan & Kerry A. Durning, *Writing the Brief—Writer's Discipline*, 41 Mass. Prac., App. Proc. §3:4 (3d ed. 2011). Scalia and Garner advise that clarity trumps all other elements of style. Scalia and Garner, *supra* note 56, at 107.

Zeal—Teddy Roosevelt

Zeal is a term familiar to lawyers. Advocating for our clients with zeal has long been part of our American legal tradition.[108] The early American ethical and professional responsibility rules used the word zeal explicitly, and the word remains a part of the preamble and commentary to the ethical rules.[109] The most familiar reference states, "A lawyer should act with commitment and dedication to the interests of the client and with zeal in advocacy upon the client's behalf."[110] Many lawyers acting in an advocacy role identify zeal as "*the* fundamental principle of the law of lawyering."[111]

---

108. Most scholars trace the idea of zealous advocacy to Henry Lord Broughman's representation of Queen Caroline in 1820. Monroe H. Freedman, *Henry Lord Broughman and Zeal*, 34 Hofstra L. Rev. 1319, 1319–20 (2006). Broughman defended Queen Caroline against a charge of adultery in a divorce proceeding by threatening to expose King George IV's own illicit marriage. *Id.* at 1320. Lord Broughman explained at the trial:

> [A]n advocate, in the discharge of his duty, knows but one person in all the world, and that person is his client. To save the client by all means and expedients, and at all hazards and costs to other persons, and, amongst them, to himself, is his first and only duty....

Id. at 1322 (quoting 2 *Trial of Queen Caroline* 3 (1821)).

109. The American Bar Association's first code of ethics, published in 1908, instructed, "[A] lawyer owes entire devotion to the interest of the client, warm zeal in the maintenance and defense of his rights and the exertion of his utmost learning and ability." The Model Code of Professional Responsibility Canon 7, published in 1969, noted, "A lawyer should represent a client zealously within the bounds of the law. The 1983 Model Rules of Professional Conduct include the word "zeal" in the preamble and commentary, but the rules themselves do not reference zeal. Lawrence J. Vilardo & Vincent E. Doyle III, *Where Did the Zeal Go?*, Litig., Fall 2011, at 53, 56.

110. Model R. Prof. Conduct 1.3 cmt. 1 (ABA 2004). The Preamble to the Model Rules of Professional Conduct contains three additional references to zeal:

   1. "As advocate, a lawyer zealously asserts the client's position under the rules of the adversary system." *Id.* at Preamble, para. 2.
   2. "Thus, when an opposing party is well represented, a lawyer can be a zealous advocate on behalf of a client and at the same time assume that justice is being done." *Id.* at para. 8.
   3. "These principles include the lawyer's obligation zealously to protect and pursue a client's legitimate interests, within the bounds of the law, while maintaining a professional, courteous and civil attitude toward all persons involved in the legal system." *Id.* at para. 9.

111. Freedman, *supra* note 108, at 1319 (quoting Geoffrey C. Hazard, Jr. & William Hodes, *The Law of Lawyering: A Handbook on the Rules of Professional Conduct*) 17 (Supp. 1998)("The authors wrote this five years after the Model Rules were adopted. In their third edition the authors changed the phrasing, but expressly equated "diligence" in Model Rule of Professional

As for zeal itself, a humorous story about Roosevelt's childhood understanding of the word "zeal" is telling. As a child, Roosevelt heard the word "zeal" during church sermons. He was afraid of "zeals," thinking they were scary spirits lurking in darkened corners. Once he finally learned what "zeal" meant, he decided that he believed in it, but he did not want to plagiarize Scripture, so he called the quality "strenuousity."[112]

A writer's zeal will help persuade the reader. Zeal is "fervor for a person, cause, or object; eager desire or endeavor; enthusiastic diligence; ardor."[113] The word zeal is not used here to reference an appeal to the emotions or passion of the reader. Instead, zeal refers to a way to convince the reader that the author actually believes what the author writes. Michael R. Smith suggests that advocates "should evince ... zeal" by "project[ing] passion, conviction, and confidence in a client's position."[114]

As a component of persuasion, zeal is part of the credibility of the writer.[115] The zealous writer receives two benefits: "first, the substance itself helps to per-

---

Conduct 1.3 with zeal, for example referring to "the basic duty of diligence (or zealousness).") (emphasis in original). There is a current debate about the use of "zeal" to describe legal representation. On one side are those claiming that a requirement of zealous representation leads to incivility among lawyers. *See, e.g.,* Paula Schaefer, *Harming Business Clients with Zealous Advocacy: Rethinking the Attorney Advisor's Touchstone,* 38 Fla. St. U. L. Rev. 251, 254 ("The complaint that is most frequently lodged against zealous advocacy is ... that lawyers use zealous advocacy as an excuse for incivility."); Allen K. Harris, *The Professionalism Crisis—The "z" Words and Other Rambo Tactics: The Conference of Chief Justices' Solution,* 53 S.C. L. Rev. 549, 569 (2001) ("The phrase 'zealous advocacy' is frequently invoked to defend unprofessional behavior and a 'Rambo,' or 'win at all costs,' attitude."), John Conlon, *It's Time to Get Rid of the "z" Words,* Feb. Res Gestae, Feb. 2011, at 50 (zealous advocacy used as excuse for rudeness, incivility, and offensive behavior). Those on the other side claim that zealous representation never allows for a violation of other ethical duties, and that our advocacy system depends on opposing parties being represented by lawyers who will zealously put their clients first. Anita Bernstein, *The Zeal Shortage,* 34 Hofstra L. Rev. 1165, 1169, 1186 (2005) (zeal is a "great ideal" and the shortage of zeal has affected law practice and impacts lawyer pro bono work); Vilardo & Doyle, *supra* note 109; *see also* Paul C. Saunders, *Whatever Happened to 'Zealous Advocacy'?,* 245 N.Y. L.J., March 11, 2011, at 4 (suggesting that New York should have had an open debate before eliminating the word "zeal" from the New York Code of Professional Responsibility). One scholar suggests that even if lawyer ethics move back toward a client-centered approach many lawyers will still consider that "lawyers have duties that go beyond those owed to their particular clients, but rather extend to third parties and the public at large as well." Steven K. Berenson, *Passion Is No Ordinary Word,* 71 Alb. L. Rev. 165, 193 (2008).

112. George William Douglas, *The Many-Sided Roosevelt* 18–19 (1907).

113. *Webster's American Dictionary, supra* note 5, at 915.

114. Smith, *Advanced Legal Writing, supra* note 30, at 136.

115. *Id.* at 136.

suade, and second, the credibility of the advocate's argument is enhanced by the zeal and commitment reflected in the advocate's effort."[116] The author's effort in researching and writing the legal document must be thorough and complete to give the reader the desired confidence. Frederick Salter noted that a zealous writer will be very thorough: "Someone said that the easy writing makes for damned hard reading; the converse is also true, and easy reading is likely to be due to the zeal with which the writer has checked and rechecked every chapter, paragraph, sentence, word, and comma."[117]

The language and tone of the written product also should reflect zeal. "An advocate generally should present his or her arguments using forceful and confident language."[118] Here is an example of such terse, direct, and vivid language from Ruth Bader Ginsburg: "*Goesaert* is a decision overdue for formal burial."[119]

The word zeal sometimes elicits a negative reaction, but only because some equate zeal with overzealous behavior. As used here, though, zeal implies conviction and passion, but it also includes honesty.[120] This honesty has two components: both a genuine belief in the merits of the case, and absolute candor about the strengths and weaknesses of the case. The lawyer can evince zeal only if convinced that the client should win.[121] And even the zealous advocate knows that there are some weaknesses on every side; zealous advocacy should never trump realism.[122]

Judges notice whether the lawyers have zeal for their case, and a lack of zeal can be revealed by the language they use. Patricia Wald, former Chief Judge, United States Court of Appeals for the D.C. Circuit, gives this advice: "Too many young lawyers today are afraid to show strong feelings of any kind; the jargon in which they write illustrates all too graphically their insecurity about

---

116. *Id.* at 137.

117. Frederick Millet Salter, *The Art of Writing* 56 (H. V. Weekes ed. 2004).

118. Smith, *Advanced Legal Writing, supra* note 30, at 137.

119. Ross Guberman, *Point Made: How to Write Like the Nation's Top Advocates* 202 (2d ed. 2014).

120. *See* Wayne Schiess, *Writing for the Legal Audience* 90 (2003) ("So in every court paper you submit to a trial judge, be honest.").

121. Scalia and Garner, *supra* note 56, at 13 (Scalia and Garner accept that it is appropriate for an advocate to believe the advocate's side should win), *see also* Aviam Soifer, *MuSings*, 37 J. Legal Educ. 20 (1987) (discussing the importance of writing about "what you genuinely believe").

122. *See* Ruggero J. Aldisert, *A Judge's Advice: 50 Years on the Bench* 240 (2011) (noting that successful advocates "are realistic about their cases and candid with the courts.") [hereinafter Aldisert, *A Judge's Advice*].

stating what they believe in."[123] Legal writers must convince readers that they have confidence in the merits of the client's case.[124] Of course, the ultimate act of persuasion is to convince the reader that the writer has reached the correct conclusion.[125]

"Whatever happened to eloquence? Do 21st century Americans not really care about rhetoric? Is rhetoric an old-fashioned word that looks backward to an earlier age?"[126] As legal writers, let's answer this lament with a resounding chorus that we lawyers care about eloquence, and we know that rhetoric, as the art of effectively using language, is critical for our persuasive writing. Then let's show that this is true by using metaphor effectively, and writing with rigor, brevity, clarity, and zeal.

---

123. Ross Guberman, *supra* note 119, at 280 (citing Patricia Wald). If that lack of conviction stems from a moral objection, then the lawyer should consider whether another lawyer could better represent the client. *See* Gregory C. Sisk, *Litigation with the Federal Government* 103(b) 24–26 (4th ed. ALI-ABA 2006) (noting that Judge Wald commented that the lawyer's discomfort is "often discernible to the court").

124. Helene S. Shapo and Marilyn R. Walter, *Writing and Analysis in the Law* 356 (6th ed. 2013) (Shapo and Walters also suggest that the author should convey positive feelings for the client); Smith, *Advanced Legal Writing*, *supra* note 30, at 135–36.

125. Aldisert, *A Judge's Advice*, *supra* note 122, at 137.

126. Ronald C. White, Jr., *The Eloquent President: A Portrait of Lincoln Through His Words* 307 (2005).

Chapter 2

The Power of Metaphor: Thomas Jefferson

(April 13, 1743–July 4, 1826)
Presidency 1801–1809

Metaphors are powerful. A metaphor has the potential for tremendous good, such as perfectly summarizing and simplifying a difficult concept. But any metaphor also has the potential for tremendous danger, such as oversimplifying or incorrectly summarizing a difficult concept. Some metaphors are so powerful that they remain the quintessential description of an abstract and complex ideal, despite attacks on their accuracy or helpfulness. This chapter examines one such powerful metaphor: Thomas Jefferson's metaphor describing the First Amendment religion clause as "building a wall of separation between Church & State."[1] Perhaps no metaphor about church-state relations has been more powerful, more controversial, or more lasting. Jefferson wrote the metaphor in a January 1, 1802, letter to the Danbury Baptist Association of Connecticut, in part to assure the Danbury Baptists that he agreed with them "that religion is a matter which lies solely between Man & his God."[2]

---

1. *See* App. 6 (Letter from Thomas Jefferson, Pres. of the U.S., to the Danbury Baptist Assn. (Jan. 1, 1802)). Dreisbach's transcriptions of the Danbury Baptist correspondence are included in his book. Daniel L. Dreisbach, *Thomas Jefferson and the Wall of Separation between Church and State* 34–35 (2002) [hereinafter Dreisbach, *Thomas Jefferson and the Wall of Separation*].

2. Jefferson revealed this intent in a letter he wrote to Attorney General Levi Lincoln while he was drafting the January 1, 1802 letter. *See* App. 4 (Letter from Thomas Jefferson, Pres. of the U.S., to Atty. Gen. Levi Lincoln (Jan. 1, 1802)).

Scholars, judges, and lawyers will long debate the accuracy of Jefferson's "wall of separation" metaphor. Learned minds take opposing views on the issue of whether the "wall of separation" metaphor is accurate in almost any sense. Some contend there is no "wall" at all. Others dispute what the wall separates.[3] I leave the debate about whether Jefferson's "wall of separation" metaphor is a brilliant, flawed, complex, or simplistic metaphor for the First Amendment religion clause to Constitutional law scholars and historians. Instead, this chapter has other goals: to study how Jefferson came to use the "wall of separation" metaphor, to consider how the metaphor developed into a doctrinal metaphor substituting for the language and meaning of the First Amendment religion clause, and to glean lessons for legal writers from Jefferson's "wall of separation" metaphor.

Jefferson's careful writing practices while he was drafting the Danbury Baptist letter should inspire us to take care in crafting or borrowing metaphors for our own writing. Jefferson carefully considered his audience, asked for advice from two Cabinet members, and revised the letter before sending it to the Danbury Baptists. Further, Jefferson wrote the letter to express his opinion about at least one church-state issue—whether presidents should declare national days of thanksgiving.

Jefferson's understanding of the First Amendment religion clause was not encapsulated entirely in the "wall of separation" metaphor. Instead, Jefferson's

---

3. Felix Frankfurter noted, "[A]greement, in the abstract, that the First Amendment was designed to erect a 'wall of separation between church and state,' does not preclude a clash of views as to what the wall separates." *McCollum v. Bd. of Educ.*, 333 U.S. 203, 213 (1948) (Frankfurter, J., concurring).

Some argue that the "wall of separation" is a broad statement applying to all levels of government. Daniel L. Dreisbach & John D. Whaley, *What the Wall Separates: A Debate on Thomas Jefferson's "Wall of Separation" Metaphor*, 16 Const. Commentary 627, 628, 673–74 (1999) (Whaley's argument). Others claim that the "wall of separation" separates only government from religion, but does not prohibit ecclesiastical authorities from engaging in all civil government formats. *Id.* at 628 (Dreisbach's view). Still others point out that "the wall of separation" is a prohibition only on actions by the federal, but not the state, government. Dreisbach, *Thomas Jefferson and the Wall of Separation, supra* note 1, at 65–66 (Dreisbach notes that the First Amendment only governed relations between religion and the national government).

John Witte, Jr. offers five early American understandings of the "wall of separation": protecting the church from the state; protecting the "liberty of conscience of the religious believer" from both church and state; protecting the state from the church; protecting individual state governments from federal government interference in local religious affairs; and protecting "society from unwelcome participation in and support for religion." John Witte, Jr., *That Serpentine Wall of Separation*, 101 Mich. L. Rev. 1869, 1889–91 (2003).

"wall of separation" metaphor was the beginning, but certainly not the end, of his position on the appropriate intersection between church and state. Jefferson likely did not intend for the "wall of separation" metaphor to be his ultimate statement about church-state relations based on several circumstances surrounding the writing of the letter: he only used the metaphor one time, he wrote the metaphor in a letter, he was not the first to use the metaphor, and the metaphor gained stature long after he penned the words in 1802. The "wall of separation" metaphor started as a stylistic metaphor. Only much later, long after Jefferson wrote the Danbury Baptist letter, did the metaphor develop into a doctrinal metaphor representing the meaning of the First Amendment religion clause.

Legal writers can learn several lessons from Jefferson's vivid metaphor. Jefferson's "wall of separation between Church & State" is so powerful that, at least in the minds of the American public and perhaps in the minds of most American lawyers, the language of the metaphor has replaced the language of the law.[4] Further, the image created by the metaphor has defined our understanding about the relationship between religion and government in America.[5] The metaphor has had such astonishing longevity because it meets all the requirements of an effective metaphor: it is simple, concrete, visual, creative, and concise. Finally, consideration of the common attacks made on metaphors in the legal context, and made against the "wall of separation" metaphor specifically, will help us craft effective metaphors. Metaphors should be used with caution, but metaphors are so effective that they should be used.

Jefferson's Classical Education

Historians study the lives of American presidents and search for important influences on each president. The inquiry often starts with the early life of the president, as scholars delve into family influences, religious training, and education or the lack of any of these. The search continues as scholars study the life of the president as he became an adolescent and young man.

Thomas Jefferson was primarily influenced by his classical education. Charles A. Miller reviews how Jefferson's classical education informed Jeffer-

---

4. Philip Hamburger, *Separation of Church and State* 1 (2002) ("In the minds of many [Americans], [Jefferson's words "separation between church and state"] have even displaced those of the U.S. Constitution, which, by contrast, seem neither so apt nor so clear.").

5. Dreisbach & Whaley, *supra* note 3, at 628.

son's understanding of metaphor.[6] Jefferson began his study of Greek and Latin at the age of nine. He entered the College of William & Mary at the age of seventeen. He heard lectures on rhetoric from Dr. William Small, who brought the Scottish Enlightenment to Virginia. He then studied law under the apprenticeship of George Wythe, who was also a classical scholar.[7] Jefferson read and admired Aristotle, Homer, Epicurus, and Tacitus.[8] Miller notes, "Jefferson had few peers either for depth or breadth in classical learning and none for the mark that an education in the classics left on his life."[9] Further, Jefferson believed that an accomplished lawyer must read and study, among other subjects, mathematics, astronomy, philosophy, history, politics, ethics, physics, rhetoric, oration, and poetry.[10]

Among the Greek philosophers, Jefferson most admired Aristotle.[11] Jefferson seemed to agree with Aristotle that metaphor did not have a place in philosophical argument, but it could be used in poetry and legal argument as an ornament and to persuade.[12] In the *Poetics*, Aristotle said that "[metaphor] alone cannot be learned from others and its use is a sign of genius, for to use metaphors well is to see resemblances."[13] Jefferson also likely read Quintilian, who wrote that metaphor was "by far the most beautiful of tropes."[14] Miller points out that John Locke's views on metaphor had the greatest influence on Jefferson.[15] In his *Essay Concerning Human Understanding*, Locke warned that metaphor and figures of speech could be dangerous and deceptive, but he also acknowledged that readers enjoy metaphor.[16] Miller concludes:

---

6. Charles A. Miller, *Ship of State: "The Nautical Metaphors of Thomas Jefferson* 2–6 (2003).

7. *Id.* at 7; *see also* David N. Mayer, *The Constitutional Thought of Thomas Jefferson* 3–11 (1994) (describing Jefferson's classical and legal educations and listing many of the texts Jefferson studied).

8. Miller, *supra* note 6, at 7.

9. *Id.* (citations omitted).

10. Morris L. Cohen, *Thomas Jefferson Recommends a Course of Law Study*, 119 U. Pa. L. Rev. 823, 824 (1970) (summarizing the letter written by Jefferson at Monticello on August 30, 1814 and addressed to General John Minor and intended for John Minor's eldest son, also named John, who was 17 years old).

11. Miller, *supra* note 6, at 18.

12. *Id.* at 19.

13. Aristotle, *Poetics* 59a4 (Allan H. Gilbert, *Literary Criticism: Plato to Dryden* 103 (Alfred Gudeman trans., 1940)).

14. Miller, *supra* note 6, at 20, n. 21 (citing *Institutio Oratio*, VIII.6.4, VIII. 6.44).

15. *Id.* at 23. Other scholars note that Locke also influenced Jefferson's views on religious toleration. Mayer, *supra* note 7, at 158–59.

16. John Locke, *An Essay Concerning Human Understanding*, bk. III, ch. X (Peter H. Nidditch ed., 1975); Miller, *supra* note 6, at 24.

Like Jefferson, Locke risked being inconsistent. But Locke wrote the creed that is also Jefferson's. A clear distinction exists between the requirements for seeking truth and the requirements for public persuasion and literary beauty. It is a distinction that goes back to Aristotle. Jefferson is in the tradition of both the ancient thinker and the modern.[17]

The 18th century thinkers did not change Jefferson's understanding of the proper use of metaphor.[18] Jefferson used his metaphors in the controlled, classical sense.

The classical works Jefferson read were replete with nautical metaphors, and he used nautical references more often than any other reference for his metaphors.[19] Among nautical references, Jefferson used variations on the ship of state metaphor most frequently.[20] That metaphor, like the "wall of separation" metaphor, did not originate with Jefferson, but was used in many classical works.[21] Jefferson's nautical metaphors were his most constrained metaphors, perhaps because they derived from these classical works.[22] Miller examines several of Jefferson's non-nautical metaphors, although not the "wall of separation" metaphor, and concludes that these metaphors "are more striking, more extended … more passionately felt … [and] are at times philosophical."[23]

The main point to be learned from Jefferson's classical education is that he was fully aware of the dangers of metaphor because all the classicists he admired pointed out those dangers. He recognized that metaphor could stand in the way of truth.[24] He thus used his metaphors for style and persuasion, but not as substitutes for complex abstract ideas.

Jefferson's Use of the "Wall of Separation" Metaphor in the Danbury Baptist Correspondence

The text of the First Amendment religion clause states, "Congress shall make no law respecting an establishment of religion, or prohibiting the free

---

17. Miller, *supra* note 6, at 24.
18. *Id.* at 25–30.
19. *Id.* at 2.
20. *Id.* at 12.
21. *Id.* at 11–17.
22. *Id.* at 56.
23. *Id.* at 43.
24. *Id.* at 31.

exercise thereof."[25] But Jefferson was not a delegate to the Constitutional Convention; he was not present during the drafting or adoption of the First Amendment.[26] Despite his physical absence from the Constitutional Convention because he was serving in Europe as the ambassador to France,[27] Jefferson's views on Constitutional issues are considered important. Jefferson scholar David Mayer noted, "Jefferson ... properly may be regarded as one of the founders because of the central role he played in the key issues that surfaced during the first four decades of government under the Constitution— issues many of which persist to this day."[28] Scholars and historians have focused on Jefferson's writings to determine his understanding of church-state relations. The Danbury letter is valuable for its potential to shed light on Jefferson's views.

One important consideration in evaluating Jefferson's views is the historical context of the 1800 presidential race, often called the "Revolution of 1800."[29] Jefferson, Vice-President, defeated President John Adams in one of the most hotly contested races for the American presidency.[30] During the election, the Federalists charged that Jefferson "was an immoral, deist, Jacobin infidel, bent on severing government from its necessary religious roots and essential clerical alliances."[31] The New England clergy, particularly the dominant Congregationalist ministers, led this attack.[32] Jefferson's Republican party countered that Jefferson was a Christian, "albeit of an unusual sort," who believed in the separation of church and state to protect religious liberty.[33] Jefferson survived as the winner of the 1800 election, but "came away with a bitter hatred for the established clergy of New England."[34]

---

25. U.S. Const. amend I.

26. *See* Mayer, *supra* note 7, at ix; *see also Reynolds v. United States*, 98 U.S. 145, 163 (1879).

27. *See* Robert A. Goldwin, *From Parchment to Power: How James Madison Used the Bill of Rights to Save the Constitution* 125 (1997); *see also* Merrill D. Peterson, *Thomas Jefferson and the New Nation: A Biography* 297–390 (1975) (describing Jefferson's years in France).

28. Mayer, *supra* note 7, at ix–x. *But see* Mark J. Chadsey, *Thomas Jefferson and the Establishment Clause*, 40 Akron L. Rev. 623, 645–46 (2007) (arguing that Jefferson played "almost no role at all" in the adoption of the Establishment clause because his church and state views were not widely known outside of Virginia).

29. *The Revolution of 1800: Democracy, Race & the New Republic* xiii (James Horn, Jan Ellen Lewis & Peter S. Onuf eds., 2002).

30. John Ferling, *Adams vs. Jefferson: The Tumultuous Election of 1800* xvii–xix (2004).

31. Witte, *supra* note 3, at 1893.

32. *Id.*

33. *Id.*

34. *Id.*

Jefferson was inaugurated as the third American president on March 4, 1801.[35] The Danbury Baptists sent a letter of congratulations to Jefferson, but the complete story of the Danbury correspondence involves six different letters.[36] The Danbury Baptists wrote their letter in October 1801. The letter reached Jefferson's desk on December 30, 1801.[37] Jefferson drafted a response letter. He sent the draft to his two New England cabinet members, Postmaster General Gideon Granger of Connecticut and Attorney General Levi Lincoln of Massachusetts.[38] His letter to Granger no longer exists, but Granger's December 31, 1801 reply letter—which did not offer any suggested changes—survives. Jefferson's January 1, 1802 letter to Lincoln asking for his advice on tone and content also survives; Lincoln responded the same day. By the end of the day on January 1, 1802, Jefferson revised the letter based on Lincoln's recommendations, signed the letter, and released it.[39] Jefferson had looked for a chance to express his views on one important church-state issue: the practice of prior presidents in declaring national days of thanksgiving and prayer.[40] He thought his response to the Danbury Baptists would be his opportunity to express his view that such proclamations were inappropriate. A few highlights from each of the six letters, with close attention paid to Jefferson's writing habits, follow.

Danbury Baptist Association to Jefferson (October 1801) (Appendix 1)

The Danbury Baptists sent their letter to Jefferson to congratulate him on the presidency and to ask Jefferson how to better secure their religious liberty in

---

35. Peterson, *supra* note 27, at 653–54.

36. Daniel L. Dreisbach, in his elegant book *Thomas Jefferson and the Wall of Separation between Church and State*, thoroughly considers the historical context behind the famous "wall of separation" metaphor. Dreisbach, *Thomas Jefferson and the Wall of Separation*, *supra* note 1, at 128. Dreisbach explains, "This volume is a sourcebook for jurists and scholars who use Jefferson's metaphor ... [t]his book is about a metaphor—a metaphor that has shaped American church-state law, politics, and discourse. Th[is] book is primarily descriptive, and it seeks to avoid the polemical and ideological cant that polarizes students of church and state." *Id.* at 6–7. The Appendices to this Article include the documents as transcribed by Dreisbach because his transcripts are the most accurate. Hamburger, *supra* note 4, at 1 n.1.

37. Dreisbach, *Thomas Jefferson and the Wall of Separation*, *supra* note 1, at 31 (noting that the reasons behind this three-month delay are unknown).

38. *See* Hamburger, *supra* note 4, at 159–60.

39. Dreisbach, *Thomas Jefferson and the Wall of Separation*, *supra* note 1, at 26.

40. App. 4.

Connecticut.[41] The Connecticut Baptists admired and supported Jefferson because they saw him as a defender of religious liberty, and they were a minority sect in a state dominated by the Congregationalist establishment.[42] The Baptists were upset about the restrictions and taxes imposed by the Congregationalist establishment.[43] Even though the Danbury Baptists understood federalism to mean that the president could not interfere with any state laws, they hoped Jefferson's views on religious liberty would spread to the states.[44] Most importantly, the Baptists "believed that religious liberty was an inalienable right, and they were deeply offended that the religious privileges of dissenters in Connecticut were treated as favors that could be granted or denied by the political authorities."[45]

Jefferson to Danbury Baptist Association (preliminary draft) (Appendix 2)

Jefferson drafted a response to the Danbury Baptists, and that draft letter with his corrections was retained as part of his presidential papers.[46] In the draft, Jefferson explained that he would not offer thanksgiving proclamations or prayers.[47] Jefferson also wrote:

> Believing with you that religion is a matter which lies solely between man & his god, that he owes account to none other for his faith or his worship, that the legitimate powers of government reach actions only and not opinions, I contemplate with sovereign reverence

---

41. Witte, *supra* note 3, at 1893.
42. Dreisbach, *Thomas Jefferson and the Wall of Separation, supra* note 1, at 25.
43. Witte, *supra* note 3, at 1893.
44. Dreisbach, *Thomas Jefferson and the Wall of Separation, supra* note 1, at 33.
45. *Id.*
46. Many of the changes Jefferson made to the letter have been obvious since he made the changes, but some words from the draft were not visible because Jefferson had inked over those words when editing the letter. In 1998, the FBI developed a new technology, described as a digital airbrush, which revealed all the original words in the letter. Irvin Molotsky, *One of Jefferson's Enigmas, So Finally the F.B.I Steps In*, N.Y. Times B7 (May 30, 1998), *available at* http://www.nytimes.com/1998/05/30/arts/one-of-jefferson-s-enigmas-so-finally-the-fbi-steps-in.html?pagewanted=1. The FBI photographed the letter and scanned the image into a computer. Once the image was enlarged, an FBI photography expert could see the difference between the ink Jefferson used to draft the letter and the ink he used to edit the letter. The FBI expert then used a new computer tool to remove the overstriking. *Id.*
47. App. 2 (Letter from Thomas Jefferson, Pres. of the U.S., to Danbury Baptist Assn. (prelim. draft) (Jan. 1, 1802)).

that act of the whole American people which declared that *their* legislature should make no law respecting an establishment of religion,
or prohibiting the free exercise thereof; thus building a wall of eternal separation between church and state.[48]

Postmaster General Gideon Granger to Jefferson (December 31, 1801) (Appendix 3)

Jefferson suspected that his draft letter might offend the New England clergy,
so he asked Postmaster General Gideon Granger of Connecticut to review the
draft.[49] Granger wrote a brief note to Jefferson, saying that he could not "wish
a Sentence changed."[50] Granger acknowledged that Jefferson's letter might offend "the established Clergy of New England," but he thought Jefferson's sentiments should not be softened.[51]

Jefferson to Attorney General Levi Lincoln (January 1, 1802) (Appendix 4)

Granger's lack of editing may have disappointed Jefferson.[52] Jefferson took
time away from entertaining the public on New Year's Day to ask Levi Lincoln, his other New England cabinet member, to review his draft. He sent a
copy of his draft letter with a cover letter explaining his objectives to Levi
Lincoln.[53]

Jefferson used two metaphors in his letter to Lincoln. Jefferson told Lincoln
that he had two main purposes in writing a response to the Danbury Baptists:
(1) to use his letter to express his views about religious liberty with the hope
that some of his views would become part of the American people's under-

---

48. *Id.*

49. Jefferson's request letter to Granger no longer exists, but it can be surmised that it
was similar to the request letter Jefferson sent to Lincoln because Granger mentions the
phrase "germinate among the People, and in time fix 'their political Tenets.'" A similar phrase
was included in Jefferson's letter to Lincoln. *See* App. 3 & App. 4.

50. *See* App. 3 (Letter from Postmaster Gen. Gideon Granger to Thomas Jefferson, Pres.
of the U.S.) (Dec. 31, 1801)).

51. *Id.*

52. Dreisbach suggests that Jefferson "perhaps desiring a more discerning view, solicited
a second opinion, this one from Lincoln, of Massachusetts." Dreisbach, *Thomas Jefferson
and the Wall of Separation, supra* note 1, at 42.

53. *Id.* at 26.

standing of religious liberty, and (2) to explain why he would not make presidential proclamations of fasting and thanksgiving.[54] In explaining his first purpose, Jefferson used a metaphor comparing the transfer of his ideas about religious freedom to a seed being planted and germinating. Jefferson told Lincoln that he was averse to receiving letters like the one sent by the Danbury Baptists, but he tried to use his answers to further his goal of "sowing useful truths & principles among the people, which might germinate and become rooted among their political tenets."[55]

Jefferson used a second metaphor in his letter to Lincoln, seeking Lincoln's specific comments about the tone he used in his Danbury letter. Jefferson compared his audience's ability to receive his message to people's receptivity to cooking flavors. Jefferson told Lincoln, "[Y]ou understand the temper of those in the North, and can weaken it therefore to their stomachs: it is at present seasoned to Southern taste only."[56]

Attorney General Levi Lincoln to Jefferson (January 1, 1802) (Appendix 5)

Unlike Granger, Lincoln offered several suggestions to Jefferson when he wrote back several hours after receiving Jefferson's request.[57] Lincoln told Jefferson that he should make several revisions to the letter to avoid offending both the New England clergy and Jefferson's fellow Republicans.[58] Lincoln noted, "The people of the five N England Governments (unless Rhode Island is an exception) have always been in the habit of observing fasts and thanksgivings in performance of proclamations from their respective Executives."[59] Lincoln suggested alterations which would tone down Jefferson's sentence about executive proclamations regarding fasts and thanksgivings. Jefferson heeded Lincoln's advice, but instead of changing tone, he eliminated the entire sentence about executive proclamations.

---

54. App. 4; *see also* Witte, *supra* note 3, at 1893–94.

55. *See* App. 4.

56. *Id.* Note that Jefferson mixed metaphors by using "temper" instead of "taste."

57. Dreisbach, *Thomas Jefferson and the Wall of Separation, supra* note 1, at 44.

58. App. 5 (Letter from Atty. Gen. Levi Lincoln, to Thomas Jefferson, Pres. of the U.S. (Jan. 1, 1802)).

59. *Id.* Lincoln's reference to Rhode Island referred to an October 1801 session when the Rhode Island legislature broke from tradition and rejected a resolution asking the Governor to proclaim a day of thanksgiving and prayer. This legislative decision generated controversy and disagreement from both Republicans and Federalists. Dreisbach, *Thomas Jefferson and the Wall of Separation, supra* note 1, at 45–46.

Jefferson to Danbury Baptist Association (January 1, 1802—final version) (Appendix 6)

Jefferson incorporated Lincoln's advice into his final draft. Most significantly, he eliminated any reference to his refusal to use the presidential office to declare days of thanksgiving or prayer.[60] Although it is sometimes difficult to tell why a writer makes editing changes, Jefferson was very clear about why he made this change. He wrote in the margin of his draft, "this paragraph was omitted on the suggestion that it might give uneasiness to some of our republican friends in the eastern states where the proclamation of thanksgivings etc by their Executive is an antient [sic] habit, & is respected."[61]

Jefferson's original draft noted that the First Amendment religion clause is "thus building a wall of eternal separation between church and state."[62] Jefferson eliminated the word "eternal" between the words "wall of" and "separation," so that the final metaphor reads that the First Amendment religion clause is "thus building a wall of separation between Church and State."[63] In this instance, there is no clear explanation of why Jefferson made this editing change. Perhaps he thought removal of the word "eternal" would make it clear that this was a fundamental principle, not just a political solution.[64] Or maybe he thought the word "eternal" connoted religion, so eliminating it would show that he did not plan to infringe on any religious rights.[65]

---

60. Dreisbach, *Thomas Jefferson and the Wall of Separation, supra* note 1, at 38.

61. App. 6 (Letter from Thomas Jefferson, Pres. of the U.S., to Danbury Baptist Assn. (final version) (Jan. 1, 1802)).

62. App. 2.

63. App. 6.

64. *See* Robert S. Alley, *Public Education and the Public Good*, 4 Wm. & Mary Bill Rights J. 277, 314 n. 232 (1995–1996) (suggesting that Jefferson struck the word "eternal" from the final draft because "separation of church and state was never simply a political solution for Jefferson, but a fundamental principle to which he was dedicated");

65. James Hutson, *A 'Wall of Separation': FBI Helps Restore Jefferson's Obliterated Draft*, 57 Lib. of Congress Info. Bull. 136, 139, 163 (June 1998) (Library of Congress Manuscript Division Chief Hutson suggests that Jefferson's striking out of both the word "eternal" as well as a draft reference to his presidential office as "merely temporal" might show "the Republican faithful" that Jefferson would not infringe on their religious rights).

Jefferson's "Wall of Separation" Metaphor Started as a Stylistic Metaphor but Developed into a Doctrinal Metaphor

The theory that the "wall of separation" metaphor developed from a stylistic metaphor to a doctrinal metaphor is supported by the earlier analysis of Jefferson's understanding of metaphor, but also by a consideration of Jefferson's intent when he wrote the metaphor. Scholars hotly debate exactly what Jefferson intended when he used the "wall of separation" metaphor. On one side of the debate are those claiming that Jefferson intended for the "wall of separation" metaphor to perfectly encapsulate his opinion about the First Amendment religion clause and, in turn, the true meaning of the First Amendment's prohibition against church and state mingling.[66] Count several United States Supreme Court justices and legal scholars on that side.[67] On the other side of the debate are those claiming Jefferson wrote the Danbury letter primarily as a political statement to appease his New England supporters, but he never meant the "wall of separation" metaphor to convey either his ultimate understanding of the First Amendment religion clauses, or the true meaning of the First Amendment's prohibition against church and state mingling. Again, count several United States Supreme Court justices and legal scholars as holding this opposing view.

Jefferson intended for his "wall of separation" metaphor to be an important stylistic metaphor, but once he released the metaphor then it developed, over

---

66. Some scholars have pointed out that Jefferson's intent is not particularly relevant in determining the true meaning of the First Amendment religion clause. Dreisbach notes, "Much of the modern controversy that surrounds Jefferson's 'wall,' by contrast, is less about the historical record than about the legal, political, and ideological uses of the metaphor in these times." Dreisbach, *Thomas Jefferson and the Wall of Separation, supra* note 1, at 127. Still, Dreisbach notes, "Jefferson's views on church-state relations have been more closely scrutinized than those of any other American." *Id.* at 7; *see also* Mayer, *supra* note 7.

67. Haig Bosmajian notes:

[N]o other judicial metaphor [as "the wall of separation between church and state"] has been so directly defended and challenged by the [Supreme Court] justices, who have been conscious that they are relying on a metaphor that has had a great impact on court decisions related to church-state issues, especially the establishment clause of the First Amendment.

Haig Bosmajian, *Metaphor and Reason in Judicial Opinions* 73 (1992). Bosmajian also notes that scholars, theologians, and others have both attacked and defended the "wall of separation." *Id.* at 77.

the last 200 years in the law, into a doctrinal metaphor.[68] The circumstances surrounding the "wall of separation" metaphor suggest that Jefferson did not intend the metaphor to be his final and all-encompassing statement about the First Amendment religion clause: Jefferson used the metaphor once, he wrote it in a letter, he did not create the metaphor, and the metaphor gained prominence long after he wrote the Danbury letter.

Jefferson has been described as an artist at metaphor.[69] As far as we know, Jefferson used the "wall of separation" metaphor only once, in the Danbury letter.[70] By contrast, he used his nautical metaphors numerous times.[71] To be fair, Jefferson used a metaphor similar to the "wall of separation" metaphor, "fences," on one occasion. In a December 4, 1790, letter to Noah Webster, Jr., Jefferson wrote that there are certain rights, such as "freedom of religion," that people "need not" surrender to the government. He continued, "[T]here are also certain fences which experience has proved peculiarly efficacious against wrong, and rarely obstructive of right, which yet the governing powers have ever shewn a disposition to weaken and remove."[72]

Jefferson's correspondence was an important part of his life, and he wrote letters almost every day, to both friends and strangers.[73] It is estimated that he

---

68. Michael R. Smith, *Levels of Metaphor in Persuasive Legal Writing*, 58 Mercer L. Rev. 919, 922 (2007) [hereinafter Smith, *Levels of Metaphor*]

69. Miller, *supra* note 6, at 5 ("A metaphor depends on artistry, not science, and at metaphor Jefferson was an artist.").

70. Dreisbach notes:

There is no evidence from the written record that he ever again used the "wall" metaphor. Its absence is particularly noteworthy in documents such as his second inaugural address and letter to the Reverend Samuel Miller that, like the Danbury letter, purportedly addressed Jefferson's views on the propriety of the executive appointment of days for religious observance. In short, there is little evidence that Jefferson considered his "wall" the quintessential symbolic expression of theme of his church-state thought.

Daniel L. Dreisbach, *"Sowing Useful Truths and Principles": The Danbury Baptists, Thomas Jefferson, and the "Wall of Separation,"* 39 J. Church & St. 455, 471 [hereinafter Dreisbach, *Sowing Useful Truths and Principles*].

71. Miller, *supra* note 6, at app. 1 (Miller lists 95 nautical metaphors in Appendix 1).

72. Dreisbach, *Thomas Jefferson and the Wall of Separation, supra* note 1, at 87–88 (citing Letter from Thomas Jefferson, Pres. of the U.S., to Noah Webster, Jr. (Dec. 4, 1970), in *The Papers of Thomas Jefferson* (Julian P. Boyd et al. eds., 28 vols. to date) (1950)).

73. Cohen, *supra* note 10, at 824. Cohen further notes that many of Jefferson's original manuscripts have survived, but Jefferson also made copies for his own files with either a copy press or the polygraph copying machine. *Id.* at 824–25. Jefferson called the polygraph copying machine the "finest invention of the present age." *Id.* at 825 n.4 (citing *The Writings of Thomas Jefferson* vol. XI, 118 (A.A. Lipscomb & A.E. Bergh eds., 1903–1904)). "The poly-

wrote 18,000 letters in his lifetime.[74] Many of Jefferson's original manuscripts have survived, but Jefferson also made copies for his own files.[75] The Danbury Baptists' letter to Jefferson and his reply were published in New England newspapers by late January 1802, the same month he wrote the letter.[76]

Based on the seriousness Jefferson attached to his correspondence and the reality that much of that correspondence was published, Jefferson's Danbury letter was not inconsequential. Still, Jefferson had formal opportunities to express his views on the First Amendment. Jefferson served two terms as president, so his views could have been expressed in his State of the Union addresses or his second inaugural.[77] Jefferson did not use these formal occasions to reemphasize his "wall of separation" metaphor.

Although Jefferson authored the Danbury letter, he was neither the first nor the last to use the "wall of separation" metaphor. At least three people, Richard Hooker, Roger Williams, and James Burgh, used the "wall of separation" metaphor in a church-state context before Jefferson.[78] Further, "[t]he image of a wall or similar barrier separating the realms of the church and civil government can be found in Western political and theological literature centuries before Jefferson penned the Danbury Baptist letter."[79] It is difficult to say with certainty whether Jefferson knew about these earlier "wall of separation" metaphors, but scholars suggest that he likely read at least one of the earlier references.[80]

More importantly, Jefferson's metaphor languished in obscurity for years after he wrote the Danbury letter and it was published in 1802. The metaphor became

---

graph copying machine was a device with one or more additional pens connected to a writer's pen," so copies were produced simultaneously while the writer wrote. *Id.* Cohen reports, "Jefferson himself made several improvements in his own version of the polygraph." *Id.*

74. Mayer, *supra* note 7, at ix.

75. Cohen, *supra* note 10, at 824 (most of Jefferson's copies are in the Library of Congress).

76. Dreisbach, *Thomas Jefferson and the Wall of Separation, supra* note 1, at 24.

77. *See* Dreisbach, *Sowing Useful Truths and Principles, supra* note 70, at 471 (pointing out the wall metaphor is missing from Jefferson's second inaugural even though he again alluded to the issue of Presidential proclamations of days of fasting and thanksgiving).

78. Dreisbach, *Thomas Jefferson and the Wall of Separation, supra* note 1, at 71.

79. *Id.* at 71–72.

80. *Id.* at 76 (Jefferson had a copy of Hooker's book in his personal library which was sold to the Library of Congress), 78 (some scholars suggest that Jefferson deliberately borrowed Williams's "wall of separation" metaphor, but others say there is no conclusive evidence that Jefferson knew about the metaphor), 79 ("A plausible source for Jefferson's 'wall' metaphor is the work of the dissenting Scottish schoolmaster James Burgh ... Jefferson read and admired the Scotsman's work and almost certainly encountered Burgh's use of the 'wall of separation' metaphor in his extensive readings.").

a doctrinal metaphor only after several Supreme Court Justices used it in their opinions. After 1802, the Danbury letter was not published again until 1853 when it was included in a collection of Jefferson's writings.[81] The "wall of separation" entered the legal vocabulary in 1879 when the Supreme Court included the entire second paragraph of the Danbury letter and wrote that the letter "may be accepted almost as an authoritative declaration of the scope and effect of the [first] amendment thus secured."[82] The "wall of separation" metaphor languished again for almost seventy years before Justice Hugo Black wrote, in *Everson v. Board of Education,* "In the words of Jefferson, the [First Amendment] clause against establishment of religion by law was intended to erect 'a wall of separation between church and State.' ... That wall must be kept high and impregnable. We could not approve the slightest breach."[83] Barbara A. Perry notes "Justice Hugo L. Black, the foremost jurisprudential interpreter of the metaphor in the Supreme Court's modern era, is arguably responsible for the public's familiarity with the 'wall' doctrine."[84] The Supreme Court cited the Danbury letter "frequently and favorably in the cases that followed *Everson.*"[85] The "wall" metaphor was used frequently during the Chief Justice Burger and Rehnquist eras.[86]

If someone creates an effective metaphor and releases it to the world, then others can use the metaphor. Michael Smith notes that if those others happen to be judges who use the metaphor in opinions to stand for a particular legal concept, then "it is also possible for the metaphor to become the rule governing the analysis of the issue—to wit, a doctrinal metaphor."[87] Jefferson's metaphor started as a stylistic metaphor which later, with substantial help from various Supreme Court Justices, developed into a doctrinal metaphor.

Lessons Legal Writers Can Learn from Jefferson's "Wall of Separation" Metaphor

Jefferson's "wall of separation" metaphor has remained in our legal lexicon. A study of Jefferson's habits in using the metaphor can help us learn how to create and use effective metaphors.

---

81. *Id.* at 96.

82. *Reynolds v. United States,* 98 U.S. 145, 164 (1879).

83. *Everson v. Bd. of Educ.,* 330 U.S. 1, 16, 18 (1947).

84. Barbara A. Perry, *Justice Hugo Black and the "Wall of Separation between Church and State,"* 31 J. of Church & St. 55, 55 (1989).

85. Dreisbach, *Thomas Jefferson and the Wall of Separation, supra* note 1, at 102.

86. *Id.* at 103.

87. Smith, *Levels of Metaphor, supra* note 68, at 941.

Use Decorative, Concrete, Analogic, Creative, and Concise Metaphors

Metaphor is critical to all humans in general and to lawyers in particular. Chad Oldfather identifies five functions of metaphor in legal analysis and discourse, which parallel the function of metaphor in all contexts.[88] First, metaphors serve a decorative function which "is more important than its name implies" because metaphor enhances persuasiveness.[89] Second, metaphors make abstract concepts more concrete.[90] Third, metaphors are a "concealed form of analogical reasoning ... [because] they ... compare[e] one concept with another."[91] Fourth, metaphors have an "almost magical capacity to unleash creative thought."[92] Oldfather explains that "metaphor provides a link between two often largely unrelated ideas," which leads to "a radically different view of the underlying subject."[93] Fifth, metaphors are concise.[94]

The classical teachers who Jefferson studied offer insights about what qualities make a metaphor particularly effective. Aristotle said, "[M]etaphor[s] ... must not be far-fetched; rather we must draw them from kindred and similar things; the kinship must be seen the moment the words are uttered."[95] Quintilian offered, "A metaphor must not be too great for its subject, or, as is more frequently the case, too little."[96]

The "wall of separation" metaphor works on all levels. It is decorative and concrete.[97] It is analogic because the metaphor helps explain that the First Amendment relationship between religion and government is a boundary— and that boundary is rigid and well-defined.[98] The metaphor is creative because it helps the reader understand the First Amendment in a new way.[99] It

---

88. *See* Chad Oldfather, *The Hidden Ball: A Substantive Critique of Baseball Metaphors in Judicial Opinions*, 27 Conn. L. Rev. 17 (1994).

89. *Id.* at 20.

90. *Id.* at 21.

91. *Id.* at 22.

92. *Id.* at 23 (citing Michael Boudin, *Antitrust Doctrine and the Sway of Metaphor*, 75 Geo. L. J. 395, 414, 414–21 (1986)).

93. *Id.*

94. *Id.* at 23–24.

95. Aristotle, *The Rhetoric of Aristotle* 188 (Lane Cooper trans., 1932).

96. Michael R. Smith, *Advanced Legal Writing: Theories and Strategies in Persuasive Writing* 237 (3d ed. 2013) (citing 3 Marius Fabius Quintilianus, *Institutio Oratoria* 309 (H.E. Butler trans., 1954)) [hereinafter Smith, *Advanced Legal Writing*].

97. Dreisbach, *Thomas Jefferson and the Wall of Separation*, *supra* note 1, at 111.

98. Oldfather, *supra* note 88, at 22.

99. *Id.* at 23.

is concise because it describes several complex legal concepts "into a few words."[100] We can see the wall and so could early Americans. No special cultural competence is required to visualize a wall.[101] The concept of a wall separating things is familiar. Both those who first read the metaphor and those who read it today can see the relationship between a wall as a way to separate things and the First Amendment as a way to separate church and state. The metaphor's image of a wall is consistent with the theme of the First Amendment as a barrier to keep church and state from mingling. Finally, the serious tone of the metaphor is appropriate for the gravity of the subject.[102]

In addition to all these strong qualities, Jefferson's "wall of separation" has one additional quality which we cannot replicate: Thomas Jefferson wrote it. Jefferson's fame no doubt played a role in the lasting quality of the metaphor.[103] But other famous Americans, like George Washington and James Madison, also wrote metaphors about the role of religion and government that never took hold like Jefferson's metaphor. Jefferson's words hold a particular gravity for Americans:

> Jefferson's words seem to have shaped the nation. Beginning with his draft of the Declaration of Independence, Jefferson's taut phrases have given concentrated and elevated expression to some of the nation's most profound ideals. Few of Jefferson's phrases appear to have had more significance for the law and life of the United States than those in which he expressed his hope for a separation of church and state.[104]

We obviously cannot be Thomas Jefferson, so we will have to use metaphors that have all the other qualities of good metaphors.

---

100. Dreisbach, *Thomas Jefferson and the Wall of Separation, supra* note 1, at 112 (quoting Steven J. Safranek.).

101. This is in contrast to several metaphors which are criticized because "the metaphor will trigger different associations for the reader and writer and thus they will no longer assign congruent meanings to the concept, nor will they be able to express fully their shared meaning through literal language." Oldfather, *supra* note 88, at 25. Oldfather suggests that baseball metaphors may fall into this category. *Id.* at 30–51. Others suggest that "because baseball is central to our culture, it is a presumptively appropriate source of metaphorical references." Michael J. Yelnosky, *If You Write It, (S)he will Come: Judicial Opinions, Metaphors, Baseball, and "The Sex Stuff,"* 28 Conn. L. Rev. 813, 817 (1996).

102. *See* Smith, *Advanced Legal Writing, supra* note 96, at 240 (suggesting that a metaphor's tone should be consistent with the discussion, and a serious tone is appropriate for most legal matters).

103. *See* Hamburger, *supra* note 4, at 1.

104. *Id.*

Take Time When Crafting or Borrowing Metaphors

Chief Justice William Rehnquist called Jefferson's Danbury letter "a short note of courtesy."[105] But any argument that Jefferson hastily wrote the "wall of separation" metaphor dissolves when one reviews how Jefferson drafted the letter, asked for editing advice, and redrafted the letter. Scholars must be careful not to make overbroad conclusions from a writer's decision to eliminate or change words during the drafting of a document unless the writer specifically indicates exactly why the change was made. Still, Jefferson's writing practices show that he took care when crafting his response to the Danbury Baptists. He carefully considered his audiences, both the Danbury Baptists and the public who he knew would read the letter once it was published in newspapers. He did not send his first draft but made several changes before sending the final draft. He consulted with two Cabinet members who he believed would have particularly helpful insights because they were from New England states. We should take that same care when we create, or borrow, metaphors for our legal writing.[106]

Consider the Common Attacks against Metaphors

Legal writers should be prepared for the common attacks against doctrinal metaphors. A doctrinal metaphor like the "wall of separation" metaphor can be defeated either by an attack on the accuracy of the metaphor or the adoption of an alternative legal analysis.[107] A third common way to defeat a doctrinal metaphor is the attempt to substitute a different metaphor. All three methods of attack have been tried in the "wall of separation" debate, but still the "wall of separation" stands. Courts continue to mention the metaphor even if only to criticize it.[108] It is a testament to its power that the "wall of separation" metaphor continues to appear in judicial opinions and scholarly articles.

---

105. *Wallace v. Jaffree*, 472 U.S. 38, 92 (1985) (Rehnquist, J., dissenting). He also called the metaphor misleading. *Id.*

106. Jefferson did borrow some of his other metaphors, most notably his nautical metaphors. Miller, *supra* note 6, at 8–17.

107. Smith, *Levels of Metaphor, supra* note 68, at 923–28.

108. *See e.g. Wallace*, 472 U.S. at 107 (Rehnquist, J., dissenting) ("Our recent opinions, many of them hopelessly divided pluralities, have with embarrassing candor conceded that the 'wall of separation' is merely a 'blurred, indistinct, and variable barrier,' which 'is not wholly accurate' and can only be 'dimly perceived.' Whether due to its lack of historical support or its practical unworkability, the *Everson* 'wall' has proved all but useless as a guide to sound constitutional adjudication.").

Many judges and scholars have long used the first attack, lamenting that the "wall of separation" metaphor does not accurately capture the meaning of the First Amendment religion clause.[109] We must be prepared for a similar criticism against any metaphors we use to describe a legal concept.

The second type of attack, that an alternative legal analysis should be used, was launched by the United States Supreme Court itself when it developed the 1971 *Lemon* test, a three-part test for evaluating whether government action is constitutional.[110] Under the *Lemon* test, a challenged governmental action (1) must have a secular legislative purpose; (2) must have a primary effect that neither advances nor inhibits religion; and (3) must not foster "an excessive government entanglement with religion."[111] This suggestion, that an alternative legal analysis is better than the metaphor, might also be used against any doctrinal legal metaphors we use.

The third type of attack is that an alternative metaphor should be used. Several alternatives to the "wall of separation" metaphor have been suggested. The proposed alternatives often take one of three forms: (1) a metaphor suggesting separation or a barrier; (2) variations on the wall metaphor; or (3) a completely different metaphor comparing church-state relations to something else.

Dreisbach notes that other early Americans used the image of a separation or barrier to explain church-state relations. George Washington wrote a letter to a Baptist association promising that he would zealously labor "to establish effectual barriers against the horrors of spiritual tyranny."[112] James Madison used the metaphor of "the great Barrier" several times to describe his understanding of religious freedom.[113] Madison also penned the metaphor "the line

---

109. Bosmajian notes that Justice Stewart criticized the "wall of separation" metaphor as not accurately reflecting the meaning of the First Amendment. Bosmajian, *supra* note 67, at 76. Bosmajian also notes that Robert Hutchins criticized the "wall of separation" metaphor by stating, "It is not a reason; it is a figure of speech." *Id.* at 77 (citing Robert Hutchins, *The Future and the Wall*, in *The Wall Between Church and State* 19 (Dallin Oaks ed., 1963)).

110. *Lemon v. Kurtzman*, 403 U.S. 602, 612–13 (1971) (citing *Walz v. Tax Comm.*, 397 U.S. 664, 674 (1970)).

111. For a thorough discussion opining that the "wall of separation" doctrinal metaphor was dismantled and replaced by the three-part test see Smith, *Levels of Metaphor, supra* note 68, at 925–28. Smith notes, "Interestingly, the third part of the *Lemon* test itself contains a metaphor: 'excessive government entanglement.'" *Id.* at 927 n. 44.

112. Dreisbach, *Thomas Jefferson and the Wall of Separation, supra* note 1, at 84 (citations omitted). Washington wrote the letter months before the First Amendment was drafted. *Id.*

113. *Id.* at 85–87 (citations omitted).

of separation, between the rights of Religion & the Civil authority."[114] Jefferson himself used the metaphor of "fences" to explain how individual rights should be protected from government encroachment.[115] Roger Williams used the metaphor of "the hedge or wall of separation between the garden of the church and the wilderness of the world."[116]

At least since the United States Supreme Court emphasized Jefferson's "wall of separation" metaphor in 1947, people have suggested variations on the wall metaphor.[117] In *Everson v. Board of Education*, Justice Hugo Black wrote that the First Amendment "wall must be kept high and impregnable."[118] Walls were important to Jefferson, who used a unique architectural feature, serpentine brick walls, on the University of Virginia campus.[119] Justice Robert H. Jack-

---

114. *Id.* at 88 (citations omitted). The line of separation metaphor has been criticized, most notably by Justice Felix Frankfurter who wrote, "Separation means separation, not something less. Jefferson's metaphor in describing the relation between Church and State speaks of a 'wall of separation,' not of a fine line easily overstepped." *McCollum*, 333 U.S. at 231 (Frankfurter, J., concurring).

115. Dreisbach, *Thomas Jefferson and the Wall of Separation*, *supra* note 1, at 87 (citations omitted).

116. *Id.* at 76–77 (citing Perry Miller, *Roger Williams: His Contribution to the American Tradition* 98 (1953)). Both a fence and a hedge suggest something less substantial than a wall. *Id.* at 88 ("A fence, although clearly a barrier and a structure of demarcation, suggests a construct less impermeable than a high, solid wall or a great and permanent barrier.").

117. Dreisbach notes, "These twentieth-century alternatives, unlike earlier metaphoric barriers suggested by Washington and Madison, were crafted with knowledge of, and response to, Jefferson's construct, as interpreted by the modern Court." *Id.* at 90.

118. *Everson*, 330 U.S. at 18. In the same case, Justice Wiley B. Rutledge did not reference the "wall of separation," but said that the First Amendment's purpose "was to create a complete and permanent separation of the spheres of religious activity and civil authority." *Id.* at 31–32 (Rutledge, J., dissent).

Dreisbach lists several other variations on the wall metaphor which have been proposed: a permeable wall; a wall with cracks, gaping holes, or a few doors; a wall punctuated with checkpoints; a single-sided wall; or a prison wall. Dreisbach, *Thomas Jefferson and the Wall of Separation*, *supra* note 1, at 90–94 (citations omitted).

119. Susan Tyler Hitchcock, *The University of Virginia: A Pictorial History* 32–33 (2003) ("Between the Lawn and the Ranges stretch ten gardens, some divided in two. The serpentine walls enclosing these gardens were designed by Thomas Jefferson after English 'crinkle-crankle walls,' whose combination of strength, efficiency of materials, and beauty he admired."). Jefferson considered his design and founding of the University of Virginia to be one of his greatest accomplishments. Jefferson requested the following inscription for his tombstone: "Here was buried Thomas Jefferson: Author of the Declaration of American Independence; Of the Statute of Virginia for Religious Freedom; and Father of the University of Virginia." Alf J. Mapp, Jr., *Thomas Jefferson: Passionate Pilgrim: The Presidency, The Founding of the University, and the Private Battle* 361 (1991).

son made a reference to these walls when he wrote that without "surer legal guidance" in church-state matters, the Justices "are likely to make the legal 'wall of separation between church and state' as winding as the famous serpentine wall designed by Mr. Jefferson for the University he founded."[120]

A few new alternatives to the "wall" metaphor have been suggested in legal opinions and scholarly articles. These include suggestions that the area where church and state intersect should be considered a zone, a permeable membrane, a parchment barrier, an iron curtain, or the public square.[121]

We could speculate about how our understanding of the religion clause would differ if Jefferson wrote about a "hedge of separation" or if the Supreme Court adopted one of the other suggested metaphors. But the real lesson is that we must be prepared to face suggestions that metaphors, other than the one we select, more accurately describe the legal doctrine.

Jefferson is considered one of our most eloquent presidents. He used metaphor to illuminate and persuade. Jefferson's classical education cautioned that metaphor could be dangerous. Jefferson might be shocked to learn that the metaphor he used once, comparing the First Amendment religion clause to a "wall of separation," remains. Dreisbach emphasized the lasting power of Jefferson's metaphor, "Given the extensive and continuing influence of Jefferson's felicitous phrase in church-state law, policy, and discourse, it can be said, in the words of John Adam's memorable deathbed declaration, that 'Thomas Jefferson still survives.'"[122]

---

120. *McCollum*, 333 U.S. at 238 (Jackson, J., concurring).

121. Dreisbach, *Thomas Jefferson and the Wall of Separation, supra* note 1, at 90–94 (citations omitted). One judge even suggested the metaphor comparing a camel sticking its nose into a tent to the court investigating the constitutionally protected area of religion. *Catholic H.S. Assn. of Archdiocese of NY v. Culbert*, 753 F.2d 1161, 1166 (2d Cir. 1985). Some of these metaphors, like the iron curtain, are politically charged. Dreisbach, *Thomas Jefferson and the Wall of Separation, supra* note 1, at 92–93 (noting that James H. Hutson uses the term as a "constructive allusion," but others use the term pejoratively and "one suspects, ... not only to emphasize the impenetrability of the modern Supreme Court's 'wall' but also to associate the Court's 'wall' with atheistic communist regimes ... and the strictly secular culture promulgated by a 'high and impregnable' barrier.").

122. Dreisbach, *Thomas Jefferson and the Wall of Separation, supra* note 1, at 128 (citations omitted). Jefferson and Adams died on the same day, July 4, 1826, the fiftieth anniversary of the American Declaration of Independence. These were reported as Adams's last words. Adams did not realize that Jefferson had died at Monticello five hours before Adams's own death. *Id.* at 242, n. 104 (citing Merrill D. Peterson, *The Jefferson Image in the American Mind* 3–6 (1960)). *See also* Bosmajian, *supra* note 67, at 73 (noting that no other judicial metaphor "has been so directly defended and challenged by the [Supreme Court] justices....").

Metaphor has been eternally criticized for its inability to capture every nuance and delicacy contained in abstract concepts. Yet, metaphor is the way all humans, including lawyers, make sense of difficult ideas. Jefferson's use of metaphor and his writing habits can inspire us. In the end, we should remember the overarching lesson from Jefferson's "wall of separation" metaphor: metaphor is powerful.

Appendix 1[123]
Address of the Danbury Baptist
Association to Jefferson, October 1801

The address of the Danbury Baptist Association, in the State of Connecticut: assembled October 7th. AD 1801.

To *Thomas Jefferson* Esq. President of the united States of America.

Sir,

> Among the many millions in America and Europe who rejoice in
> your Election to office; we embrace the first opportunity
> which we have enjoy,d in our collective capacity, since your
> Inauguration, to express our great satisfaction, in your
> appointment to the chief Magistracy in the United States: And
> though our mode of expression may be less courtly and
> pompious than what many others clothe their addresses with,
> we beg you, Sir to believe, that none are more sincere.

> Our Sentiments are uniformly on the side of Religious
> Liberty—That Religion is at all times and places a Matter
> between God and Individuals—That no man ought to suffer in
> Name, person or effects on account of his religious
> Opinions—That the legitimate Power of civil Government
> extends no further than to punish the man who *works ill to
> his neighbour*: But Sir. our constitution of government is not
> specific. Our antient charter, together with the Laws made
> coincident therewith, were adopted as the Basis of our
> government, At the time of our revolution; and such had been
> our Laws & usages, & such still are; that Religion is
> consider,d as the first object of Legislation; & therefore
> what religious privileges we enjoy (as a minor part of the
> State) we enjoy as favors granted, and not as inalienable
> rights: and these favors we receive at the expence of such

---

123. Correspondence included in the Appendices is reprinted with permission from and follows the format of the original: Documents from the Papers of Thomas Jefferson, Correspondence with the Danbury Baptist Association, 1801–1802, Daniel L. Dreisbach, *Thomas Jefferson and the Wall of Separation between Church and State*, app. 6 (2002) © 2002 by New York University.

degrading acknowledgements, as are inconsistent with the rights of fre[e]men. It is not to be wondered at therefore; if those, who seek after *power* & *gain* under the pretence *of government* & *Religion* should reproach their fellow men—should reproach their chief Magistrate, as an enemy of religion Law & good order because he will not, dares not assume the prerogative of Jehovah and make Laws to govern the Kingdom of Christ.

Sir, we are sensible that the President of the united States, is not the national Legislator, & also sensible that the national government cannot destroy the Laws of each State; but our hopes are strong that the sentiments of our beloved President, which have had such genial Effect already, like the radiant beams of the Sun, will shine & prevail through all these States and all the world till Hierarchy and tyranny be destroyed from the Earth. Sir, when we reflect on your past services, and see a glow of philanthropy and good will shining forth in a course of more than thirty years we have reason to believe that America,s God has raised you up to fill the chair of State out of that good will which he bears to the Millions which you preside over. May God strengthen you for the arduous task which providence & the voice of the people have cal,d you to sustain and support you in your Administration against all the predetermin,d opposition of those who wish to rise to wealth & importance on the poverty and subjection of the people—

And may the Lord preserve you safe from every evil and bring you at last to his Heavenly Kingdom through Jesus Christ our Glorious Mediator.

Signed in behalf of the Association,

Neh,h Dodge   )
Ephm Robbins   )   The Committee
Stephen S. Nelson   )

Appendix 2
Jefferson to Danbury Baptist Association (preliminary draft)

To messrs. Nehemiah Dodge, Ephraim Robbins, & Stephen S. Nelson a committee of the Danbury Baptist association in the state of Connecticut.

Gentlemen

The affectionate sentiments of esteem & approbation which you are so good as to express towards me, on behalf of the Danbury Baptist association, give me the highest satisfaction, my duties dictate a faithful & zealous pursuit of the interests of my constituents, and, in proportion as they are persuaded of my fidelity to those duties, the discharge of them becomes more & more pleasing.

Believing with you that religion is a matter which lies solely between man & his god, that he owes account to none other for his faith or his worship, that the legitimate powers of government reach actions only and not opinions, I contemplate with sovereign reverence that act of the whole American people which declared that their legislature should make no law respecting an establishment of religion, or prohibiting the free exercise thereof; thus building a wall of *eternal* separation between church and state. [Congress thus inhibited from acts respecting religion, and the Executive authorised only to execute their acts, I have refrained from prescribing even *those* occa-

prescribed indeed legally where an

sional performances of devotion, *practised indeed by the* Executive *of another*

a national

*nation as/*is the legal head of *it's* [sic] church, but subject here, as religious exercises only to the voluntary regulations and discipline of each respective sect.] *confin-*

adhering to this expression of the supreme will of the nation in half of the rights of conscience,

ing myself therefore to the duties of my station, which are merely temporal, adhering to, concurring with this great act of national legislation in behalf of the rights of be assured that your religious rights shall never be infringed by any act conscience   sincere satisfaction

of mine, and that I shall see with *friendly dispositions* the progress of those sentiments which tend to restore to man all his natural rights, convinced he has no natural right in opposition to his social duties.

I reciprocate your kind prayers for the protection and blessing of the common father and creator of man, and tender you for yourselves and
your religious
the Danbury Baptist association, assurances of my high respect & esteem.

Th: Jefferson
Jan. 1. 1802

Dreisbach's Note: In the manuscript of this draft letter, the italicized text is linked out. In addition, a line is drawn around the sentence bracketed in this transcription, and the following comment in the same hand is written in the left margin:

> this paragraph was omitted on the suggestion that it might give uneasiness to some of our republican friends in the eastern states where the proclamation of thanksgivings etc by their Executive is an antient habit, & is respected.

The manuscript of this draft letter reveals that Jefferson wrote and rewrote the last sentence of the second paragraph. He first wrote:

> confining myself therefore to the duties of my station, which are merly temporal, be assured that your religious rights shall never be infringed by any act of mine, and that I shall see with friendly dispositions the progress of those sentiments which tend to restore to man all his natural rights, convinced he has no natural right in opposition to his social duties.

He then apparently amended this sentence to read: "concurring with this great act of national legislation in behalf of the rights of conscience" (Jefferson apparently intended this sentence to continue with "I shall see with friendly dispositions the progress of those sentiments ..." from the initial draft). The opening words "concurring with" were replaced with "adhering to." Both of these versions were inked out before Jefferson wrote the final version, which reads:

> adhering to this expression of the supreme will of the nation in behalf of the rights of conscience, I shall see with sincere satisfaction the progress of those sentiments which tend to restore to man all his natural rights, convinced he has no natural right in opposition to his social duties.

At some point, Jefferson replaced "friendly dispositions" in the initial version with "sincere satisfaction."

Appendix 3
Postmaster General
Gideon Granger to Jefferson

G. Granger presents his compliments to The Presidt. and assures him he has carefully & attentively perused the inclosed Address & Answer—The answer will undoubtedly give great Offence to the established Clergy of New England while it will delight the Dissenters as they are called. It is but a declaration of Truths which are in fact felt by a great Majority of New England, & publicly acknowledged by near half of the People of Connecticut; It may however occasion a temporary Spasm among the Established Religionists yet his mind approves of it, because it will "germinate among the People,, and in time fix "their political Tenets,,—He cannot therefore wish a Sentence changed, or a Sentiment expressed equivocally—A more fortunate time can never be expected.—

Appendix 4
Jefferson to Attorney General Levi Lincoln

Th: J. to mr. Lincoln

Averse to recieve [*sic*] addresses, yet unable to prevent them, I have generally endeavored to turn them to some account, by making them the occasion,
by way of answer, of sowing useful truths & principles among the people, which
might germinate and become rooted among their political tenets. the Baptist
address now inclosed admits of a condemnation of the alliance between church
and state, under the authority of the Constitution. it furnishes an occasion
too, which I have long wished to find, of saying why I do not proclaim fast-
ings & thanksgivings, as my predecessors did. the address to be sure does not
point at this, and it's [*sic*] introduction is awkward. but I foresee no opportunity of doing it more pertinently. I know it will give great offence to the New
England clergy: but the advocate for religious freedom is to expect neither
peace nor forgiveness from them. will you be so good as to examine the answer and suggest any alterations which might prevent an ill effect, or promote
a good one among *the people*? you understand the temper of those in the North,
and can weaken it therefore to their stomachs: it is at present seasoned to the
Southern taste only. I would ask the favor of you to return it with the address
in the course of the day or evening. health & affection.

Jan. 1. 1802

Appendix 5
Attorney General Levi Lincoln to Jefferson

The President   )   Jany 1s. 1802—
of the U. States   )

    Sir I have carefully considered the subject you did me the honor of submiting to my attention. The people of the five N England Governments (unless Rhode Island is an exception) have always been in the habit of observing fasts and thanksgivings in performance of proclamations from their respective Executives. This custom is venerable being handed down from our ancestors. The Republicans of those States generally have a respect for it. They regreted very much the late conduct of the legislature of Rhode Island on this subject. I think the religious sentiment expressed in your proposed answer of importance to be communicated, but that it would be best to have it so guarded, as to be incapable of having it construed into an implied censure of the usages of any of the States. Perhaps the following alteration after the words "but subject here" would be sufficient, vis [?], only to the voluntary regulations & discipline of each respective sect, as mere religious exercises, and to the particular situations, usages & recommendations of the several States, in point of time & local circumstances. With the highest esteem & respect.

          yours,   Levi Lincoln

Appendix 6
Jefferson to Danbury Baptist Association
(final version)

To messrs. Nehemiah Dodge, Ephraim Robbins, & Stephen S. Nelson, a committee of the Danbury Baptist association in the state of Connecticut.

Gentlemen

The affectionate sentiments of esteem and approbation which you are so good as to express towards me, on behalf of the Danbury Baptist association, give me the highest satisfaction. my duties dictate a faithful & zealous pursuit of the interests of my constituents, & in proportion as they are persuaded of my fidelity to those duties, the discharge of them becomes more and more pleasing.

Believing with you that religion is a matter which lies solely between Man & his God, that he owes account to none other for his faith or his worship, that the legitimate powers of government reach actions only, & not opinions, I contemplate with sovereign reverence that act of the whole American people which declared that *their* legislature should "make no law respecting an establishment of religion, or prohibiting the free exercise thereof," thus building a wall of separation between Church & State. adhering to this expression of the supreme will of the nation in behalf of the rights of conscience, I shall see with sincere satisfaction the progress of those sentiments which tend to restore to man all his natural rights, convinced he has no natural right in opposition to his social duties.

I reciprocate your kind prayers for the protection & blessing of the common father and creator of man, and tender you for yourselves & your religious association, assurances of my high respect & esteem.

Th: Jefferson
Jan. 1. 1802.

Chapter 3

The Power of Rigor: James Madison

(March 16, 1751–June 28, 1836)
Presidency 1809–1817

We lawyers promise to represent our clients with both competence[1] and diligence.[2] That means we will be thorough, prepared, and diligent. In essence, we will be rigorous. We will do our homework about our legal writing audience — the judges we want to persuade. We will assemble the strongest arguments available on behalf of our client. We will anticipate all our opponent's counterarguments, and we will have answers for those counterarguments. We will consider the practical consequences of our proposed solutions to legal problems. We will summarize our position with eloquence and persuasion so that our readers agree that our position is the best possible solution.

James Madison's work is an example of effective rigor in writing. Madison's physical characteristics made him an unlikely candidate as a model for power and persuasiveness in communication. At 5'4" tall, he was the shortest of our

---

1. Model Rules of Prof'l Conduct R. 1.1 (2010) ("A lawyer shall provide competent representation to a client. Competent representation requires the legal knowledge, skill, thoroughness and preparation reasonably necessary for the representation.").

2. *Id.* R. 1.3 ("A lawyer shall act with reasonable diligence and promptness in representing a client.").

presidents.[3] He was shy, some say painfully so.[4] His speaking voice was weak.[5] He was physically frail, and many thought he would not live past young adulthood. Yet no less than Chief Justice John Marshall concluded that if eloquence—"the art of persuasion"—"includes persuasion by convincing, Mr. Madison was the most eloquent man I ever heard."[6] Madison showed enviable rigor in his preparation and work habits, perhaps in spite of his physical limitations. He did his homework. He took detailed notes during important events including his classes at Princeton and during the Constitutional Convention.[7] He thought of arguments and counterarguments. He puzzled out the logical conclusions and practical consequences of both those arguments and counterarguments. As for the written product that emerged, admittedly it was not always rigorous in the sense of containing tight analysis, logic, or syntax.[8] Madison's writings could be unformed,[9] workmanlike,[10] or sentimental.[11] But at his best, Madison's rigorous approach did produce rigorous content: writings that were precise, accurate, logical, anticipatory of other arguments, and persuasive. Fortunately for us Americans, his habit of rigor helped him develop some of the most significant political theories—and practical proposals—shaping our government.

---

3. Natl. Park Serv., U.S. Interior Dept., *Celebrating the American Presidency in America's*, https://web.archive.org/web/20100301211958/http://www.nps.gov/pub_aff/pres/trivia.htm (last visited Aug. 31, 2016). Madison, at about 100 pounds, was also the lightest president. *Id.*

4. *See* Garry Wills, *James Madison* 5 (2002) (Madison's "social relations were such that he did not even try to woo a woman until he was thirty-one, and then he chose an apparently easy target").

5. Robert Allen Rutland, *The Presidency of James Madison* 2 (1990).

6. Louis C. Schaedler, *James Madison, Literary Craftsman*, Wm. & Mary Q., 3d Ser., Vol. 3, No. 4, 515, 524 (Oct. 1946) (quoting Rives, *History of the Life and Times of James Madison*, II, 612n).

7. Ralph Ketcham, *James Madison* 30, 195 (1990).

8. Madison's First Inaugural has been called "unremarkable." Sean Wilentz, *The Rise of American Democracy: Jefferson to Lincoln* 139 (2005).

9. In college, Madison "fell into bad literary company" and wrote "in clumsy, scurrilous, boyish verses," but he abandoned that style and "was himself never again guilty of such bumptiousness." Schaedler, *supra* note 6, at 517–18.

10. As "our best committeeman," much of Madison's writing necessarily reflected his legislative talent and ability to simply finish the necessary work. *See* Wills, *supra* note 4, at 36.

11. Sometimes, when Madison was writing for the public, he descended "to the level of the popular." Schaedler, *supra* note 6, at 521. Schaedler notes that, after writing *The Federalist*, Madison "finally succumbed to the rising popular taste for inflated, elephantine diction." *Id.* at 533.

Lawyers should emulate Madison, even though he was not a lawyer.[12] In the ironic way that history often plays out, he is (next to Abraham Lincoln) perhaps the most lawyer-like president in his writing habits and style. This likely resulted in part from his classical education, which included some study of law.[13] Some scholars suggest that his legal study was extensive.[14] He needed to know law to succeed as a landowner and political leader, but he never wanted to become a lawyer.[15] Madison was always "[c]ognizant of legal arguments"[16] and approached problems with a lawyer's mentality.[17] Madison wrote like an accomplished lawyer: he was thorough, he was prepared, he viewed each problem from every side, and he knew the answers to all the questions about his position before his opponents had even formulated those questions. Jack N. Rakove emphasizes, "Madison … dissect[ed] issues and alternatives with a rigor that even his opponents respected. When he was done briefing an issue, it was hard for anyone to avoid perceiving the problem in the terms he had used."[18] In sum, Madison's writing was lawyer-like in the very best sense of that word.

Other scholars have thoroughly analyzed Madison's writings; they dissect Madison's writings to determine his intent and beliefs in an effort to discern the underlying meaning of those critical works.[19] This chapter does not purport to offer new historical analysis of either Madison himself or of Madison's writings,

---

12. *See America's Lawyer Presidents* 37 (Norman Gross ed. 2004) (noting that thirty-three of the fifty-five delegates to the Constitutional Convention were lawyers, but not the "Father of the Constitution"—James Madison).

13. *Id.*

14. For a fascinating article about Madison's study of law and a strong argument that he did perhaps study law in great depth, see Mary Sarah Bilder, *James Madison, Law Student and Demi-Lawyer*, 28 L. & Hist. Rev. 389 (2010).

15. Andrew Burstein & Nancy Isenberg, *Madison and Jefferson* 12 (2010) ("[A]lthough [Madison] never had any intention of becoming an attorney, he began the study of law in late 1773.").

16. John T. Noonan, Jr., *The Lustre of Our Country: The American Experience of Religious Freedom* 83 (1998).

17. Joseph J. Ellis recognizes all of Madison's qualities, "Though he had the demeanor and disposition of a scholar, he had the mentality of a lawyer defending a client, which in this case was a fully empowered American nation-state." Joseph J. Ellis, *American Creation: Triumphs and Tragedies at the Founding of the Republic* 103 (2007) [hereinafter Ellis, *American Creation*].

18. Jack N. Rakove, *Original Meanings: Politics and Ideas in the Making of the Constitution* 37 (1997) [hereinafter Rakove, *Original Meanings*].

19. Louis Schaedler points out that "Judgment of [Madison's] literary qualities is further confused by the fact that both the praise and the blame his style has received have been inspired by approval or disapproval of his political content rather than by literary judgment." Schaedler, *supra* note 6, at 515.

but instead focuses on when Madison's rigorous approach did result in writings that demonstrated that rigor—and could stand on their own as severely exact, precise, logical, and thorough. Madison's rigor in the task of writing, and the resultant rigor evident in his work product, was the key to his persuasiveness. Madison's story will likely be familiar to many, but the focus on his rigor will bring new insight to that story. Any lawyer would consider Garrett Ward Sheldon's assessment of Madison as the highest compliment: "His was a learned, rigorous mind producing tightly reasoned, persuasively argued texts."[20]

Madison's Biography and Writing Habits

Madison was born on March 16, 1751, into a line of Virginians who had owned plantations for over a century.[21] He spent his youth in Orange County.[22] Although formal education was scarce in the middle of eighteenth-century Virginia, eleven-year-old Madison attended a school where he received a robust education in subjects such as logic, philosophy, mathematics, astronomy, and French.[23] Under the direction of the Scottish-born Donald Robertson, this education was a complement to Madison's intellectual eagerness in the context of an agrarian upbringing.[24]

At age eighteen Madison "broke ranks with Virginia tradition" and attended the College of New Jersey (now Princeton) instead of the College of William and Mary.[25] Madison was already familiar with the ancients and "fashionable" writers such as Swift, Addison, and Steele.[26] The Reverend John Witherspoon, a Scottish Presbyterian clergyman professing the value of the Scottish Enlightenment, and Princeton's president during Madison's attendance, "warned his students against imitation of any author" and counseled familiarity with the "excellences of all the best writers."[27] Developing a unique style from his scholarship helped prevent Madison from becoming another one of the "justly forgotten imitators of Addison and of Pope."[28]

---

20. Garrett Ward Sheldon, *The Political Philosophy of James Madison* 2 (2001).

21. Wills, *supra* note 4, at 11.

22. Conover Hunt-Jones, *Dolley and "the Great Little Madison"* 1 (1977).

23. Jack N. Rakove, *James Madison and the Creation of the American Republic* 3 (3d ed. 2007) [hereinafter Rakove, *James Madison*].

24. Ketcham, *supra* note 7, at 19; *see also* Rakove, *James Madison, supra* note 23, at 9–11.

25. Hunt-Jones, *supra* note 22, at 2.

26. Ketcham, *supra* note 7, at 39.

27. Schaedler, *supra* note 6, at 515.

28. *Id.* at 518.

Madison's scholarship was rigorous before, during, and after his time at Princeton, where he compressed three years of coursework into two and remained for an additional year of study.[29] Madison took detailed notes and composed his own 122-page compilation entitled *A Brief System of Logick*.[30] In his notes, he frequently referred to "miscellaneous reading." For Madison, "miscellaneous" meant delving into subjects such as chemistry and agriculture.[31]

Although Madison did not make a strong first impression, he always impressed anyone who had further contact with him that he was quite sickly.[32] Conover Hunt-Jones noted:

> In terms of physical appearance alone, few famous men have suffered more at the hands of observers than James Madison. Comments on his smallness, sickly nature, awkward manner, and sallow complexion abound in the historic record, and one harsh critic even compared him to a "country schoolmaster in mourning for one of his pupils whom he had whipped to death."[33]

Sickness kept Madison from travels or work when little else could. His delicate form was a reason for pause to some: "No one ever described a personal encounter with James Madison as an inspirational moment."[34] Yet his precarious physique and his social awkwardness were not indicative of his talents or the respect he commanded after a first impression. Frances Few, Representative Albert Gallatin's sister-in-law, noted, " '[A] few moments in his company and you lose sight of these defects and will see nothing but what pleases you— his eyes are penetrating ... his smile charming ... his conversation lively and interesting.' "[35] Louisa Catherine Adams, John Quincy Adams's wife, also found him "a *very* small man in *person*" but "a 'lively' and 'playful' conversationalist."[36] Alexander Hamilton "described Madison as 'a clever man' who was 'uncorrupted and incorruptible.' "[37]

Princeton was not only a place for Madison to grow in intellectual rigor and knowledge, but it also influenced his interests and convictions. Madison's time

---

29. Rakove, *James Madison, supra* note 23, at 3; Ketcham, *supra* note 7, at 28.

30. Ketcham, *supra* note 7, at 32.

31. *Id.* at 519.

32. Madison's poor health included epileptic-like attacks. Wills, *supra* note 4, at 6.

33. Hunt-Jones, *supra* note 22, at 11.

34. Burstein & Isenberg, *supra* note 15, at 470.

35. Ketcham, *supra* note 7, at 476 (citing the *Diary of Frances Few, 1808–1809* (Ga. Dept. of Archives & History, Mar. 3, 1809)).

36. Rutland, *supra* note 5, at 21 (emphasis in original).

37. Rakove, *James Madison, supra* note 23, at 104.

at Princeton exposed him to a setting in which religious freedom was not simply tolerated, but defended.[38] As a young adult he cared about religious freedom more than any political issue, perhaps because most of his classmates were Presbyterians and thus dissented from Virginia's officially established Anglican Church. In a letter written at age twenty-two to his closest college friend, Madison complained bitterly about the imprisonment of unlicensed Baptist preachers near his family's home. He spoke of the "diabolical Hell conceived principle of persecution" and added, "I have squabbled and scolded[,] abused and ridiculed about it so long, to so little purpose that I am without common patience."[39]

Madison's interest in religious liberty, combined with his eye for subtlety and precision, led him to successfully liberalize conscience protection in The Virginia Declaration of Rights. He was twenty-five when he was elected to the Virginia Convention and "demonstrated for the first time what would be his greatest strength in committee, prior preparation."[40] This, his first important public act, was centered on the meaning of a single word and its unspoken implications.[41] The removal of the word "toleration" from George Mason's original draft of the Declaration happened at Madison's suggestion.[42] Madison's suggested language that "all men are equally entitled to the free exercise of religion according to the dictates of conscience" was ultimately adopted.[43] Ralph Ketcham, Madison's chief biographer, noted,

> The change was crucial ... because it made liberty of conscience a substantive right, the inalienable privilege of all men equally, rather than a dispensation conferred as a privilege by established authorities. Madison had made possible the complete liberty of belief or unbelief, and the utter separation of church and state.[44]

Madison's rigor during that Virginia Convention proved to be a lifelong, and formidable, quality. When writing to persuade, Madison achieved rigor through three habits: he considered his audience, he was always prepared, and he thought practically about real-world consequences.

---

38. Wills, *supra* note 4, at 16.

39. Letter from James Madison to William Bradford (Jan. 24, 1774), in *James Madison, Writings* 5, 7 (Jack N. Rakove ed. 1999) [hereinafter *James Madison, Writings*]). *See* Bernard Bailyn, *The Ideological Origins of the American Revolution* 260 (Enlarged Ed. 1992).

40. Wills, *supra* note 4, at 17.

41. Schaedler, *supra* note 6, at 516.

42. Ketcham, *supra* note 7, at 73.

43. Wills, *supra* note 4, at 17–18.

44. *Id.*

Considering Audience

Madison always considered his audience. He knew exactly who was likely to read his writing, and he wrote to address their concerns. He lined up rows of arguments and recapitulated them as he proceeded so that the audience would feel carried along to the inevitable conclusion. He thought of the objections his audience might raise, and he refuted those objections and counterarguments before the audience even had time to fully form them. Further, he knew who the important decisionmakers would be when the most important political questions had to be decided. In many instances he went to extreme lengths to ensure that the group of decisionmakers included those sympathetic to his position. Most notably, he convinced George Washington to come out of retirement to join the Constitutional Convention.[45] Washington "happened to be the only man in America whose sheer prestige instantly transformed a lost cause [the Constitutional Convention] into a viable contender."[46] Madison, in his habitual way, anticipated all of Washington's objections to representing Virginia at the convention and presented convincing arguments to counter all of Washington's concerns.[47] Madison did not stop there; he lobbied his fellow Virginia delegates to support his plan before the Constitutional Convention convened.[48]

Preparation

Madison was thoroughly prepared—indeed, he was typically the most prepared person in the room. Perhaps this was a result of his weakness as an orator.[49] Madison's voice was so soft that stenographers complained they could not hear him.[50] In contrast to the flamboyant oratorical styles of many other Virginia statesmen, "Madison stood out by being self-consciously inconspicuous. His style, in effect, was not to have one."[51] Madison did not like to im-

---

45. Ellis, *American Creation*, *supra* note 17, at 97–99.

46. *Id.* at 97.

47. *Id.* at 98. ("Madison's response to this litany of protestations [from Washington] was the political equivalent of guerrilla warfare.").

48. *Id.* at 108.

49. *Id.* at 101.

50. *Id.* at 100. The ratification debates in Virginia, in particular, frequently contain the notation that Madison spoke too low to be understood. *James Madison, Writings*, *supra* note 39, at 354, 387, 390, 400; *see* Burstein & Isenberg, *supra* note 15, at 179 (noting that Madison's voice was inaudible because he was recovering from a serious bout of illness).

51. Ellis, *American Creation*, *supra* note 17, at 100.

provise, and his thorough preparation meant that he rarely had to speak extemporaneously.[52] Joseph Ellis explains,

> [Madison was] always ... the most fully prepared participant, the kind of frustrating opponent who always had more relevant information at his fingertips and who also somehow understood the logical implications of your argument better than you did.[53]
>
> If God was in the details, so the saying went, Madison was usually there to greet him upon arrival.[54]

Madison's habit of preparation served him very well in another way: he was ready when political issues ripened. Madison is commonly regarded as the "father of the Constitution." But the reason he was able to write so many constitutional provisions, or their first drafts, was because he had "steeped himself in constitutional issues" since age 22.[55]

Madison worked hard, harder even than his hardworking contemporaries like Thomas Jefferson.[56] He valued the discipline his father exhibited on his Virginia plantation, and he lived his own life with discipline because he believed that discipline would prolong his life.[57] Madison's hard work began when he started thinking through a problem very early on. Part of that puzzling out of a problem happened while Madison took copious notes, a habit he prac-

---

52. Wills, *supra* note 4, at 14 ("And he was methodical in preparing his responses to situations beforehand, which meant that he rarely had to improvise on the spot.").

53. Ellis, *American Creation*, *supra* note 17, at 101.

54. Joseph J. Ellis, *Founding Brothers: The Revolutionary Generation* 54 (2000) [hereinafter Ellis, *Founding Brothers*].

55. Wills, *supra* note 4, at 37. Burstein and Isenberg sum up the persuasive power that Madison had developed, through preparation and credibility, by the time of the first Congress:

> He never aimed to convince by harangue or bluster. He did not make loud, disapproving signs, and he rarely made exaggerated claims.... He concentrated his thoughts and spoke to influence.... Madison was all about note-taking, thinking through his points in advance. Since he had years in the state legislature and national congresses to his credit, and with a well-earned reputation for meticulousness and thoroughness, others allowed him to set the agenda.

Burstein & Isenberg, *supra* note 15, at 191.

56. *See* Noonan, *supra* note 16, at 4 ("Overshadowed by Jefferson, Madison was the better workman.").

57. Wills, *supra* note 4, at 14–15 (Wills explains, "Madison's lifelong admiration of his father's plantation regimen dovetailed with his own great need for personal discipline, based on concern for this health.... He lived to be eighty-five thanks to that regimen.").

ticed throughout his lifetime.[58] He became the "unofficial chronicler" of the Constitutional Convention.[59]

Madison's preparation and discipline took the form of a scholarly approach. When faced with a problem, he read, studied, considered all sides, and anticipated all arguments. He was a diligent scholar and "omnivorous reader."[60] Historians often describe Madison as having done his "homework."[61] The most famous example of Madison's research was the study of confederacies, ancient and modern, that he undertook in the spring of 1787 in an effort to develop solutions to the increasing chaos in the American states under the Articles of Confederation.[62] He had received a "literary cargo" of books on government from Jefferson, then in Paris, in 1786.[63] Historian Douglass Adair described Madison's work in the spring of 1787 as "probably the most fruitful piece of scholarly research ever carried out by an American."[64] The research convinced him that the problems of confederacies of states were insurmountable, and it

---

58. Again, this may be attributed in part to his personality. A person who is uncomfortable interacting with others can avoid some of that interaction by furiously writing notes. Still, at least in some situations like during the Constitutional Convention, Madison knew that the notes would be valuable for American history. Sheldon, *supra* note 20, at 53–54. Madison also had an intellectual curiosity about how governments were formed. Schaedler, *supra* note 6, at 522 ("Madison's decision to keep a journal of the constitutional Convention was prompted partly by his scholarship and partly by his sense of the importance of the proceedings.").

59. Sheldon, *supra* note 20, at 53. Sheldon explains Madison's notetaking process: Madison was the unofficial chronicler of the convention and chose a seat in the front of the meeting room, in the center, where he could hear every delegate speak. Using shorthand during the sessions, Madison would write out completely each day's debates within a day or two of having recorded them.... The result, *Debates in the Federal Convention*, was not published until fifty years later, when Congress authorized its release in 1840. In it, Madison had recorded all the arguments over every aspect of the U.S. Constitution as well as the sectional and philosophical sources of those arguments. His own comments at the convention, [were] recorded in the third person....
Id. at 53–54.

60. *Id.* at 5.

61. *Id.* at 19.

62. *Id.* at 43.

63. Letter from James Madison to Thomas Jefferson (Mar. 18, 1786), *in* 2 *The Writings of James Madison: Comprising His Public Papers and His Private Correspondence* 224, 226 (Gaillard Hunt ed., 1910). Sheldon, *supra* note 20, at 49.

64. Douglas Adair, *Fame and the Founding Fathers* 134 (Trevor Colbourn ed. 1974) (*quoted in* Wills, *supra* note 4, at 26–27).

energized him to work at creating a central government that would act directly on the people rather than through the states.

Thinking Practically and Institutionally

Madison's persuasiveness also benefited from his habit of thinking through the practical consequences of ideas and how the ideas would need to be translated into institutions to be successful. This intellectual habit may have been encouraged by the Scottish "common sense" humanism that the Reverend Witherspoon taught at Princeton, which "became popular in late eighteenth-century America in large part because of its pragmatic outlook."[65] In the central example of Madison's translation of theory to practice, his study of confederacies—motivated by a practical desire to reform American government—led him to propose the structure of a new government that would act directly on the people and that would, at least in part, be directly elected. The Virginia Plan, of which he was the chief architect, became the basic structure for the Constitution, even though it was significantly changed along the way, and he was central to almost every major debate over the Constitution's provisions. Madison's *Federalist* writings, especially *No. 10* and *No. 51*, are viewed as classics of political theory.

> [But] [t]hese essays were not the work of an "ingenious theorist" toiling away in splendid isolation.... They were far more the product of experience and reflections on it.... Madison was an actor—indeed, more than—a thinker or writer, and his ideas grew out of his action.... His publications supporting the Constitution were not his chief political legacy.... That greater legacy was the Constitution, ... [n]ot so much the text itself as the deliberations that made it possible.[66]

Like lawyers, Madison started with concrete rather than abstract goals and, like good lawyers, he thought in concrete terms, translating theories into practice.

His pragmatism showed even in his response to the major defeats he suffered in the Constitutional Convention: the rejection of his proposed congressional veto over state laws and the delegates' decisions that the Senate should represent each state equally rather than (as Madison advocated) by population and be elected by state legislatures rather than (as he advocated) by the House

---

65. Terance S. Morrow & Terence A. Morrow, *Common Sense Deliberative Practice: John Witherspoon, James Madison, and the U.S. Constitution*, 29 Rhetoric Society 25, 30 (1999).

66. Jack Rakove, *Revolutionaries* 344 (2010) [hereinafter Rakove, *Revolutionaries*].

of Representatives. When his initial measures to restrict state power failed, Madison did not give up. "[R]ealizing that he would have to work with what he was given, he regrouped" and, for the remainder of the convention, sought to strengthen the power of other federal institutions besides the Senate, most notably the presidency.[67] His dogged pragmatism led him to take the lead in producing a Constitution that achieved his basic goal—strengthening central government—even if several of its particulars disappointed him.

Madison's Rigor at Work

The elements of Madison's rigor at work are visible in documents concerning three achievements in which he was most influential: the adoption of religious liberty in Virginia, the original Constitution, and the Bill of Rights. Not every Madison writing habit outlined above (consideration of audience, preparation, and thinking practically and institutionally) is present in the writings analyzed here. But each document shows multiple aspects of Madison's rigorous approach and the document's resulting contextual rigor. In the *Memorial and Remonstrance Against Religious Assessments*, Madison carefully thought of his audience and all counterarguments others might raise, explained the practical consequences of the proposed bill, and included many different, but well-developed arguments. Madison wrote *Federalist No. 10* only after years spent studying democracies, with a goal of drafting and defending the Constitution. He guided his audience to see that alternatives to an extensive republican government were not workable in the real world. He strengthened this appeal to readers by subtly reminding them of a small democracy's inherent faults, which helped convince them of his position. In his letter to Jefferson, Madison showed his rigor in considering all arguments both for and against the Bill of Rights, including the pragmatic consideration of what competing principle should, in the end, take precedence in light of the most pressing evil.

(The) Memorial and Remonstrance against Religious Assessments

Virginia made advances in religious freedom during the Revolution, enacting "free exercise of religion" in its Declaration of Rights over mere "toleration" at Madison's initiative. It also eliminated preferential tax support for

---

67. Burstein & Isenberg, *supra* note 15, at 161–62.

Anglican clergy in the late 1770s. But in 1784 Patrick Henry introduced a bill for a new state property tax "Establishing a Provision for Teachers of the Christian Religion."[68] More liberal than its predecessor, this tax would reimburse Christian ministers of all denominations; each taxpayer could designate which church should receive his payment.[69] Madison stemmed the bill's momentum by getting the vote in the House of Delegates delayed.[70] He then published the anonymous *Memorial and Remonstrance Against Religious Assessments* to persuade Virginia voters to pressure their legislators.[71] Voters signed both Madison's petition and others opposing the assessment bill, which was handily defeated.[72] From this success, Madison went on to convince the Virginia Assembly to pass Jefferson's Bill for Religious Freedom.[73]

The *Memorial and Remonstrance* is Madison's quintessential argument for religious liberty: for free exercise of religion according to individual conscience and for disestablishment of religion in the sense of ending not just government support for one faith, but government interference in religion generally. It is "probably the fullest and most thoughtful exposition of disestablishmentarian thinking at the time of the founding," one with "enduring appeal" for the cause of religious liberty.[74] In fifteen separately numbered paragraphs, each containing at least one argument, Madison set forth a case that was concise but also complete and rigorous.[75]

The *Memorial and Remonstrance* especially shows Madison's attention to his audience. He carefully considered what would persuade a range of Virginia voters that the assessment bill was a "dangerous abuse of power."[76] His first ar-

---

68. Noonan, *supra* note 16, at 71. Henry was responding to "concern at the seeming decline in public virtue and religion" after the Revolutionary War. John A. Ragosta, *James Madison's Memorial and Remonstrance against Religious Assessments*, Milestone Documents in American History 212, *available at* www.milestonedocuments.com.

69. Noonan, *supra* note 16, at 72.

70. *Id.*

71. Rakove, *Original Meanings*, *supra* note 18, at 310. "While the Memorial and Remonstrance is nominally addressed to the General Assembly of Virginia, the audience for Madison was the Virginia populace." Ragosta, *supra* note 68, at 215.

72. The *Memorial and Remonstrance* had 1552 signatories. Noonan, *supra* note 16, at 74.

73. Rakove, *Original Meanings*, *supra* note 18, at 311.

74. Michael W. McConnell, Thomas C. Berg & Christopher C. Lund, *Religion and the Constitution* 43, 47 (4th ed. 2016).

75. The fact that the *Memorial and Remonstrance* was a legislative petition limited the length and depth of arguments Madison could make. *See* Schaedler, *supra* note 6, at 522.

76. James Madison, *A Memorial and Remonstrance against Religious Assessments* preamble (1785) (reprinted in *James Madison, Writings, supra* note 39) [hereinafter Madison, *Memorial and Remonstrance*].

gument appealed to legal authority—that the tax would violate the Virginia Declaration of Rights—which Madison quoted:

> Because we hold it for a fundamental and undeniable truth, "that religion or the duty which we owe to Our Creator and the manner of discharging it, can be directed only by reason and conviction, not by force or violence."[77]

Madison wanted voters to recognize the value of the rule of law and the dire consequences that could result if it were not respected. He reminded them that Americans had recently fought for freedom from an oppressive government,[78] and he echoed the revolutionary language:

> The preservation of a free Government requires not merely, that the metes and bounds which separate each department of power be invariably maintained; but more especially that neither of them be suffered to overleap the great Barrier which defends the rights of the people. The Rulers who are guilty of such an encroachment ... are Tyrants.[79]

Tyrannical governments, he later emphasized, have often used established religions.[80]

Madison had to appeal both to relatively secularized, rationalist Virginian leaders and to the growing evangelical sects of Baptists and Presbyterians, dominant in the state's center and west, whose chief concern was keeping the Christian faith vital and pure. He knew the Baptists would oppose the assessment bill, but Presbyterians were initially divided and a cause of concern.[81] His first paragraph spoke to both rationalists and evangelicals by upholding both "reason and conviction" and by setting forth clearly the proposition that religion was outside government's authority and the social compact:

---

77. *Id.* ¶ 1.

78. *Id.* ¶ 3. Rakove notes the *Memorial and Remonstrance* "echoed the rhetoric of the earlier Revolutionary conflict, and thus evoked the conventional image of an ongoing struggle between the power of rulers and the liberties of the ruled." Rakove, *Original Meanings, supra* note 18, at 42.

79. Madison, *Memorial and Remonstrance, supra* note 76, ¶ 2.

80. *Id.* ¶ 8.

81. Mark S. Scarberry, *John Leland and James Madison: Religious Influence on the Ratification of the Constitution and on the Proposal of the Bill of Rights*, 113 Penn. St. L. Rev. 733, 751–52 (2009) (Virginia Baptists "vehemently opposed" the assessments bill); Thomas J. Curry, *The First Freedoms: Church and State in America to the Passage of the First Amendment* 144 (1986) (describing Madison's anger at the Hanover Presbytery's 1784 support of the assessment bill).

It is the duty of every man to render to the Creator such homage, and such only, as he believes to be acceptable to him. This duty is precedent both in order of time and degree of obligation, to the claims of Civil Society. Before any man can be considered as a member of Civil Society, he must be considered as a subject of the Governor of the Universe.... [E]very man who becomes a member of any particular Civil Society, [must] do it with a saving of his allegiance to the Universal Sovereign.[82]

The idea that religion lay outside government's cognizance could appeal both to the rationalist, for whom religion was a private matter, and the evangelical, for whom religious duties came first. Referring to the "Governor of the Universe" could appeal both to the deist, who believed that an impersonal God created the universe and then stepped aside, and to the evangelical, who believed that God directed the affairs of everyday life.

Madison appealed specifically to Christians. In one passage he warned all Christians, even those belonging to the current majority sects, that passage of the assessment bill could one day mean that their own sect would be persecuted:

Who does not see that the same authority which can establish Christianity, in exclusion of all other Religions, may establish with the same ease any particular sect of Christians, in exclusion of all other Sects?[83]

He reminded Christians that the assessment bill would likely discourage the spread of Christianity:

Instead of Levelling as far as possible every obstacle to the victorious progress of Truth [Christianity], the Bill with an ignoble and unchristian timidity would circumscribe it with a wall of defence against the encroachments of error.[84]

---

82. Madison, *Memorial and Remonstrance*, *supra* note 76, ¶ 1. Noonan points out that Madison remained consistent in this belief that the right of conscience was not surrendered to the state, "It was his consistent, coherent, bold position. If Mr. Madison had been a lawyer, it would be questioned as a lawyer's too close reading of language." Noonan, *supra* note 16, at 83.

83. Madison, *Memorial and Remonstrance*, *supra* note 76, ¶ 3.

84. *Id.* at ¶ 12 (adding that by discouraging nonbelievers from coming to Virginia, the tax would discourage them from seeing "the light of [revelation]") (brackets in original). Madison believed that the entanglement between religion and government would inhibit religion's growth. He explained this belief to Edward Everett: "[A] connexion between [government and religion] is injurious to both; that there are causes in the human breast, which ensure the perpetuity of religion without the aid of the law." He gave specific examples, in-

Perhaps resonating most with evangelicals was his argument "that ecclesiastical establishments, instead of maintaining the purity and efficacy of religion, have had a contrary operation," producing "pride and indolence in the Clergy; ignorance and servility in the laity; in both, superstition, bigotry, and persecution."[85]

With these concerns for the health of religion, Madison interwove concerns about the health of government and society. Most passionately, he warned that state interventions into religion had historically caused violence and suffering:

> Torrents of blood have been spilt in the old world, by vain attempts of the secular arm to extinguish Religious discord, by proscribing all differences in Religious opinions. Time has at length revealed the true remedy. Every relaxation of narrow and rigorous policy, wherever it has been tried, has been found to assuage the disease.... [If] we begin to contract the bonds of Religious freedom, we know no name that will too severely reproach our folly.[86]

He warned that the bill would undermine civic equality—the "equal title to the free exercise of Religion"[87] for non-Christians as well as Christians—and that by undermining America's promise of religious freedom, the bill would discourage immigration:

> Because the proposed establishment is a departure from that generous policy, which, offering an Asylum to the persecuted and oppressed of every Nation and Religion, promised a lustre to our country, and an accession to the number of its citizens.[88]

For the same reasons, it would trigger emigration.[89] Madison also suggested another civic danger: that laws "obnoxious to a great proportion of citizens, tend to enervate the laws in general."[90] And he threw in a procedural objection

---

cluding the thriving of the Episcopal Church in Virginia after it was no longer supported by the state, and concluded, "This proves rather more than, that the law is not necessary to the support of religion." Letter from James Madison to Edward Everett (Mar. 19, 1823), in *James Madison, Writings, supra* note 39, at 796.

85. Madison, *Memorial and Remonstrance, supra* note 76, ¶ 7. Madison was thinking, among other things, of "[t]he decadent and truncated religion of the Anglican establishment, which suppressed lively, vital Christianity." Sheldon, *supra* note 20, at 33.

86. Madison, *Memorial and Remonstrance, supra* note 76, ¶ 11.

87. *Id.* ¶ 4.

88. *Id.* ¶ 9.

89. *Id.* ¶ 10.

90. *Id.* ¶ 13.

based on the lack of fair representation in the Assembly, a particular complaint of voters in the underrepresented western part of Virginia.[91] Until Virginia had a democratic representation system, the proposed assessment bill could not represent the will of the people that the legislature had claimed to seek.[92] At the end of the argument, he returned to the theme of tyranny, warning that the principle underlying the bill would authorize the legislature to "swallow up the Executive and Judiciary Powers of the State" and "sweep away all our fundamental rights."[93]

The sheer number of arguments also demonstrates Madison's habit of thoroughly preparing with rigor. Judge John T. Noonan Jr. groups the arguments into theological (seven arguments), civic (ten arguments), and historical (two arguments)[94] and concludes that this topical arrangement "illustrates most graphically the nature and range of the considerations driving him."[95] Much of the "enduring appeal" of *Memorial and Remonstrance* comes because "it draws on such a broad range of disestablishmentarian thought."[96]

One might object to all these arguments on the ground that Madison was making a mountain out of a molehill: the assessment was small and, in a state where practically every citizen was Christian, highly ecumenical. Madison anticipated that objection early in the document, with one of the single best constructed arguments for constitutional vigilance in small matters:

> [I]t is proper to take alarm at the first experiment on our liberties. We hold this prudent jealousy to be the first duty of citizens, and one of the noblest characteristics of the late Revolution. The freemen of America did not wait till usurped power had strengthened itself by exercise, and entangled the question in precedents. They saw all the consequences in the principle, and they avoided the consequences by denying the principle.[97]

---

91. Ragosta, *supra* note 68, at 215.
92. Madison, *Memorial and Remonstrance, supra* note 76, ¶ 14.
93. *Id.* ¶ 15.
94. Noonan, *supra* note 16, at 72–74.
95. *Id.* at 72.
96. McConnell et al., *supra* note 74, at 47. Madison was also typically rigorous in thinking early about the issue, making notes in opposition to the bill as soon as it was introduced. Noonan, *supra* note 16, at 61–64, 72.
97. Madison, *Memorial and Remonstrance, supra* note 76, ¶ 3; *see also id.* ¶ 9 ("Distant as it may be in its present form from the Inquisition, it differs from it only in degree. The one is the first step, the other the last in the career of intolerance.").

He concluded the paragraph with the famous image that "the same authority which can force a citizen to contribute three pence only" for an establishment "may force him to conform to any other establishment in all cases whatsoever."[98]

This paragraph is rigorous in anticipating and confronting a counterargument. It is worth taking a moment, however, to note another aspect that could be called rigorous: its lean and powerful style. The sentence, "The freemen of America did not wait till usurped power had strengthened itself by exercise, and entangled the question in precedents" captures briskly what Eugene Volokh has labeled one of the "mechanisms of the slippery slope": a law that is enacted based on narrow justifications might later be seen "as endorsing a much broader principle" or power.[99] Madison's sentence describing government usurpation rushes by quickly, packed with meaning that one must study in order to comprehend. Its style therefore reinforces and dramatizes the warnings that he makes: that the assessment bill could rush through to enactment because it seemed innocuous and that it had to be scrutinized with suspicion for the precedent it would set. Like much great writing, the sentence has power because its form reinforces its substantive claims.

In passages like this, the *Memorial and Remonstrance* soars with eloquence.[100] As a general matter, Madison's detailed-oriented approach, its "studied distinctions and qualifications," did not lend itself to great phrasemaking like that of his friend Jefferson.[101] Sometimes, as in his first inaugural address as president, Madison was practically incomprehensible.[102] But he produced many elegant, eloquent phrases. For example, in just two paragraphs on separation of powers in *Federalist No. 51*, we find "Ambition must be made to counteract ambition," "If men were angels, no government would be necessary," and "th[e] policy of supplying by opposite and rival interests, the defect of better motives."[103] The *Memorial and Remonstrance* too is filled with memorable phrases—"It is proper

---

98. *Id.* ¶ 3.

99. Eugene Volokh, *Mechanisms of the Slippery Slope*, 116 Harv. L. Rev. 1026, 1089 (2003).

100. Eloquence sometimes results from a rigorous approach to writing, but most importantly it is another valuable writing quality. We can learn from Madison's rigor; but while we are studying him, we can also learn from those passages of his that are eloquent.

101. Rakove, *Revolutionaries, supra* note 66, at 341 ("Jefferson ... wrote more vividly, concisely, directly. Madison by contrast had a deserved reputation for prudence and thoughtfulness.").

102. *See* Wilentz, *supra* note 8, at 139 (Madison "mumbled through an unremarkable inauguration address").

103. *Federalist*, No. 51 (James Madison) (reprinted in *James Madison, Writings, supra* note 39, at 294, 295) (hereinafter *Federalist*, No. 51].

to take alarm at the first experiment on our liberties," and "Torrents of blood have been spilt in the old world"—and is worth reading in full.

The *Memorial and Remonstrance* was only one petition against the assessment bill; the evangelicals who provided most of the opposition presented petitions with more signatures.[104] Much of Madison's distinctive contribution came in legislative maneuvering and organization. But the elegance and comprehensiveness of his document have given it lasting effect. Today's Supreme Court cites it again and again[105] not just because of Madison's status as the First Amendment's prime mover, but because of the power of his rigorous arguments.

Federalist No. 10

Undoubtedly, Madison's most famous writing is No. 10 of *The Federalist*, which "has been called the 'most often anthologized, taught, studied, and remembered' of all American political writing."[106] It was the distillation of Madison's effort over several years to understand the weaknesses of American government and to design and enact a better alternative.

The immediate context for *The Federalist* was the ratification process after the Constitutional Convention, in which Madison had played a pervasive role. Proponents of the new Constitution and Union had to convince States that their best interest lay in surrendering some powers to a national government and sharing others. Several "states, or groups within states, saw no need, in terms of the matters then facing them, for a stronger central government."[107] Alexander Hamilton and John Jay approached Madison and asked him to help

---

104. Douglas Laycock, *Religious Liberty as Liberty*, 7 J. Contemp. Leg. Iss. 313, 345 (1996) ("[T]he single most common petition, with more than twice as many signatures as the *Memorial and Remonstrance*, came from evangelical Christians of unidentified affiliation.").

105. The *Memorial and Remonstrance* has been cited in thirty-two Supreme Court cases on religious liberty from 1947 to the present, including the vast majority of the Court's Establishment Clause cases. It is reprinted in full as an appendix to the dissent in the first modern Establishment Clause case, *Everson v. Bd. of Educ.*, 330 U.S. 1, 63–72 (1947) (appendix to dissent of Rutledge, J.). It is quoted for authority and persuasiveness by majority opinions and dissents, and by proponents of both sides on current issues. *Compare e.g. Rosenberger v. Rector & Visitors of U. of Va.*, 515 U.S. 819, 854–58 (1995) (Thomas, J., concurring) *with e.g. id.* at 868–74 (Souter, J., dissenting) (debating whether *Memorial and Remonstrance*'s principles would permit state university subsidies for student publications to extend to a student religious publication).

106. Michael I. Meyerson, *Liberty's Blueprint* 163 (2008) (quoting Albert Furtwangler, *The Authority of Publius: A Reading of the Federalist* 112 (1984)).

107. Ketcham, *supra* note 7, at 237.

draft a series of essays to tout the Constitution's merit.[108] Most of the essays were published in great haste—so great, Madison recalled, that there was "seldom time for even a perusal of the pieces by any but the writer before they were wanted at the press, and sometimes hardly by the writer himself."[109]

Federalist No. 10's famous argument is that an extensive republic—like the new federal government—is the most effective form of government to provide for liberty and neutralize self-interest and oppression. Madison reversed "[t]he conventional assumption, most famously articulated by Montesquieu, … that republics worked best in small geographic areas, where elected representatives remained close to the interests of the citizens,"[110] who in turn acted with civic-mindedness because they identified closely with the polity. Madison's experience with chaotic and squabbling state governments in the 1780s convinced him this assumption was wrong. In *Federalist No. 10*, and a series of writings leading to it, he "reversed the conventional logic."[111] No advantage of the new union, the essay began, "deserves to be more accurately developed than its tendency to break and control the violence of faction": the instability, conflict, and oppression in popular governments.[112] He defined faction as "a number of citizens, whether amounting to majority or a minority of the whole, who are united and actuated by some common impulse of passion, or of interest, adverse to the rights of other citizens, or to the permanent and aggregate interests of the community."[113] The first significant move was to define factions to include majorities—indeed, to identify majority oppression as the greatest danger under popular governments, since minorities seeking to oppress others would be quashed, in a democracy or republic, by majority rule.[114]

Madison then argued that faction would be better controlled in a republic (a representative system) than in a direct democracy, and in a large rather than a small republic. Representatives could "refine and enlarge" the views of the popular majority, and a large republic would be more conducive to electing

---

108. *Id.* at 239.

109. Letter from James Madison to Thomas Jefferson (Aug. 10, 1788), *in* 5 *The Writings of James Madison* (Gaillard Hunt ed. 1904) *available at* http://oll.libertyfund.org/?option=com_staticxt&staticfile=show.php%3Ftitle=1937&chapter=118843&layout=html&Itemid=27.

110. Ellis, *American Creation*, *supra* note 17, at 105.

111. *Id.*

112. *Federalist*, No. 10 (James Madison) (reprinted in *James Madison, Writings*, *supra* note 39, at 160) [hereinafter *Federalist*, No. 10].

113. *Id.* at 161.

114. "If a faction consists of less than a majority, relief is supplied by the republican principle, which enables the majority to defeat its sinister views by regular vote." *Id.* at 163.

worthy representatives.[115] But Madison quickly passed from the virtue of legislators to the "principa[l] [reason] which renders factious combinations less to be dreaded" in a large republic:

> The smaller the society, the fewer probably will be the distinct parties and interests composing it; ... the more frequently will a majority be found of the same party; and ... the more easily they will concert and execute their plans of oppression. Extend the sphere, and you take in a greater variety of parties and interests; you make it less probable that a majority of the whole will have a common motive to invade the rights of other citizens; or if such a common motive exists, it will be more difficult for all who feel it to discover their own strength, and to act in unison with each other.[116]

A single religious sect, or a group advocating "paper money," "an abolition of debts," or "any other improper or wicked project"—Madison showed his economic and class perspective here—would be more likely to be checked when decisionmaking was at the national level.[117] "In the extent and structure of the union, therefore, we behold a republican remedy for the diseases most incident to republican government."[118]

Before identifying the power of rigor in *Federalist No. 10*, it should be acknowledged that the essay's immediate effect was limited. *The Federalist* as a whole had "little impact on the struggle for ratification."[119] Moreover, *No. 10*'s specific argument was not picked up, or perhaps even understood, by many others at the time.[120] Indeed, Madison's belief in the structural advantages of the federal over state governments led him to make proposals that were rejected. He strenuously advocated that the Senate should have the power to veto state laws "in all cases whatsoever."[121] When he introduced what became the Bill of Rights—restrictions on the federal government—he included a pro-

---

115. Madison argued that worthier candidates would be elected in a large republic because the representatives in such a republic would be more distant from factions and because the larger electorates in a large republic would be less subject to the "vicious arts" of unworthy candidates. *Id.* at 165.

116. *Id.* at 166.

117. *Id.* at 167.

118. *Id.*

119. Rakove, *James Madison, supra* note 23, at 87.

120. *See e.g.* Larry Kramer, *Madison's Audience*, 112 Harv. L. Rev. 611 (1999).

121. *See* Rakove, *James Madison, supra* note 23, at 58–59 (describing this as "his most radical conclusion").

posal to bar states from violating rights of conscience, the press, or jury trial. That proposal, he argued, would be "the most valuable amendment on the whole list."[122] Both efforts failed; Madison was far more nationalistic at the time than most citizens or political leaders.

But *Federalist No. 10* remains worth studying. Its features of rigor characterized Madison's entire project of drafting and defending the Constitution, and those features are worth emulating. He achieved a huge amount, even if it was not everything he wanted. Moreover, eventually Madison's insight about the dangers of local majorities became embodied in the Constitution through the Fourteenth Amendment, which restricted state action, and its incorporation of the Bill of Rights against state government.[123]

The first feature of rigor in *Federalist No. 10* is preparation: it reflects years of study and analysis, refined in stages. It was not written under the same severe time pressure as later contributions, but if it had been Madison would have been ready anyway. Many earlier works illustrate Madison's preparation for the content of *Federalist No. 10*. After reading through the "literary cargo" from Jefferson in the winter of 1786, Madison drafted "Notes on Ancient and Modern Confederacies" and then a memorandum outline of "Vices of the Political Systems of the United States."[124] The "Vices" is "one of those rare documents in the history of political theory in which one can literally observe an original thinker forge his major discovery."[125] It catalogued the problems within and among the state governments under the Articles of Confederation—selfish parochial interests, disorganization, inadequate foreign relationships, and the internal oppression of minorities[126]—and led him to conclude the problems could be cured only by a central government that acted independent of the states. It also included, in effect, a draft version of Madison's argument for an extended republic, suggesting that "an enlargement of the sphere [might] lessen the insecurity of private rights" because "[t]he Society becomes broken into a greater variety of interests, of pursuits, of passions, which check each other."[127] By this time, April 1787, Madison had helped lead the charge for a convention to tackle the problems of the Articles, and he went to the Convention in May

---

122. James Madison, Remarks in Congress (Aug. 17, 1789), *in James Madison, Writings, supra* note 39, at 470.

123. Rakove, *James Madison, supra* note 23, at 233.

124. Sheldon, *supra* note 20, at 49.

125. Rakove, *James Madison, supra* note 23, at 52.

126. *Id.* at 50.

127. James Madison, *Vices of the Political System of the United States* (Apr. 1787), in *James Madison, Writings, supra* note 39, at 78–79.

"intent on seizing the initiative from the opening moments."[128] He arrived in Philadelphia nine days before the scheduled opening, "the first on the scene from any state other than the host," to have still more time to prepare.[129]

What Madison did not do in "Vices," but did do in *Federalist No. 10*, was add another level of rigor: addressing and countering alternatives to an extensive republic that opponents of a new union would raise. He drafted *No. 10* in a tight structure, presenting, at each stage of his argument, a dichotomy of possible solutions. First, Madison stated that faction can be dealt with "either by removing its causes" or "by controlling its effects."[130] To achieve the first solution, removing faction's causes, "[t]here are again two methods: the one, by destroying the liberty" to disagree, and "the other, by giving to every citizen the same opinions, the same passions, and the same interests."[131] But the former is "worse than the disease," since liberty "is essential to political life," and "[t]he second expedient is as impracticable as the first would be unwise. As long as the reason of man continues fallible, and he is at liberty to exercise it, different opinions will be formed."[132] Faction's causes cannot be removed; only its effects can be controlled. With this, Madison eliminated a slew of potential alternatives to a republican form of government. The essay continues to present dichotomies between a republican government and direct democracy, and between large and small republics.

This writing technique of creating and analyzing dichotomies, as Michael Meyerson has noted, "can be linked directly to a methodology for reasoning first introduced by Plato" in his dialogues *The Sophist* and *The Statesman*.[133] That technique has been described as "an elaborate tree-like system of roads" where "at each fork [readers] must choose which branch to take."[134] Using this method, Madison anticipates and answers counterarguments by presenting alternative possibilities to a large republic. He subtly yet forcefully guides his reader to his conclusion by presenting and answering alternative solutions.

Federalist No. 10 is also rigorous because it is practical: focused on the consequences of proposals and on how they will work in the real, rather than an

---

128. Rakove, *James Madison*, *supra* note 23, at 49.
129. *Id.* at 62.
130. *Federalist*, No. 10, *supra* note 112, at 161.
131. *Id.*
132. *Id.*
133. Meyerson, *supra* note 106, at 166.
134. *Id.* (quoting Mary Louise Gill, *Method and Metaphysics in Plato's "Sophist and Statesman,"* in *The Stanford Encyclopedia of Philosophy* (Edward N. Zalta, ed., Winter 2005)).

ideal, world. Clashes of interests are inevitable, because "[t]he latent causes of faction are sown in the nature of man," in "the connection ... between his reason and his self-love."[135] And "[i]t is in vain to say, that enlightened statesman will be able to adjust these clashing interests" for the public good. "Enlightened statesmen will not always be at the helm."[136] Madison, unlike many of his peers who were preoccupied with ideals about man's virtue, took an arguably realistic view of man's nature.[137] He looked to the structure and scope of the proposed republic to mitigate the negative effects on human nature. He did the same in *Federalist No. 51*, on the separation of powers, in which he argued that the natural human tendency to seek power meant that "[a]mbition must be made to counter ambition," and therefore the different branches must be not only separated but each armed with the power to "be a check on the other."[138]

The final section of *Federalist No. 10* focuses on how to control majority faction by controlling its effects. There, Madison conceives of two methods to achieve this end: first, to prevent a majority from ever having the same passion or interest; or, second, to disable a majority sharing a passion or interest "by their number and local situation."[139] Unlike the possible ways to suppress the causes of majority faction, Madison does not question the practicability or wisdom of these two ways to control the effects. Rather, accepting them, he demonstrates their legitimacy by showing how an extensive republic can achieve them, and he thereby legitimizes the extensive republic.

Before doing so, however, Madison shows how a pure democracy[140] cannot control the effects of majority faction: "A common passion or interest will, in almost every case, be felt by a majority of the whole; a communication and concert result from the government itself; and there is nothing to check the inducements to sacrifice the weaker party or obnoxious individual."[141] Within a pure democracy, which would necessarily be small, passions would spread like a fire and consume a majority. Under such circumstances, when "the impulse and the opportunity be suffered to coincide," Madison warns, "neither

---

135. *Federalist*, No. 10, *supra* note 112, at 161.

136. *Id.* at 163.

137. The well-known theologian Reinhold Niebuhr commended Madison: "[Madison] had no hope of resolving [social] conflicts by simple prudence. With the realists of every age he knew how intimately man's reason is related to his interests." Reinhold Niebuhr, *The Irony of American History* 98 (1952) (citing *Federalist*, No. 10, *supra* note 112).

138. *Federalist*, No. 51, *supra* note 103, at 290.

139. *Federalist*, No. 10, *supra* note 112, at 164.

140. Madison wrote, "a pure democracy, by which I mean a society, consisting of a small number of citizens, who assemble and administer the government in person...." *Id.*

141. *Id.*

moral nor religious means can be relied upon as an adequate control."[142] With
a propensity to be consumed by passion and no means to limit such a majority, Madison concludes that a pure democracy "can admit no cure for the mis-
chiefs of faction."

   To read Madison's attack on pure democracy in *No. 10* within the political
context of the eighteenth century should give pause to the trained eye.[143] Most
everyone in Madison's time was already fully aware of pure democracy's inherent faults and impracticability. Madison's strategy, Paul Peterson argues,
was the fruit of thoughtful consideration about his audience: "The reason
Madison discusses pure democracy is that ultimately his reader will see that
the defects of pure democracy [which he would likely concede] are also the defects of a small republic."[144] Because Madison's readers had a strong rational
and emotional attachment to small republics, they might not have been open
to seeing their defects if he had not started with a pure democracy.[145] The conventional wisdom of the time, based on Montesquieu and Aristotle, held that
a republic needed to be small to preserve the common good.[146] Antifederalists, opposed to ratification, argued that an extensive republic "[could not] be
governed on democratic principles," but required despotism.[147] Madison knew
that his audience needed to be eased into a discussion of the defects of what
they held dear. He first juxtaposed pure democracy and representative government, and then showed that a small republic was subject to the same ills
that everyone perceived in pure democracy.

   Madison gives three asserted deficiencies of a small, versus a large, republic. Two of them involve the greater difficulty of finding enlightened representatives.[148] The third, the "principa[l]" difference, most directly connects a
small republic to the accepted flaws of pure democracy, and Madison's phrasing bears repeating:

> The smaller the society, the fewer probably will be the distinct parties
> and interests composing it; the fewer the distinct parties and inter-
> ests, the more frequently will a majority be found of the same party;
> and the smaller the individuals composing a majority, and the smaller

---

142. *Id.*
143. *See* Paul Peterson, *The Rhetorical Design and Theoretical Teaching of* Federalist *No. 10*, 17 Pol. Science Reviewer 193, 206 (1987).
144. *Id.* at 206.
145. *Id.* at 207.
146. *See id.* at 195.
147. *Id.* at 196 (quoting "Centinel," in *The Antifederalists* (Cecilia Kenyon ed., 1966)).
148. *See Federalist*, No. 10, *supra* note 112, at 164.

the compass within which they are placed, the more easily they will concert and execute their plans of oppression.[149]

With this marvelously, rigorously constructed sentence, Madison draws the chain of reasoning especially tightly: note how each step in the argument begins with a repetition of the conclusion of the previous step. Having maneuvered his readers methodically into this position, Madison then springs the trap on those readers who opposed democracy but favored a small republic: "Hence it clearly appears, that the same advantage, which a republic has over a democracy, ... is enjoyed by a large over a small republic — is enjoyed by the union over the states composing it."[150]

Madison's method here was far more cunning and tactful in light of his audience than was Hamilton making the same point in *No. 9*:

> The opponents of the plan proposed have, with great assiduity, cited and circulated the observations of Montesquieu on the necessity of a contracted territory for a republican government. But they seem not to have been appraised of the sentiments of that great man expressed in another part of his work, nor to have adverted to the consequences of the principle to which they subscribe with such ready acquiescence.[151]

Hamilton continues by observing that Montesquieu had republics in mind that were already far smaller than many in existence among the States: "Neither Virginia, Massachusetts, Pennsylvania, New York, [nor] North Carolina can by any means be compared with the models from which he reasoned and to which the terms of his description apply."[152] Although Hamilton's point was valid, and was not even addressed by Madison in *No. 10*, Hamilton's bluntness in a hostile environment may be part of why *No. 10* stands out as the principal federalist document arguing for an extended republic. Indeed, throughout the two essays Madison wrote more subtly than Hamilton: "Madison's [introduction] suggested a subject for exploration and discussion," drawing the reader in; "Hamilton's introduction stated a proposition to be proved."[153]

And so Madison carried his reader to the conclusion — with several good lessons for persuasive writing. First, through a rigorous examination of dif-

---

149. *Id.* at 166.

150. *Id.*

151. *Federalist*, No. 9 (Alexander Hamilton) (reprinted in *The Federalist Papers* 41 (Clinton Rossiter ed., 1961)).

152. *Id.*

153. Schaedler, *supra* note 6, at 527.

ferent alternatives, he created the impression that he was covering every conceivable one. This is in part because he did cover many bases, and in part because he increased his credibility by doing so. Because of this, even if there are still more directions in which the reader might go, the reader experiences the text as if there is not. Second, Madison carefully considered his audience's sensitivities in favor of small republics, the object of his attack. He eased and led readers into supporting his position, rather than lambasting them with a series of blunt assaults. Bernard Bailyn, acknowledging that Madison was not the only federalist arguing for an extended republic, reflected that "[t]he difference between Madison and the other federalist writers who tackled the problem of size lay not in the point of the arguments but in the style and quality of argumentation. No other writer had Madison's cogency, penetration, knowledge, and range."[154] This rigor could only be the fruit of forethought and enabled him to address well the needs of his audience.

Madison to Jefferson on the Bill of Rights

One of Madison's many letters to Thomas Jefferson is a third example of Madison's rigor. Their thirty-year collaboration—"the most successful political partnership in American history," Joseph Ellis calls it[155]—produced religious disestablishment in Virginia, mobilized opposition to the Alien and Sedition Acts of 1798, and led to Jefferson's election as president over John Adams in 1800 and ultimately the demise of the Federalist Party. By the early 1790s, Madison had turned fearful of federal power as it was being exercised by Hamilton and had joined Jefferson in political war against Hamilton's centralist program. Usually Jefferson was the general, and Madison the lieutenant who drafted documents or tried to outmaneuver the Federalists in the legislature.[156] But the letter comes from 1788, the earlier period of the Constitution's creation and ratification: "Madison's most singularly creative moment,"[157] when he was driving the nation's agenda and Jefferson was far away as ambassador in Paris. The subject was the Bill of Rights, enacted as the first ten amendments to the Constitution, for which Madison played as central a role as he had with the original document.

Several of Madison's important letters to Jefferson over the years showed rigor in their attention to detail and their pragmatism. Although Madison often followed Jefferson's lead, he also frequently moderated Jefferson's extreme or

---

154. Bailyn, *supra* note 39, at 368.
155. Ellis, *Founding Brothers*, *supra* note 54, at 172.
156. *Id.* ("Jefferson was the grand strategist, Madison the agile tactician.").
157. *Id.*

impractical visions by subjecting them to lawyer-like analysis. For example, when Jefferson floated the idea that every constitution, law, and debt should expire after nineteen years—based on his famous dictum that "the earth belongs to the living and not to the dead"[158]—Madison rebuffed it, as politely as he could manage, "as not in *all* respects compatible with the course of human affairs."[159] He argued that, in both practice and theory, the "uncertainty" the measure would create would "subver[t] the foundations of civil society."[160] Madison's response exemplifies, as a dual biography of the two men remarks, how he "was predisposed to a structure that bent but did not break. No matter the issue, he always sought to uphold the usefulness of civil institutions."[161]

On a more pressing, practical issue, when Jefferson and Madison drafted protests by state legislatures against the Alien and Sedition Acts, Madison was careful to choose more measured language than Jefferson to characterize a state's right to challenge unconstitutional federal laws. Precision in word choice is central to the effectiveness of rigorous writing. Careful phrasing anticipates the effect of words on the audience and bolsters one's argument by anticipating the practical effect of arguments in future cases. Madison was careful in drafting his resolutions of protest. Jefferson's Kentucky Resolutions asserted the right of any single state to formally "nullify" such laws;[162] Madison's Virginia Resolutions invited other states to join as group to "interpose for arresting the progress of the evil."[163] Madison's terms were both "gentler" and "intentionally ambiguous"—to "interpose" meant "to mediate" a dispute, but it did not explain exactly how the states would intervene[164]—and this allowed him to challenge federal power without proposing, as Jefferson had, the chaotic course of allowing each state to refuse to follow federal law. Madison also was careful, unlike Jefferson, to include an argument that the antisedition law violated First Amendment freedoms of speech and press—thereby appealing to the supremacy of federal law rather than attacking it.[165] Shortly thereafter, in

---

158. Letter from Thomas Jefferson to James Madison (Sept. 6, 1789), *in Thomas Jefferson, Writings* 959, 963 (Merrill D. Peterson ed., 1984).

159. Letter from James Madison to Thomas Jefferson (Feb. 4, 1790), *in James Madison, Writings, supra* note 39, at 473, 474.

160. *Id.* at 476.

161. Burstein & Isenberg, *supra* note 15, at 207.

162. Thomas Jefferson, *Draft of the Kentucky Resolutions* (before 4 Oct. 1798), *in Thomas Jefferson, Writings, supra* note 158, at 450.

163. Va. Res. Against the Alien and Sedition Acts (Dec. 21, 1798), *in James Madison, Writings, supra* note 39, at 589.

164. Burstein & Isenberg, *supra* note 15, at 340.

165. *See* Ellis, *Founding Brothers, supra* note 54, at 200.

a face-to-face meeting, he talked Jefferson out of circulating ideas about the right of states to secede from the Union—a step whose consequences Madison would always regard as too dire.[166]

Madison's letter on the Bill of Rights came ten years earlier, on October 17, 1788, when he wrote from New York to tell Jefferson about the newly ratified Constitution and the amendments being proposed to it. Madison's position on a Bill of Rights was evolving. Along with other defenders of the Constitution, he had at first claimed such provisions would be unnecessary and perhaps even counterproductive: "Can the general government exercise any power not delegated to it?" he had asked Virginia's ratifying convention. "If an enumeration be made of our rights, will it not be implied, that everything omitted, is given to the general government?"[167] Once some states had ratified the Constitution without a bill of rights, he adamantly opposed Virginia or other states making their ratification conditional on amendments, which would trigger a whole new process.[168]

After ratification, Madison began to consider the possibility of a Bill of Rights, partly because it would help reconcile some of the Constitution's opponents and skeptics to the new system, and partly because he began to see benefits in it. Eventually, with his typical industry, he would become the prime mover behind the Bill of Rights.[169] His October 1788 letter to Jefferson shows his thought in transition, as he listed systematically the considerations for and against amendments. "My own opinion has always been in favor of a bill of rights," he said, because "it might be of use" provided it were drafted carefully; but he had "never thought [its] omission a material defect, nor been anxious to supply it ... for any other reason than that it is anxiously desired by others."[170] He set forth four reasons against amendments, three of which reiterated the earlier points that federal powers were already limited by enumeration and that the rights explicitly adopted would be too narrow.

---

166. *See* Burstein & Isenberg, *supra* note 15, at 345; Rakove, *James Madison, supra* note 23, at 153; Ellis, *Founding Brothers, supra* note 54, at 200 & n. 65.

167. James Madison, Speech in the Virginia Ratifying Convention on Ratification and Amendments (June 24, 1788), *in James Madison, Writings, supra* note 39, at 405.

168. *Id.*

169. Ellis, *Founding Brothers, supra* note 54, at 53 (after leading the campaign for the Constitution, Madison, "to top it off, ... drafted and ushered the Bill of Rights through the first Congress"); *see also* Paul Finkleman, *James Madison and the Bill of Rights: A Reluctant Paternity*, 1990 S. Ct. Rev. 301 (1990) (describing Madison's evolution and efforts).

170. Letter from James Madison to Thomas Jefferson (Oct. 17, 1788), *in James Madison, Writings, supra* note 39, at 418, 420.

His final negative argument, made in much more detail, was that bills of rights had proven ineffective when they were most needed: "Repeated violations of these parchment barriers have been committed by overbearing majorities in every State."[171] For example, he said, the religious-assessment bill would have passed in Virginia, despite the state's Declaration of Rights, had the majority not been turned against it.[172] Madison was still driven by his flash of insight that the majority could be more dangerous than a "usurping" set of rulers:

> In our Governments the real power lies in the majority of the Community, and the invasion of private rights is *chiefly* to be apprehended, not from acts of Government contrary to the sense of its constituents, but from acts in which the Government is the mere instrument of the major number of the constituents.[173]

Where the tyranny was the popular majority, rather than a few rulers, bills of rights would have limited value because "the tyrannical will ... is not to be controuled by the dread of an appeal to any force within the community."[174] This was why Madison thought the greatest threat to rights came from states, where a faction could more easily make a majority, and why he sought the congressional veto over state laws.

Nevertheless, Madison listed two arguments for a bill of rights, beyond the fact that many honorable citizens wanted it. First, "political truths declared in that solemn manner acquire by degrees the character of fundamental maxims of free Government" and might begin to moderate the majority: "as they become incorporated with the national sentiment, [they may] counteract the impulses of interest and passion."[175] Second, although the danger of oppression usually flowed from "interested majorities," "there may be occasions" when it would flow from "usurping" rulers, and in such cases "a bill of rights will be a good ground for an appeal to the sense of the community."[176] This was Madison's sober, balanced case for a bill of rights.

Madison's concern about the ineffectiveness of "parchment barriers" had an obvious answer, which Jefferson pointed out when he replied in March 1789. "You omit one [argument in favor of a bill of rights] that has great weight with

---

171. *Id.* at 420.
172. *Id.*
173. *Id.* at 421 (emphasis in original).
174. *Id.*
175. *Id.* at 422.
176. *Id.*

me; the legal check which it puts into the hand of the judiciary."[177] Majorities would not have their way as long as the Constitution was applied by judges insulated from electoral pressure. For some reason Madison had ignored the power of judicial review in limiting majorities, perhaps because he had focused so on his idea of a congressional veto over state laws. But Madison accepted the point, and when he introduced the bill of rights in Congress in June 1789, he argued that it would have "a salutary effect" because "independent tribunals of justice will consider themselves in a peculiar manner the guardian of those rights," resisting "every assumption of power in the legislative or executive."[178]

The letter to Jefferson is therefore only a way station toward Madison's final position on the Bill of Rights. When he introduced the proposals in June, he showed his typical rigor—in the sense of thoroughness—by making a speech accumulating multiple arguments, including the fact that the judiciary would enforce the provisions and that many respectable citizens wanted them.[179] The letter to Jefferson is also important, however, for a more general reason related to rigor in thought. It expresses Madison's pragmatism: his lawyer-like commitment to assess particular circumstances, to recognize that evils may come from different sources and that the right response depends on judging where the greater threat lies at a given time. He suggested that his own focus on majority tyranny came from seeing the problems of popular government in America, while Jefferson's fear of usurping rulers came from living in monarchical France:

> Wherever the real power in a Government lies, there is the danger of oppression. [The danger of majority tyranny] is probably more strongly impressed on my mind by facts, and reflections suggested by them, than on yours which has contemplated abuses of power issuing from a very different quarter.[180]

Later in the letter, Madison worried that the danger in the America of the 1780s was not too much government, but too little:

> Power when it has attained a certain degree of energy and independence goes on generally to further degrees. But when below that degree, the direct tendency is further degrees of relaxation, until the abuses of liberty beget a sudden transition to an undue degree of

---

177. Letter from Thomas Jefferson to James Madison (Mar. 15, 1789), *in Thomas Jefferson, Writings, supra* note 158, at 943.

178. James Madison, *Speech in Congress Proposing Constitutional Amendments* (June 8, 1789), *in James Madison, Writings, supra* note 39, at 437, 449.

179. *Id.*

180. *Id.* at 421.

power.... [I]n the latter sense only is [the danger of government power] in my opinion applicable to the Governments in America. It is a melancholy reflection that liberty should be equally exposed to danger whether the Government have too much or too little power, and that the line which divides these extremes should be so inaccurately defined by experience.[181]

The sense of precarious balance between liberty and order echoes his statement in *Federalist No. 51* that "the great difficulty in government lies in this: You must first enable the government to control the governed; and in the next place, oblige it to control itself."[182] Striking the balance, he suggests, involves good judgment and strenuous—rigorous—attention to detail and circumstances.

Madison shifted his judgments throughout his life. He later joined Jefferson in believing passionately that the greatest threats in America came from ruling cabals (led by Hamilton) rather than the people, and from the federal government rather than the states. Some observers, then, and in the years since, have found his positions irreconcilable under any principle—a product, perhaps, of his desire to protect Virginia's interests, particularly its ability to continue slavery, from whatever threatened them at the moment. But in his old age, Madison wrote several letters against Southern doctrines of secession, nullification, and disregard of federal-court decisions: he defended the Union while still emphasizing that federal power was limited.[183]

In any event, whether Madison's judgments were wrong or excessive at various times, his writing points to one of the public servant's crucial tasks: to consider competing principles and judge which is more applicable, or consider competing evils and judge which is more pressing, in a given situation. To carry out that task effectively, the public servant must employ rigor. Anthony Kronman has written of the ideal "lawyer-statesman" who combines public-spiritedness with the common-law skill of "practical wisdom": a "subtle and discriminating sense of how the (often conflicting) generalities of legal doctrine should be applied in particular disputes."[184] The "subtle and dis-

---

181. *Id.* at 422.

182. *Federalist*, No. 51, *supra* note 103, at 294, 295.

183. *See e.g.* Letter from James Madison to Edward Everett (Aug. 28, 1830), *in James Madison, Writings, supra* note 39, at 842, 847 ("[I]t is perfectly consistent with the concession of this power to the Supreme Court ... to maintain that the power has not always been rightly exercised."); *id.* at 850 (nullification); Letter from James Madison to Nicolas P. Trist, *id.* at 861; Letter from James Madison to William Cabell Rives, *id.* at 863.

184. Anthony T. Kronman, *The Lost Lawyer: Failing Ideals of the Legal Profession* 21 (1995).

criminating" approach to disputes is essentially the same as the "studied distinctions and qualifications"[185] that Madison, the founding statesman, made. He drew subtle distinctions not for their own sakes, but in order to manage the difficult choices between liberty and order, between central and local power, between popular government and minority rights. Lawyers, too, in the more typical tasks of representing or advising clients, must judge which course of action follows the principles that are most applicable and avoids the harms that are most dangerous or immediate. Making those fine judgments calls for rigorous, precise distinctions, in thought and in writing. Lawyers can therefore benefit from absorbing the best writings, and emulating the habits, of the founder who paid lawyerly attention to detail precisely because he recognized the challenge of making legal and political decisions in a complex world.

Madison's life should be a source of encouragement to lawyers who think they lack physical presence or personal charisma. "The great little Madison" overcame those limitations to become one of the most influential public figures in American history. He did so, like all successful professionals, by relying on and cultivating his distinctive strengths. He had an analytical mind that he cultivated to see and clearly express arguments, counterarguments, and distinctions. He had, despite poor health, an appetite for work that he cultivated in order to out-prepare others. And he had a sensitivity to surrounding circumstances that he cultivated to address his audience's concerns and to envision the practical consequences of various actions. The key habits of Madison that lawyers should emulate—attention to audience, careful preparation, and attention to consequences—are difficult to summarize in one concept, but "rigor" best fits the bill. Rigor in this sense can make a lawyer forceful who lacks other qualities. Madison, unprepossessing and soft-speaking, was still eloquent. Remember the verdict of Chief Justice Marshall: "If [eloquence] includes persuasion by convincing, Mr. Madison was the most eloquent man I ever heard."[186]

---

185. Rakove, *Revolutionaries*, *supra* note 66, at 341.

186. Schaedler, *supra* note 6, at 524 (quoting Rives, *History of the Life and Times of James Madison*, II, 612*n*).

Chapter 4

The Power of Brevity: Abraham Lincoln

(February 12, 1809–April 15, 1865)
Presidency 1861–1865

Abraham Lincoln is often lauded as our most eloquent president, and "Lincoln's eloquence may prove to be his most lasting legacy."[1] Picking one specific quality of Lincoln's writing talent, his use of brevity, certainly does not mean this was his only literary skill. Lincoln used many rhetorical devices very effectively including alliteration, rhyme, repetition, contrast, balance, and metaphor.[2] Lincoln loved poetry from his childhood to the time of his death.[3] Both the Gettysburg Address and the Second Inaugural have been called prose poems.[4] Lincoln often chose to forego brevity in favor of another rhetorical device. Still, Lincoln's eloquence was grounded in his ability to express much with few words—and brevity is the focus here because it is so critical for legal writers.

---

1. Ronald C. White, Jr., *The Eloquent President: A Portrait of Lincoln Through His Words* 308 (2005) [hereinafter White, *The Eloquent President*].

2. Theodore C. Sorenson, *A Man of His Words*, Smithsonian 102–03 (Oct. 2008).

3. Douglas L. Wilson, *Honor's Voice: The Transformation of Abraham Lincoln* 71 (1998) [hereinafter Wilson, *Honor's Voice*]. Lincoln loved all forms of literature. Fred Kaplan, *Lincoln: The Biography of a Writer* 292 (2008) (noting that Lincoln was an avid reader of literary anthologies, Shakespeare, Bryon, Burns, and the Bible). Kaplan contends that John Quincy Adams is the only other president who loved literature as much as Lincoln. *See id.* at 346.

4. Douglas L. Wilson, *Lincoln's Sword: The Presidency and the Power of Words* 266 (2006) [hereinafter Wilson, *Lincoln's Sword*].

Lincoln scholars point out that Lincoln could have had a very successful career as a professional writer.[5] But what many Lincoln scholars fail to acknowledge is that Lincoln, like all lawyers, WAS a professional writer. That is one reason why he is the ideal hero for legal writers. Not only was he one of us, but he also learned the persuasive power of brevity while practicing law. The other reason he is an ideal hero is because Lincoln never fails to fascinate. Over 16,000 books have been written about Lincoln, and more titles appear every week.[6] Examining anything about Lincoln is considered a "mother lode" for writers and publishers, and "an old joke proclaimed that the ideal surefire best-seller would be a book entitled Lincoln's Doctor's Dog."[7]

Lincoln used brevity to persuade in the First Inaugural, the Gettysburg Address, and the Second Inaugural, and those three speeches continue to inspire and persuade us. We fellow lawyers should adopt Lincoln's habits of writing early, visualizing audience, and ruthlessly editing. Lincoln worked hard for his eloquence and persuasiveness, and by adopting his habits we lawyers can also increase our eloquence and persuasiveness.

Lincoln as Lawyer: Learning the Value of Brevity

Other writing professionals use brevity to persuade. One of the most poignant examples comes from literature. According to legend, friends bet Ernest Hemingway that he could not write a short story in six words. Supposedly, Hemingway returned the next day with his six-word masterpiece, "For sale: Baby shoes. Never used."[8]

---

5. Douglas L. Wilson notes, "Lincoln has thus become one of the most admired of all American writers. 'Alone among American presidents,' Edmund Wilson has written, 'it is possible to imagine Lincoln, grown up in a different milieu, becoming a distinguished writer of a not merely political kind.'" Wilson, *Lincoln's Sword, supra* note 4, at 4 (quoting Edmund Wilson, *Patriotic Gore: Studies in the Literature of the American Civil War* 122 (1962)). Lincoln Biographer Fred Kaplan notes that Lincoln and Thomas Jefferson were the American presidents who most eloquently expressed the national concerns, but nothing Jefferson wrote during his presidency has "a permanent place in the literary or political canon." Kaplan, *supra* note 3, at 320–21.

6. Frank J. Williams, *Abraham Lincoln: Commander in Chief or "Attorney in Chief?*," 18 Spring Experience 12, 13 (Spring 2008) [hereinafter *"Attorney in Chief?"*] (Frank J. Williams is retired Chief Justice of the Rhode Island Supreme Court and a lifelong Lincoln scholar).

7. Maury Klein, *Book Review*, 9 Roger Williams U. L. Rev. 213, 215 (2003) (reviewing *Judging Lincoln* by Frank J. Williams).

8. In some versions the last word in the short story is "worn" instead of "used." *See* https://web.archive.org/web/20091226094521/http://www.cliffsnotes.com/WileyCDA/Section/ In-which-Hemingway-short-story-is-the-saying-Childrens-shoes-for-sale-.id-305403,article

Lincoln's particular skill in persuading with brevity was honed during his days practicing law.[9] It was during this critical time that he developed his "judgment, lucidity of expression, and unforgettable prose."[10] Lincoln spent 25 years practicing law before becoming President of the United States, but his legal career was initially ignored by historians.[11] This oversight is somewhat surprising because, even though over half of the American presidents have been lawyers, "no other president spent quite so much time inside a courtroom; and the law had never exercised quite so exclusive an influence over a chief executive."[12] One notable exception was Benjamin P. Thomas, who wrote a 1952 biography of Lincoln, and described how Lincoln's life as a lawyer influenced his presidency. Mark Steiner explains, "Thomas ... concluded that Lincoln's presidential speeches and writings were a product of his legal training. In Lincoln's state papers, he 'manifested that capacity to understand an opponent's point of view, and to present his own case clearly and simply, which he had so painstakingly acquired as a circuit lawyer.'"[13]

More is known today about Lincoln's legal practice than in any previous time.[14] Research into Lincoln's legal career has been greatly enhanced by the Lincoln Legal

---

Id-41062.html (archived Dec. 26, 2009) (noting that Hemingway scholars are not able to confirm that he wrote this story, but neither are they able to prove that he did not write the story). This myth inspired one new book, Larry Smith & Rachel Fershleiser, *Not Quite What I Was Planning: Six-Word Memoirs by Writers Famous & Obscure* (SMITH Magazine 2008). *See* http://litpark.com/2008/02/06/smith-magazine/ (last visited Aug. 31, 2016).

9. Without specifically mentioning brevity, Justice Williams notes,
    This goal [political leadership] remained primary in the imperatives which animated his very being. But, having said that, it is clear that devotion to the law was a significant aspect of Abraham Lincoln's life. As I hope to demonstrate in this article, in achieving his political goals, he constantly utilized skills and tactics honed in the courtroom and in other phases of his legal life.
Williams, *"Attorney in Chief?," supra* note 6, at 13–14.

10. Mark Steiner, *An Honest Calling: The Law Practice of Abraham Lincoln* 23 (2006) (citing John J. Duff, *A. Lincoln, Prairie Lawyer* 345, 368–69 (1960)).

11. For an excellent discussion of the early books discussing Lincoln's legal career, *see id.* at 5–25 (chapter one of Steiner's book is entitled, "Lawyer Lincoln in American Memory"). In 1906, a book review in the Yale Law Journal became the first to cite a book about Lincoln's career as a lawyer. *Book Review*, 16 Yale L.J. 154 (1906) (reviewing Frederick Trevor Hill's *Lincoln the Lawyer* and noting that "little attention has been given to [Lincoln's] professional career"); *see also* Duff, *supra* note 10; Robert Littler, *Book Review*, 15 Stan. L. Rev. 146 (1962) (reviewing John P. Frank's *Lincoln as a Lawyer);* John Maxcy Zane, *Lincoln, the Constitutional Lawyer* (1932).

12. Brian Dirck, *Lincoln the Lawyer* 171 (2007).

13. Steiner, *supra* note 10, at 15 (quoting Benjamin P. Thomas, *Abraham Lincoln: A Biography* 410 (1952)).

14. Williams, "Attorney in Chief?," supra note 6, at 13.

Papers project which compiled all the available court records from Lincoln's state and federal cases. The researchers for the project went to 88 Illinois counties, other states, and Washington, D.C. to study Lincoln's legal career, which lasted from 1836 to 1861.[15] As a result of this project which was completed in 2000 after 15 years of work, several new books about Lincoln the lawyer are available.[16]

Studying Lincoln's career as a lawyer raises several questions, and competing scholars take opposing views on many issues. Was he a masterful lawyer[17] or merely an average practitioner whose legal career would not be studied or found significant if he had never become President of the United States?[18] Did Lincoln have a special insight into the hearts and minds of people,[19] or did he practice law with an intentional distance from both his clients and his colleagues?[20] Was Lincoln the lawyer a champion of freedom, a supporter of slaveholders' rights, a frontier philosopher, a gifted student of human nature, or a practical lawyer who worked to reduce friction by resolving disputes?[21]

One fact is not contested: "Lincoln was a lawyer, and he thought and spoke like a lawyer."[22] Lincoln used clear, simple language when arguing a case be-

---

15. Abraham Licoln Online, *Lincoln Legal Practice DVD-ROM Released,* abrahamlincoln.org, http://showcase.netins.net/web/creative/lincoln/news/dvdrom.htm (last visited Aug. 31, 2016).

16. Dirck, *supra* note 12; Julie M. Fenster, *The Case of Abraham Lincoln* (2007); Allen D. Spiegel, *Lincoln, Esquire: A Shrewd, Sophisticated Lawyer in His Time* (2002); Steiner, *supra* note 10; Frank J. Williams, *Judging Lincoln* (2002).

17. *See* Steiner, *supra* note 10, at 18 ("Abraham Lincoln is one of the great heroes of the American legal profession.").

18. Dirck, *supra* note 12, at 142 ("Lincoln the great American was in reality a pretty ordinary attorney."); Steiner, *supra* note 10, at 55 ("While Lincoln had an extraordinary life, he also had a relatively ordinary law practice. If Lincoln hadn't become president, it's doubtful that his law practice would have been noticed by later historians.").

19. Doris Kearns Goodwin, *Team of Rivals* 703 (2005).

20. Dirck, *supra* note 12, at 7. Dirck also emphasizes the professional balance lawyers need because of the changing nature of the profession when adversaries one day can become co-counsel or even judge and advocate the next day. *Id.* at 43.

21. *Id.* at 154–55. Dirck explains his new theory about Lincoln as "grease":

[Lincoln's law practice] taught him about the value of grease—that unglamorous, often overlooked but vital substance that lubricates and reduces friction to acceptable levels, that slips between the cogs and devices of machines and allows continuous movement without malfunction.

Lincoln's age sorely needed grease....

Abraham Lincoln the attorney applied his own form of grease, in a multitude of visible and not so visible ways.

Id. at 155.

22. Jerry J. Phillips, *Uncommon Predicates: Notes on Lincoln's Second Inaugural Address,* 72 Tenn. L. Rev. 807, 810 (2005).

fore a jury.[23] He avoided technical language but instead used a conversational tone.[24] Lincoln the lawyer used a common language to appeal to the average person.[25] He did not quibble over nonessential matters and was known to say he "reckoned" it was fair to allow a certain piece of evidence or admit the truth if he knew something was true.[26] He never yielded anything essential, and, "Many a rival lawyer was lulled into complacency as Lincoln conceded, say, six out of seven points in argument, only to discover that the whole case turned on the seventh point."[27] Lincoln did not waste his arguments. He saved his words, and used just the necessary number of those words, for essential matters.

Lincoln's years spent practicing law "shaped his use of language at various points throughout his political career, giving him a high degree of clarity and a judicious use of words."[28] It might be entertaining to consider whether Lincoln would have turned out differently had he been a farmer or teacher,[29] but his skillful use of brevity was tied particularly to his choice to become a lawyer.

Lincoln as President: Using the Power of Brevity

Lincoln continued to use brevity's persuasive power when writing some of his great presidential speeches. Lincoln wrote for the live audience who would listen to his speeches. He lived at a time when the spoken word was prioritized, so "Lincoln worked hard to learn the dynamics of the spoken word.... His personal magnetism came to life through the ear, not the eye."[30] Yet Lincoln also wrote for the reader, knowing that his speeches would be transcribed in newspapers across the country, and his message could reach thousands of people.[31] The spoken and written words were identical because newspaper reporters used shorthand to record the speech exactly as it was delivered.[32]

---

23. David Herbert Donald, *Lincoln* 145 (1995).

24. *Id.* at 98.

25. *See* Kaplan, *supra* note 3, at 234–35.

26. Donald, *supra* note 23, at 149. Lincoln did not yield essentials. Leonard Swett, a Bloomington lawyer who traveled the circuit with Lincoln, said that Lincoln only gave away what he could not get and keep.

27. *Id.*

28. Dirck, *supra* note 12, at 152.

29. *Id.* at 12–13.

30. *See* Ronald C. White, Jr., *Lincoln's Greatest Speech: The Second Inaugural* 69, 72 (2002) [hereinafter White, *Lincoln's Greatest Speech*].

31. *Id.* at 187.

32. *Id.* at 70.

The speed at which Lincoln's printed speeches spread across the country changed dramatically during his four years as president. The First Inaugural made its way to California via the Pony Express,[33] while The Second Inaugural traveled the day after it was delivered from New York to California via the just completed transcontinental telegraph line.[34]

Lincoln valued both speaking and writing, but believed that writing was "the supreme artifact of human genius."[35] Lincoln also praised printing for its ability to distribute the written word to thousands.[36] Throughout his life, Lincoln relied on newspapers for his education.[37] While in his 20s, he often read newspapers out loud to others.[38] He learned by reading out loud, and he also believed that reading out loud "made him more retentive by giving him the sound as well as the sight of the words."[39] A complete understanding of Lincoln's eloquent use of brevity cannot be gleaned from analyzing only three speeches.[40] Still, a review of the First Inaugural, the Gettysburg Address, and the Second Inaugural gives us at least a glimpse into the importance of brevity in Lincoln's work.

Editing for Brevity — The First Inaugural

Lincoln's First Inaugural was delivered from Lincoln, the lawyer, making a case to the jury, the people of the North and South.[41] This first speech Lincoln gave as president is an example of how he valued brevity while he was

---

33. The First Inaugural reached California by both telegraph and the Pony Express. "The speech was first telegraphed from New York to Kearney, Nebraska. Lincoln's words were then placed in the saddlebags of Pony Express riders for their relay across plains and mountains to Folsom, California. The [First] inaugural was then telegraphed to Sacramento and from there to other points in the far West." White, *The Eloquent President, supra* note 1, at 94.

34. White, *Lincoln's Greatest Speech, supra* note 30, at 183 (Western Union connected the telegraph wired from New York to San Francisco on March 5, 1865, the day after Lincoln delivered the Second Inaugural).

35. Kaplan, *supra* note 3, at 291.

36. White, *Lincoln's Greatest Speech, supra* note 30, at 187.

37. Wilson, *Honor's Voice, supra* note 3, at 62.

38. *Id.*

39. *Id.*

40. White notes that "[a] purpose of this book is to see Lincoln's speeches as a string of pearls. Each pearl, although of different color and size, possesses its own beauty." White, *Lincoln's Greatest Speech, supra* note 30, at 224.

41. White, *The Eloquent President, supra* note 1, at 97 (noting also that Lincoln relied on precedent by referring to his previous political speeches, his own precedential legal arguments, dating back into the late 1850s).

editing.[42] Lincoln asked several people to read and comment on a draft of his First Inaugural. He asked Judge David Davis from Springfield, Illinois, to read the speech, but Judge Davis made no suggested changes. He also asked fellow lawyer Orville H. Browning who offered a single suggestion that Lincoln delete the clause "to reclaim the public property and places which have fallen" which might provoke the South. Francis P. Blair, Sr. also read the speech "and enthusiastically commended the whole address."[43] Fortunately, Lincoln also sought editing help from William H. Seward, who would become his Secretary of State. Seward, who had a reputation as an excellent speaker, took his role as an editor very seriously—he even submitted both a long version and short version of edits.[44] He made 49 suggestions, and Lincoln, working from Seward's short version, incorporated 27 of those when rewriting the First Inaugural.[45]

The most fascinating changes to the First Inaugural occur in the way Lincoln handled Seward's suggestions for the Conclusion:

SEWARD	LINCOLN
1. I close.	I am loth [sic] to close.
2. We are not, we must not be, aliens or enemies, but fellow-countrymen and brethren.	We are not enemies, but friends. We must not be enemies.
3. Although passion has strained our bonds of affection too hardly, they must not, I am sure they will not, be broken.	Though passion may have strained, it must not break our bonds of affection.
4. The mystic chords which, proceeding from so many battlefields and so many patriot graves, pass through all the hearts and all the hearths in this broad continent of ours, will yet again harmonize in their ancient music when breathed upon by the guardian angel of the nation.	The mystic chords of memory, stretching from every battlefield, and patriot grave, to every living heart and hearthstone, all over this broad land, will yet swell the chorus of the Union, when again touched, as surely they will be, by the better angels of our nature.

42. The First Inaugural was a long speech, but Lincoln effectively edited the concluding paragraph for brevity. A word count of the official copy of the First Inaugural reveals it is 3,633 words long. *See* http://www.ushistory.org/documents/lincoln1.htm (last visited Aug. 31, 2016). Lincoln delivered the First Inaugural in 35 minutes. White, *Lincoln's Greatest Speech*, *supra* note 30, at 22.

43. White, *The Eloquent President*, *supra* note 1, at 68–69.

44. *Id.* at 90.

45. *Id.* at 69.

For three of the four suggested changes, Lincoln used a shorter version than Seward suggested. In the third sentence, he used 13 words instead of Seward's suggested 21 words. He also eliminated redundant words by changing Seward's "aliens or enemies" to "enemies" and Seward's "fellow-countrymen and brethren" to "friends."[46] In only one instance, the first suggested change, did Lincoln add words. He changed Seward's "I close" to "I am loth [sic] to close." This change is an example of Lincoln not choosing brevity over all other goals. White explains that "the result of expanding Seward's first sentence, "I close," to Lincoln's "I am loth [sic] to close" was to achieve a pleasing assonance in bringing together "loth [sic]" and "close."[47] Other scholars have noted that the additional three words improved the cadence, but also make "the sentence throb with connotative meanings and emotive force."[48] The last sentence is admittedly long, but Lincoln needs all those words to convey his final thoughts about warmth and conciliation, "Thus stretched, the 'mystic chords of memory' become something like a musical instrument, capable of producing a harmonious music that will return us to our commonality.... This can occur ... by the 'better angels' of our own natures."[49] Lincoln biographer Fred Kaplan calls Lincoln's changes to Seward's suggested closing a transformation from "the adequate to the brilliant."[50]

In the First Inaugural, Lincoln used other legal skills. He argued his case, relied on his precedential political speeches, used logic and reason, and supported the Constitution.[51] He also concluded the speech with brevity, which would become an even more key factor in the persuasive power of the Gettysburg Address and the Second Inaugural. Many historians consider these two "quite short" speeches as not only Lincoln's greatest, but the greatest speeches given by any president.[52]

---

46. *Id.* at 91.

47. *Id.*

48. *Id.* at 66–67 (citing Don e. Fenhrenbacher, "The Words of Lincoln," *Lincoln in Text and Context* 285 (1987)).

49. *Id.* at 68.

50. Kaplan, *supra* note 3, at 326.

51. White, *The Eloquent President, supra* note 1, at 97.

52. Sorenson, *supra* note 2, at 102. Part of that greatness is attributable to the content of the speeches which both deal with the largest and most important ideals. *Id.*

"Startlingly Brief for What It Accomplished"— The Gettysburg Address[53]

The Gettysburg Address summarized the Civil War in 10 sentences and 272 words.[54] It took President Lincoln, a slow speaker,[55] between two and three minutes to deliver the speech.[56]

Historians often compare the brevity of Lincoln's speech favorably to Edward Everett's two-hour-long speech dedicating Gettysburg National Cemetery.[57] Everett's speech is largely forgotten, but in fairness to Everett, the audience both expected and looked forward to a long address because a long address was customary at that time.[58] Lincoln was not expected to make a long speech, yet even so the Gettysburg Address is "startlingly brief for what it accomplished."[59]

Of the 272 words, 203 are one syllable long.[60] The Gettysburg Address, now engraved on a wall in the south chamber of the Lincoln Memorial, is familiar to Americans.[61] The following version italicizes the single-syllable words:

> *Four score and* seven *years* ago *our* fathers *brought forth on this* continent, *a new* nation, conceived *in* Liberty, *and* dedicated *to the* proposition *that all men are* created equal.

> *Now we are* engaged *in a great* civil *war,* testing whether *that* nation, *or* any nation *so* conceived *and so* dedicated, *can long* endure. *We are met on a great* battle-*field of that war. We have come to* dedicate *a por-*

---

53. Garry Wills, *Lincoln at Gettysburg: The Words That Remade America* 35 (1992).

54. *Id.* at 20.

55. *See* White, *The Eloquent President, supra* note 1, at xxii ("Lincoln's pattern was to speak or read his addresses slowly. The average person speaks at about 150 or 160 words per minute. Lincoln spoke 105 to 110 words per minute.").

56. This time of between two and three minutes is an estimate. *See* Wills, *supra* note 53, at 36 ("Read in a slow, clear way to the farthest listeners, the speech would take about three minutes.").

57. *See* Donald, *supra* note 23, at 464.

58. *See* Wills, *supra* note 53, at 23.

59. *Id.* at 35.

60. Wills points out that the speech was 272 words long, but the final word count is dependent on whether "battle-field" is counted as two words instead of one word. Wills, *supra* note 53, at 20. "Field" is italicized above and counted as a one-syllable word.

61. http://www.nps.gov/linc/historyculture/lincoln-memorial-design-and-symbolism. htm (last visited Aug. 31, 2016) (stating that the Gettysburg Address was chosen "for its familiarity to many, but also because it displayed the president's strength and determination to see a successful conclusion to the American Civil War").

tion *of that field, as a* final resting *place for those who here gave their lives that that* nation *might live. It is* altogether fitting *and* proper *that we should do this.*

But, in a larger *sense, we can not* dedicate—*we can not* consecrate— *we can not* hallow—*this ground. The brave men,* living *and dead, who* struggled *here, have* consecrated *it, far* above *our poor* power *to add or* detract. *The world will* little *note, nor long* remember *what we say here, but it can* never forget *what they did here. It is for us the* living, rather, *to be* dedicated *here to the* unfinished *work which they who fought here have thus far so* nobly advanced. *It is* rather *for us to be here* dedicated *to the great task* remaining before *us—that from these* honored *dead we take* increased devotion *to that cause for which they gave the last full* measure *of* devotion—*that we here* highly resolve *that these dead shall not have died in vain—that this* nation, under *God, shall have a new birth of* freedom—*and that* government *of the* people, *by the* people, *for the* people, *shall not* perish *from the earth.*[62]

Lincoln used ordinary vocabulary to persuade his listening and reading audiences. Lincoln had long endeared himself to Americans with his homespun stories and expressions.[63] These common and ordinary words gave "greater dignity" to the speech.[64] Garry Wills calls the Gettysburg Address "a stunning verbal coup" and "an open-air sleight-of-hand" resulting in a new founding of the nation, with a resulting new interpretation of the Constitution.[65] In these 272 words, Lincoln created a new Constitution based on its spirit instead of its words—one that valued equality and did not tolerate slavery.[66]

---

62. There is some dispute about the final version of the Gettysburg Address. The version used here is Lincoln's final version, called the Bliss text. *See* Wills, *supra* note 53, at 18, App. III D 2.

63. *See* Wilson, *Lincoln's Sword, supra* note 4, at 281.

64. *See id.*

65. Wills, *supra* note 53, at 38–40.

66. *Id.* at 38.

"Grand Simplicity and Directness"—
The Second Inaugural[67]

Lincoln considered his Second Inaugural Address his finest speech.[68] In a letter to Thurlow Weed, Lincoln commented, "I expect the latter [The Second Inaugural] to wear as well—perhaps better than anything I have produced."[69] Even so, he added the caveat, "but I believe it is not immediately popular."[70]

The Second Inaugural was expected to be short, after the Associated Press reported it would be "brief."[71] Only one witness reported about Lincoln's composition of the Second Inaugural. Artist Francis C. Carpenter spent six months in residence at the White House. Carpenter reported that he was sitting in Lincoln's office with two other men when Lincoln came in holding a manuscript and stating, "Lots of wisdom in that document, I suspect. It is what will be called my second inaugural, containing about six hundred words. I will put it in my drawer until I want it."[72]

The Second Inaugural Address was 701 words long.[73] Lincoln delivered it in about six minutes.[74] Lincoln was concluding the speech even as people were still arriving to hear the Address.[75]

The Second Inaugural, now engraved on a wall in the north chamber of the Lincoln Memorial,[76] reads:

> Fellow Countrymen,
>
> At this second appearing, to take the oath of the presidential office, there is less occasion for an extended address than there was at the

---

67. Charles Francis Adams, Jr., a descendant of John Adams and John Quincy Adams, wrote to his father after hearing the Second Inaugural, "This inaugural strikes me in its grand simplicity and directness as being for all time the historical keynote of this war." White, *Lincoln's Greatest Speech*, *supra* note 30, at 184.

68. *Id.* at 200.

69. *Id.* at 197.

70. *Id.*

71. *Id.* at 22–23.

72. *Id.* at 49 (quoting Francis B. Carpenter, *The Inner Life of Abraham Lincoln: Six Months at the White House* 234 (1874)).

73. White, *The Eloquent President*, *supra* note 1, at 282. The speech is 703 words long if the later addition of "Fellow Countrymen" is counted. *Id.*

74. White, *Lincoln's Greatest Speech*, *supra* note 30, at 48.

75. *Id.* at 180.

76. Nat'l Park Serv., *Lincoln Memorial Design and Symbolism*, nps.gov, http://www.nps.gov/linc/historyculture/lincoln-memorial-design-and-symbolism.htm (last visited Aug. 31, 2016).

first. Then a statement, somewhat in detail, of a course to be pursued, seemed fitting and proper. Now, at the expiration of four years, during which public declarations have been constantly called forth on every point and phase of the great contest which still absorbs the attention, and engrosses the enerergies [sic] of the nation, little that is new could be presented. The progress of our arms, upon which all else chiefly depends, is as well known to the public as to myself; and it is, I trust, reasonably satisfactory and encouraging to all. With high hope for the future, no prediction in regard to it is ventured.

On the occasion corresponding to this four years ago, all thoughts were anxiously directed to an impending civil war. All dreaded it—all sought to avert it. While the inaugeral [sic] address was being delivered from this place, devoted altogether to *saving* the Union without war, insurgent agents were in the city seeking to *destroy* it without war—seeking to dissole [sic] the Union, and divide effects, by negotiation. Both parties deprecated war; but one of them would *make* war rather than let the nation survive; and the other would *accept* war rather than let it perish. And the war came.

One eighth of the whole population were colored slaves, not distributed generally over the Union, but localized in the Southern part of it. These slaves constituted a peculiar and powerful interest. All knew that this interest was, somehow, the cause of the war. To strengthen, perpetuate, and extend this interest was the object for which the insurgents would rend the Union, even by war; while the government claimed no right to do more than to restrict the territorial enlargement of it. Neither party expected for the war, the magnitude, or the duration, which it has already attained. Neither anticipated that the *cause* of the conflict might cease with, or even before, the conflict itself should cease. Each looked for an easier triumph, and a result less fundamental and astounding. Both read the same Bible, and pray to the same God; and each invokes His aid against the other. It may seem strange that any man should dare to ask a just God's assistance in wringing their bread from the sweat of other men's faces; but let us judge not that we be not judged. The prayers of both could not be answered; that of neither has been answered fully. The Almighty has his own purposes. "Woe unto the world because of offences! for it must needs be that offences come; but woe to that man by whom the offence cometh!" If we shall suppose that American Slavery is one of those offences which, in the providence of God, must needs come, but which, having continued through His appointed time, He now wills to remove, and that He gives to both North and South, this terrible war, as the woe due to those by whom the offence came, shall we discern therein any departure from those divine attributes which the believers in a Living God always ascribe to Him? Fondly do we hope—fervently do we pray—that this mighty scourge of war may speedily pass away. Yet, if God wills that it continue, until all the wealth piled by the bondsman's two hundred and fifty years of unrequited toil shall be sunk, and until every drop of blood drawn with the lash, shall be paid by another drawn with the sword, as was said three thousand years ago, so still it must be said "the judgments of the Lord, are true and righteous altogether[."]

With malice toward none; with charity for all; with firmness in the right, as God gives us to see the right, let us strive on to finish the work we are in; to bind up the nation's wounds; to care for him who shall have borne the battle, and for his widow, and his orphan—to do all which may achieve and cherish a just, and a lasting peace, among ourselves, and with all nations.[77]

A total of 505 of the words are only one syllable long.[78] In Lincoln's handwritten draft he underlined just five words (which are italicized above): "saving," "destroy," "make," "accept," and "cause." Three of the words—saving, destroy, and accept—are two syllables long. The remaining two words—make and cause—are one syllable long. Lincoln, even when choosing points to emphasize, knew that short and forceful words were most likely to persuade.

The last paragraph of the Second Inaugural is the shortest paragraph, but at seventy-five words, also contains the longest sentence. During his final editing, Lincoln pasted a slip over the last section following his dash so that it read "to do all which may achieve and cherish a just, and a lasting peace, among ourselves, and with all nations" instead of the earlier version's ending "to achieve and cherish a lasting peace among ourselves, and with our world."[79] Again, Lincoln's change focuses more on rhythm and sound than on any literal change in meaning.[80] Furthermore, this is another example that Lincoln did not value brevity over all other persuasive and rhetorical devices. He added seven words to achieve "the rhetorical device he … most perfectly mastered

---

77. White, *Lincoln's Greatest Speech*, supra note 30, at 17–19.
78. White, *The Eloquent President, supra* note 1, at 282.
79. Wilson, *Lincoln's Sword, supra* note 4, at 274.
80. *Id.* at 275.

over the years, the measured antithesis" to convey his ideal that magnanimity should guide a victorious nation.[81]

The Second Inaugural is remembered today for its timelessness, sacredness, and theme of reconciliation.[82] Some lament that the Second Inaugural has always been overshadowed by the Gettysburg Address.[83] Both are masterful examples of the power of brevity. Both are short and use short words, and yet still convey universal and lasting ideals and values.

Brevity played a role in why the Gettysburg Address and the Second Inaugural, from all of Lincoln's work, were selected for the Lincoln Memorial. Architect Henry Bacon included these two speeches as important features when he submitted his Lincoln Memorial design to the Lincoln Memorial Commission. Bacon wrote:

> From the beginning of my study I believed that this Memorial of Abraham Lincoln should be composed of four features—a statute of the man, a memorial of his Gettysburg speech, a memorial of his second inaugural address, and a symbol of the Union of the United States, which, he stated, it was his paramount object to save, and which he did save.... I believe these two great speeches made by Lincoln will always have a far greater meaning to the citizens of the United States and visitors from other countries than a portrayal of periods or events by means of decoration. I think, however, some reliefs and decoration designed in conjunction with these memorials and representing in allegory Lincoln's qualities, such as charity, patience, intelligence, patriotism, devotion to high ideals, and humaneness, will emphasize the effect of the speeches.[84]

Lincoln's ability to write with such breathtaking brevity allowed Bacon to incorporate the entire speeches into his Memorial. At one point, the Lincoln Memorial Commission asked Bacon to submit alternative designs. He then submitted three alternatives: two with the "two great speeches" and one design with "tablets inscribed with quotations from Lincoln's speeches."[85] Because of the brevity of the Gettysburg Address and the Second Inaugural, Bacon did

---

81. *Id.*

82. *Id.* at 164–65, 203.

83. *See* Phillips, *supra* note 22, at 808; White, *Lincoln's Greatest Speech, supra* note 30, at 201.

84. Lincoln Memorial Commission Report, Sen. Doc. 965, 62d Cong. (1912), Appendix G.

85. *See id.* at Appendix D (Bacon's Report of the Architect on Alternative Designs for the Potomac Park Site).

not have to select only quotations. Instead he was able to use the speeches in their entirety.

Bacon's prediction that the two speeches would have great meaning and significance to visitors has proven accurate. Douglas L. Wilson notes:

> This may help to explain the way millions of Americans, and a surprising number of people around the world, are affected by Abraham Lincoln's most inspired writing. It perhaps illuminates what visitors commonly experience at the Lincoln Memorial in Washington, where they typically stand in silence and read the words of the Gettysburg Address and the Second Inaugural, both of which are inscribed in their entirety on facing marble walls.... In experiencing these two "high moments," something important is somehow affirmed ... On one wall it says there must first be ideals, then dedication, then a willingness to sacrifice and to persevere. On the other wall it says that even in triumph, the victors share complicity with the vanquished.[86]

Adopt Lincoln's Habits to Achieve Brevity

Lincoln worked hard for brevity and eloquence. William Herndon, Lincoln's law partner in Springfield, Illinois, noted that Lincoln was a slow writer "who liked to sort out his points and tighten his logic and his phrasing."[87] Lincoln wrote, rewrote, and edited his speeches. One story from Lincoln's personal life attests to Lincoln's tendency to labor over complex problems:

> Willie [Lincoln's son] was bright, articulate, and exceptionally sensitive toward the feelings of others. Lincoln believed the child's mind was much like his own. Watching Willie solve a difficult problem, he told a visitor, "I know every step of the process by him, as it is by just such slow methods I attain results."[88]

Lincoln also compared his slow way of thinking to a long-bladed jack knife, telling Herndon, "Just so with these long convolutions of my brain ... they have to act slowly—pass as it were through a greater space ... I commence way back like the boys do when they want to get a good start. My weight and speed get momentum to jump far."[89] Yet once he learned something, Lincoln did not

---

86. Wilson, *Lincoln's Sword*, *supra* note 4, at 284.
87. Wills, *supra* note 53, at 28.
88. Donald, *supra* note 23, at 159.
89. *Id.* at 102.

forget it. Lincoln noted, "My mind is like a piece of steel—very hard to scratch anything on it and almost impossible after you get it there to rub it out."[90]

Lincoln's hard work, as demonstrated in these stories, explains his great success as a persuasive speaker and writer. Lincoln's son Robert Todd Lincoln knew that diligence played a role in his father's eloquence. He conceded that his father was a slow and deliberate writer, but remembered that Lincoln was not daunted by the labor of writing.[91] Despite the challenge, Lincoln often took refuge in his writing.[92] Wills emphasizes, "The spare quality of Lincoln's prose did not come naturally but was worked at.… This, surely, is the secret of Lincoln's eloquence. He not only read aloud, to think his way into sounds, but wrote as a way of ordering his thoughts."[93]

It may disappoint some to learn that Lincoln did not possess a creative muse allowing him to quickly dash off speeches that continue to inspire. However, the truth that Lincoln worked, and worked hard, to compose his speeches should be a source of inspiration to the brief writer. We cannot hope to match Lincoln's eloquence, but by adopting his habits of writing in advance, visualizing audience, and ruthlessly editing, we can improve the persuasiveness of our own briefs.[94]

Start Writing Early

Lincoln always started writing his speeches early, at least by making notes on scraps of paper.[95] No early handwritten drafts of the First Inaugural Ad-

---

90. Kaplan, *supra* note 3, at 33 (quoting *Recollected Words* 413 (Donald E. Fehrenbacher and Virginia Fehrenbacher eds.,1996)).

91. Wilson, *Lincoln's Sword*, *supra* note 4, at 5.

92. *Id.* at 7.

93. Wills, *supra* note 53, at 161, 162.

94. Incidentally, like anyone, Lincoln developed both good and bad habits as a lawyer. He was notoriously disorganized. His desk contained an overstuffed envelope with the following words written in his hand, "When you can't find it anywhere else look in this." *See* Dirck, *supra* note 12, at 38. His office was a mess. Charles Wood, *Abraham Lincoln: Corporate Lawyer*, 27 Mont. Lawyer 13 (Oct. 2001). One of Lincolns' clients "even claimed to have seen seeds sprouting in accumulated dust along the edges of the walls of [his] somewhat dilapidated second-story office." *See* Kelly Anderson, *Lincoln the Lawyer*, 58 Or. St. B. Bull. 13 (Feb./March 1998); *see also* Dirck, *supra* note 12, at 38 (attributing the story of "plants from a half-open bag of bean seeds sprouting in a dirt-encrusted corner" to a young man studying for the bar under Lincoln and Herndon). Lincoln was also a poor speller. *See* copies of the Gettysburg Address and The Second Inaugural; *see also* White, *Lincoln's Greatest Speech*, *supra* note 30, at 206. *But see* Kaplan, *supra* note 3, at 7–8 (contending that Lincoln was a good speller and noting that a classmate said Lincoln won spelling bees).

95. Wilson, *Lincoln's Sword*, *supra* note 4, at 44–45.

dress, except for one scrap related to the first sentence, survive, but Lincoln likely worked on the ideas in it for several months, and drafted in earnest at least two weeks before leaving Springfield, Illinois, for Washington.[96] When he left Springfield for Washington, he had drafted and revised several printed copies.[97] Lincoln drafted the First Inaugural far enough in advance to seek advice from several colleagues.[98] A witness observed Lincoln putting his Second Inaugural Address into a drawer six days before it was to be delivered.[99]

A common but misguided myth is that Lincoln quickly composed the Gettysburg Address on a discarded piece of paper while riding the train to Gettysburg.[100] This story started with several unreliable sources, grew more fanciful, and was perpetuated when the tale was printed as a book, *The Perfect Tribute*, which sold 500,000 copies and was included on several required high school course reading lists.[101] The myth is not true. Lincoln was formally invited to speak at Gettysburg just 17 days before the November 19, 1863, event,[102] but he was not cavalier in preparing the Gettysburg Address.[103] Instead, he wrote and rewrote the speech several times.[104] White concludes, "Lincoln's genius grew not from spontaneity but from hard, painstaking work with words."[105]

Lincoln worked very hard to learn anything new, and he learned by reading. Lincoln was a devoted student, "The intensity with which Lincoln laid siege to certain subjects stamped itself indelibly on the memories of his New Salem acquaintances."[106] Lincoln pursued his vocational interests of surveying

---

96. *Id.* at 45.

97. *Id.* at 59.

98. White, *The Eloquent President, supra* note 1, at 96.

99. White, *Lincoln's Greatest Speech, supra* note 30, at 49.

100. White, *The Eloquent President, supra* note 1, at 232.

101. *Id.* at 233–34.

102. *Id.* at 229. Some scholars note that Lincoln was probably informally invited before October 30. Wills, *supra* note 53, at 25.

103. Wills notes,

> The silly, but persistent myth is that he jotted his brief remarks on the back of an envelope. Better-attested accounts have him considering it on the way to a photographer's shop in Washington, writing it on a piece of cardboard as the train took him on the eighty-mile trip, penciling it in David Wills's house on the night before the dedication, writing it in that house on the morning of the day he had to deliver it, or even composing it in his head as Everett spoke, before Lincoln rose to follow him.

Id. at 27.

104. For a meticulous and fascinating account of the details surrounding Lincoln's writing of the Gettysburg Address see Martin P. Johnson, *Writing the Gettysburg Address* (2013).

105. White, *The Eloquent President, supra* note 1, at 234.

106. Wilson, *Honor's Voice, supra* note 3, at 4.

and the law, but even his study of English grammar was intense—probably because he knew he needed to improve his English skills so that he could make a better public impression.[107] Interestingly, Lincoln's studiousness, which sometimes took precedence over his duties, was seen as laziness by some of his contemporaries.[108] Lincoln's father Thomas also showed impatience with Lincoln's reading because he needed Abraham for field work.[109]

Lincoln emphasized the importance of diligence for lawyers.[110] In 1860, when he was a candidate for president, he responded to a young man's question about the best way to learn the law, "The mode is very simple, though laborious and tedious. It is only to get the books, and read, and study them carefully.... Work, work, work, is the main thing."[111] He knew that diligence in refining his work would pay off with increased persuasiveness.

Legal writers should follow Lincoln's lead and start writing early. Professor Linda Edwards emphasizes, "Good writing takes time—almost always more time than the writer first expects."[112] Plus, writing the brief is an essential step in understanding the case. The act of writing forces the writer to think about and develop the legal arguments, to notice strengths and weaknesses, and to craft an organized structure.[113] Finally, writing the brief early ensures enough time for editing.[114]

Visualize Audience

Lincoln learned to visualize his audience when he litigated cases.[115] He "ordinarily ended [his summation] with a low-key, logical argument that jurors

---

107. *Id.* at 62–63.

108. *Id.* at 57.

109. Kaplan, *supra* note 3, at 19–20.

110. Dirck, *supra* note 12, at 4. Lincoln's notes about practicing law are often referred to as "Notes for a Law Lecture," but there is no record where, when, or even if Lincoln ever delivered such a lecture. *Id.* at 1.

111. Wilson, *Honor's Voice*, *supra* note 3, at 106.

112. *See* Linda Edwards, *Legal Writing and Analysis* 71 (4th ed. 2015).

113. *See id.* at 68 ("Your working draft is where you 'grasp the case.' It guides, deepens, and tests your analysis, and it forms your ideas into the kind of structured, linear reasoning that lawyers must master."); Richard K. Neumann, Jr., J. Lyn Entrikin & Sheila Simon, *Legal Writing* 317 (3d ed. 2015) (urging writers to start writing before finishing research because once you begin writing you will know where you need more authority).

114. Richard K. Neumann, Jr. & Kristen Konrad Tiscione, *Legal Reasoning and Legal Writing* 46 (7th ed. 2013) (suggesting that writers allow a day or two between drafting and revising).

115. *See* Donald, *supra* note 23, at 151.

could readily understand."[116] When Lincoln the Lawyer became Lincoln the President, he knew he must write and speak both for those in the live audience and for those who would read his speeches in newspapers. Antebellum America changed "from a society of small, independent communities to a mass society ... a thousand people might hear the orator but tens of thousands would read the speech."[117]

Lincoln was well aware of the strategy of considering his audience. His First Inaugural focused on both Southerners and those of the loyal public, particularly those Unionists who needed convincing that Lincoln was a capable leader.[118] Lincoln engaged in the "artful enterprise" of "[s]peaking to one audience as a way of getting through to another."[119] Lincoln's speech rejected Southern claims, but he did not use the First Inaugural to respond to the secessionist's most important arguments, instead he used his words to show he was a reasoned and firm leader opposed to secession.[120]

The audience at Gettysburg, estimated between 15,000 and 20,000 people, had waited for hours for the dedication.[121] Lincoln knew that there would be a crowd, and that the crowd would include several state governors.[122] He knew the audience was becoming war weary. He wanted to use this speech to define the war outside his usual reports to Congress.[123] He cleansed the bloody battlefield and said that the physical residue of the battle was a test of whether a "government can maintain the *proposition* of equality."[124] He used the Gettysburg Address to define his war aims, which included winning the Civil War on both ideological and military terms.[125]

---

116. *Id.*

117. White, *Lincoln's Greatest Speech, supra* note 30, at 71–72. Lincoln's speeches were written for live audiences. White, *The Eloquent President, supra* note 1, at xx.

118. Wilson, *Lincoln's Sword, supra* note 4, at 54–55.

119. *Id.* at 54.

120. *Id.* at 55.

121. White, *The Eloquent President, supra* note 1, at 240; Wills, *supra* note 53, at 51. White marvels at the number of people in attendance:

> There were far too many people for beds, even with the accepted custom of two and three in a bed. The American House, Eagle, and McClellan hotels, as well as all the boardinghouses, were full. Where there were no beds, people slept in hotel lobbies and boardinghouse parlors. Churches opened their doors so that people could sleep on pews.

White, *The Eloquent President, supra* note 1, at 231.

122. Wills, *supra* note 53, at 25.

123. *See id.*

124. *Id.* at 37 (emphasis in original).

125. *Id.*

The audience for the Second Inaugural was even more war weary, and many citizens felt both anger and hope as the "death and despair [from the Civil War] reached into nearly every home."[126] The audience wondered what Lincoln would say about the conquered Confederates, the slaves, and suffrage.[127] Between 30,000 and 40,000 people crowded into Washington to hear the speech.[128] Lincoln knew his audience would include dignitaries, soldiers, African Americans, his supporters, and those who despised him.[129] He spoke to all, asking them to think with him about the war, its cause, and its aftermath.[130] At the inauguration reception later in the day, Lincoln himself told Frederick Douglass that he saw him in the crowd during his Second Inaugural address. Lincoln asked Douglass what he thought of the speech, "[T]here is no man in the country whose opinion I value more than yours. I want to know what you think of it?" "Mr. Lincoln, that was a sacred effort," Douglass replied.[131]

Some wonder how Lincoln would fare in the modern political climate with an audience preference for sound bites. Lincoln admirer Theodore Sorenson has no doubt that Lincoln would appeal to a modern audience, "He had a talent for getting to the point."[132]

Many writers struggle to write for their audience because they are not exactly sure who may read their work. In this regard, we lawyers have it easy. We know our primary audience is the judge or judges, and their law clerks, who will read the brief and make the decision.[133] Judges are human,[134] with the same limited attention span and preference for brevity as all other humans.[135] They

---

126. White, *Lincoln's Greatest Speech*, *supra* note 30, at 23.

127. *See id.* at 23.

128. *Id.* at 29–30.

129. *Id.* at 24–25, 30, 32, 38–39.

130. *Id.* at 59.

131. *Id.* at 199.

132. Sorenson, *supra* note 2, at 102.

133. Even though judges are the primary audience, many briefs are also shared with clients. *But see* Ruggero J. Aldisert, *Winning on Appeal* 19 (2d ed. 2003) (noting that judges and their law clerks are the only audience).

134. Senior judges advise new judges to remember their humanness. *See* Pamela Ann Rymer, *The Trials of Judging*, 4 Green Bag 2d 57, 61 (2000) (advising new judges not to "think of yourself as any different now from what you were before, except, perhaps, that the demands of honor and civility, humility and sensitivity, are more exacting than ever.").

135. *See* Edwards, *supra* note 112, at 72 ("Judges share the characteristics of other law-trained readers. Their attention is finite. They are busy and impatient with delay in getting to the bottom line"). Judges also do not like to start reading something they cannot finish. Antonin Scalia & Bryan A. Garner, *Making Your Case: The Art of Persuading Judges* 25 (2008)

are persuaded by a writer who includes enough so that the argument and facts are understandable but does not include anything that is not essential.[136]

Let's visualize those overworked and underpaid judges. The judicial workload statistics are shocking. In 1992, one federal appellate judge estimated that he read 3,500 pages of briefs a month.[137] The case filings in the appellate courts have increased 55 percent since 1990, and the district court filings have increased 29 percent over those same 18 years.[138] This caseload works out to an astonishingly heavy workload of 464 cases per district court judge and 1,230 cases per three-judge appellate panel.[139]

Judges are busy, brief reading competes with other demands on a judge's time, and "briefs are not read at a leisurely pace and their contents savored and digested in a contemplative environment."[140] Brief writers may be tempted to imagine a judge reading a brief in her robes, and that may be true, but the robes worn may be bathrobes instead of judicial robes because there simply is not time in the day to complete all the brief reading.[141]

(citing Susan Bell, *Improving Our Writing by Understanding How People Read Personally Addressed Household Mail*, 57 Clarity 40 (2007)).

136. *See* Michael R. Smith, *Advanced Legal Writing* 175 (3d. ed. 2013). Smith calls this quality "reader empathy." The brief writer "must be sensitive to the judge's lack of familiarity with the case." *Id.* at 175–76.

137. *Id.* at 327.

138. https://web.archive.org/web/20100203123512/http://leahy.senate.gov/press/200803/031308c.html (last visited Aug. 31, 2016).

139. *Id.* In an effort to make the federal judges' workload more manageable, Senator Patrick Leahy, Chairman of the Senate Judiciary Committee, introduced the "Federal Judgeship Act of 2008" on March 13, 2008, to add several permanent and temporary judges. The bill would add 12 permanent circuit court judges, 38 permanent district court judges, 14 temporary district court judges, two temporary circuit court judges; convert five existing temporary judges into permanent positions; and extend one existing temporary district court judge. Sen. 2774.RS, 110th Cong. (March 13, 2008). Chief Justice John Roberts is also leading the charge for higher federal judicial salaries. *See* Linda Greenhouse, *Chief Justice Advocates Higher Pay for Judiciary*, N.Y. Times (Jan. 1, 2007) (http://www.nytimes.com/2007/01/01/us/01scotus.html). Several other groups have joined the effort advocating for increased salaries for the federal judiciary including the American Bar Association, state and local bar associations, the General Counsels of several large corporations, law school deans, editorial staffs, and the American College of Trial Lawyers, https://web.archive.org/web/20100410121445/http://www.uscourts.gov/judicialcompensation/support.html (archived Apr. 10, 2010). The act has not yet passed, but efforts continue to add more federal judges due to a heavy workload. United States Courts, *The Federal Bench in 2015-Annual Report 2015*, uscourts.gov, http://www.uscourts.gov/statistics-reports/federal-bench-2015-annual-report-2015.

140. Aldisert, *supra* note 133, at 20.

141. Paul H. Anderson, Associate Justice, Minnesota Supreme Court, Suggestions for

We know that judges value brevity, so we lawyers need not wait for a clearer signal. Perhaps we think the judges are wrong in asking for brevity. The judges are not wrong, but even if Court rules and preferences do not make sense, we follow those rules and preferences to maximize persuasiveness. If a Court requires a brief writer to affix a white feather to the cover page of every brief, then we should start looking for white feathers. Perhaps we think the judges are referring to everyone but us. Maybe we view ourselves as such brilliant writers that a judge finds it enjoyable to read as many words from our golden pens as possible. Maybe we believe that brevity works for everyone else's simple case, but not our complex cases. This thinking is simply wrong. Even the most brilliant writer will be more persuasive when writing with brevity. If the case is complex, brevity is even more essential because "[t]he substance of legal analysis is complicated enough without adding to the confusion by using unnecessarily complex sentence structure and complicated wording."[142]

Finally, perhaps we think it is just too hard or takes too much time to write with brevity. Many are familiar with the adage, "If I had more time, I would write a shorter letter."[143] Writing with brevity admittedly requires diligence, but diligence is what we promise to our clients.[144] Beware of seeing yourself as an exception to the brevity preference. The judges are talking to you because they are talking to all of us.

Ruthlessly Edit for Brevity

Brevity does not come naturally in the initial drafting stage for most legal writers. Like so many other aspects of persuasive legal writing, the best way to improve writing is with editing. Editing for brevity works at every level of the legal brief: the complete brief, individual sections of the brief, paragraphs, sen-

---

Legal Writers (U. of St. Thomas Sch. of L., Mar. 24, 2006). Professor Mary Beth Beazley made the same observation. Remarks, *Divine Secrets of the Ha-Ha Sisterhood* (Legal Writing Institute 13th Biennial Conf., July 15, 2008).

142. Smith, *supra* note 136, at 182.

143. The quote probably originated with Blaise Pascal, *The Provincial Letters*, Provincial Letter 16 ("The present letter is a very long one, simply because I had no leisure to make it shorter."). Woodrow Wilson is quoted as saying, "If you want me to talk for ten minutes, I need two weeks to prepare. If you want me to speak for half an hour, I need a day. If you have no time limit, I am ready right now." *Quote It Completely* 986 (Eugene C. Gerhart ed., 1998) (citing McMillian Lewis, *Woodrow Wilson of Princeton* 65 (1962)). A similar quote is often attributed to Mark Twain or Winston Churchill.

144. Model Rules of Prof'l Conduct R. 1.3 (2004) ("A lawyer shall act with reasonable diligence and promptness in representing a client.").

tences, and especially words.[145] Shorter is almost always better in almost every situation. If you have time to edit for only one single problem, edit for brevity. This is the most consistent preference expressed by judges.

One caveat for the legal writer is to write so that the reader remains interested. If every section within a brief is the exact same length, every sentence has the same number of words, or every word has the same number of syllables, you will lull your reader into boredom.[146] Write with brevity, but do not forget the value of variety.

Lincoln did not always use short speeches, short sentences, or short words. Not every word or sentence in the Gettysburg Address or the Second Inaugural is short. Both end with very long sentences — the Gettysburg Address with an 83-word sentence, almost a third of the speech's length,[147] and the Second Inaugural with a 75-word sentence.[148]

Still, Lincoln deliberately chose short sentences and short words whenever possible. He preferred "short words to long, words of Anglo-Saxon origin to those of Latin derivation."[149] Saxon words are briefer and have more punch.[150] White gives several examples of the differences between the Saxon and Latinate form of words: "lie" instead of "prevaricate"; "stop" instead of "desist"; and "end" instead of "terminate."[151] Lincoln also drew on his memory when writing and did not try to use novel language.[152] He used each word carefully and precisely.[153]

---

145. The term "editing" often encompasses three very distinct processes: revising (looking at the big picture), editing (looking at smaller issues like sentence structure and word choice), and proofreading (looking for errors). Laurel Currie Oates & Anne Enquist, *The Legal Writing Handbook* 569–73 (4th ed. 2006).

146. *See* Neumann & Tiscione, *supra* note 114, at 208 (suggesting that one cure for singsongy sentences is to vary the type of sentence (simple, compound, or complex), the lengths of sentences (long, short, medium) and the way sentences begin (subject, prefatory word or phrase, dependent clause)); *see also* Richard C. Wydick, *Plain English for Lawyers* 36 (5th ed. 2005) (recommending variations in sentence construction to maintain reader interest).

147. Wills, *supra* note 53, at 157.

148. White, *Lincoln's Greatest Speech*, *supra* note 30, at 165. White notes, "[A]lthough Lincoln often crafted short sentences, some of his most memorable prose was rendered in long and complex sentences." *Id.* at 166. White adds, "Lincoln's closing sentence [to the Gettysburg Address], in a speech known for its brevity, was a surprising, long, complex sentence of eighty-two words. The simplicity of Lincoln's speeches has often been oversold." White, *The Eloquent President*, *supra* note 1, at 249.

149. Donald, *supra* note 23, at 461.

150. White, *The Eloquent President*, *supra* note 1, at 254.

151. *Id.*

152. *Id.* Wills also notes that Lincoln, in the Gettysburg Address, often used the same word in different contexts to further his themes. Wills, *supra* note 53, at 173–74.

153. Klein, *supra* note 7, at 220.

Legal brief writers should follow Lincoln's lead and write short briefs, using short sentences and short words as often as possible. The "plain English" movement has long urged legal writers to write in short sentences and use concrete and familiar words.[154] A persuasive legal writer recognizes that writing with brevity, simple language, and simple sentences helps clarify the complexity of the legal analysis.[155]

Lincoln was ruthless when editing for brevity in his First Inaugural, but he made changes and revisions in all his writings.[156] With the advent of word processing, ruthless editing is even more necessary today.[157] We are faced with the strange phenomenon of seeing our first drafts in a polished format. We struggle to start drafting, but finally think, "Oh, I'm just going to get started. I'll change it all later, but I need to get something, anything, down on paper." We then start spewing words, sentences, whole paragraphs into a Word™ document. Fast forward to the moment when the writer is ready to edit the work. Reading through the drafted material the writer thinks, "Hey, this is really not that bad. In fact, if I must say so myself, this looks pretty good. Maybe even brilliant." The moment the writer thinks to herself, "I don't even have to edit this brief" is the moment when the "Danger! Danger!" warning should be going off in her head.[158]

We must resist the temptation to believe that our first drafts are adequate, let alone brilliant. Instead, edit with a ruthless spirit. Pretend you didn't write the first draft. Imagine that the first draft was written by someone with a particularly annoying trait—writing without brevity. Your job is to notice everything that is not absolutely essential and then delete it. Simplify sentences and words. The original author will thank you. Even more importantly, the judge deciding the case is more likely to be persuaded.

---

154. Wydick, *supra* note 146, at 35–39, 57–63.

155. *See* Smith, *supra* note 136, at 182 (describing this as the trait of an intelligent and articulate legal writer). Another advantage of short sentences is that short sentences keep the verb and subject close to each other. Long sentences can be difficult to understand. Neumann & Tiscione, *supra* note 114, at 208 ("If a sentence is too long to be understood easily on the first reading, express the sentence's ideas in fewer words, or split the sentence into two (or more) shorter sentences, or do both.").

156. Wilson, *Lincoln's Sword, supra* note 4, at 8.

157. Lincoln, of course, drafted his speeches in longhand. Donald, *supra* note 23, at 238.

158. Richard Neumann and Kristen Konrad Tiscione advise, "Don't be afraid to delete material from your first draft, even if it hurts to take it out. The fact that you've written something doesn't mean you have to keep it." Neumann & Tiscione, *supra* note 114, at 46. Laurel Currie Oates and Anne Enquist add, "Don't let yourself fall in love with a particular phrase or sentence." Oates & Enquist, *supra* note 145, at 572.

For our inspiration in writing with brevity, we should look to Abraham Lincoln. Lincoln was self-confident, but he did not consider himself a great writer.[159] His personal secretaries John G. Nicolay and John Hay declared that Lincoln would have been surprised to "hear himself called a man of letters."[160] We know better—Lincoln was a brilliant writer. We can find inspiration from Lincoln's compelling and extraordinary use of the virtue of brevity.

Brevity is a virtue like many other virtues. Common wisdom advises that practicing virtues makes them easier. This is true of the virtue of writing with brevity. In the beginning it is painful to delete unnecessary pages, arguments, and words. But one day you will find yourself noticing and valuing brevity. On that day, you may find yourself editing your opponent's brief and cutting it by 30% without eliminating anything essential, but instead improving the brief's persuasiveness. Ultimately, you will acquire the virtue of brevity. Short mantras can guide us in our efforts to develop virtues. Michael Pollan developed a seven-word mantra about healthy eating, "Eat food. Not too much. Mostly plants."[161] We lawyers can adopt a seven-word mantra, too, "Brevity persuades. I will adopt Lincoln's habits."

---

159. *See* Wilson, *Lincoln's Sword, supra* note 4, at 9.

160. *Id.* at 9 (citing John G. Nicolay and John Hay, *Abraham Lincoln: A History*, vol. 10, 351. (1904)).

161. Michael Pollan, *In Defense of Food* 1 (2008).

Chapter 5

The Power of Clarity: Ulysses S. Grant

(April 27, 1822–July 23, 1885)
Presidency 1869–1877

It may come as a surprise that Ulysses S. Grant makes anyone's list of eloquent writers. Most will recall that Grant led the Union army to victory in the Civil War. But then, many will likely remember a couple of unflattering things. Didn't he have a serious drinking problem?[1] Wasn't he called the "butcher" for his willingness to sacrifice Union soldiers?[2] Wasn't his Presidency noted for its corruption?[3] Didn't he die penniless?[4] These vague memories are likely a result of our generation's lack of knowledge about Grant's accomplishments.[5] Frankly, many of us don't know much about Grant at all.

---

1. Joan Waugh noted that "as almost every Civil War history professor can testify, one of the most commonly asked questions from students and public alike is, 'Was Ulysses S. Grant a drunk?'" Joan Waugh, *U.S. Grant: American Hero, American Myth* 40 (2009).

2. James M. McPherson, *Introduction* in Ulysses S. Grant, *Personal Memoirs of U.S. Grant* xiii, xxiv (Penguin Bks. 1999); *see also* Josiah Bunting III, *Ulysses S. Grant* 3, 5–6 (2004) (Bunting's book is part of The American Presidents series, edited by Arthur M. Schlesinger Jr.).

3. *Presidential Leadership: Rating the Best and the Worst in the White House* 98 (James Taranto & Leonard Leo eds., 2004).

4. Grant was financially ruined at the end of his life, but the posthumous publication of his *Personal Memoirs* netted $450,000 for his family. McPherson, *supra* note 2, at xv.

5. Joan Waugh was inspired by this ignorance to write her book about Grant:

My project began with a question about Grant's life, and his death. Why did Grant's star shine so brightly for Americans of his own day, and why has it has

Part of the problem is that Grant is perplexing. For much of his life he was considered a failure,[6] yet he is recognized as one of the most accomplished military leaders in world history.[7] Thousands of Union soldiers were killed under his command,[8] but he could not stand the sight of blood.[9] He was determined and deliberate in achieving his goal of victory over the Confederacy, but he was magnanimous in his treatment of Southerners both during and after the Civil War.[10] He was probably an alcoholic (today we would label him a binge drinker),[11] but his drinking was the only "element of the spectacular" in Grant's otherwise calm, self-contained, and modest personality.[12] He was the most

---

[sic] been eclipsed so completely for Americans since at least the mid-twentieth century? Most Americans indisputably are ignorant of the *extent* of the once-powerful national legacy of Ulysses S. Grant.
Waugh, *supra* note 1, at 2.

6. The first chapter of William B. Hesseltine's Grant biography is labeled simply, "Forty Years of Failure." William B. Hesseltine, *Ulysses S. Grant: Politician* 1 (1935) (Hesseltine says that Grant's first forty years of "dismal failure" were "neatly severed" from the second half of his career, which began in the Civil War). Josiah Bunting noted that Hesseltine's biography of Grant is often condescending toward Grant. Bunting, *supra* note 2, at 2–3 .

7. William S. McFeely notes,
[Grant] had been through a lifetime of great contrasts between anonymous failure and vast public acclaim, and only a relentless plunge into the obscene exhilaration of war enabled him to achieve what others perceived to be a steady grasp on the world.
William S. McFeely, *Grant* 3 (1981).

8. Bunting, *supra* note 2, at 34 ("The Civil War was the most terrible in our history.... Deaths attributable to combat, both sides together, were 698,000; adding in the wounded, the casualty total is 1,168,000...."); *see also* Michael Korda, *Ulysses S. Grant: The Unlikely Hero* 56–57 (2004) (Grant recognized that the Civil War "would be incalculably more bloody than anyone supposed, and would be won only by brute force and killing on a scale that would eclipse all previous wars."); Waugh, *supra* note 1, at 8 (Grant believed the Civil War was worth its cost.).

9. Korda, *supra* note 8, at 20 (Grant avoided eating meat whenever possible, and ate only meat that was burned because he could not stand the sight of blood on his plate.).

10. Waugh, *supra* note 1, at 5, 252–53; Bunting, *supra* note 2, at 70 ("[The Appomattox surrender] was Ulysses Grant's finest hour, as it was Lee's.").

11. Grant was "a sporadic and then spectacular drunk." John Keegan, *The Mask of Command* 204 (1987).

12. *Id.* McPherson points out that excessive drinking in Grant's day was "considered a moral defect and a matter of deep shame," but that "[Grant] should have felt pride rather than shame" because he overcame his alcoholism "to achieve success and fame." McPherson, *supra* note 2, at xxv. Grant drank when he was lonely; he did not drink when surrounded by his family. Keegan, *supra* note 11, at 204.

popular man in America when he died in 1885, but he is remembered only vaguely today. He was flat broke at age 62, but his *Personal Memoirs* were a huge financial and literary success. He was in pain and dying from throat cancer in his final year of life, but he rallied to start and complete his *Personal Memoirs*. So historians debate whether Grant was gifted or ordinary,[13] a butcher or a savior,[14] a success or a failure.[15]

Notwithstanding these apparent inconsistencies, not everything about Grant is seriously debated; everyone seems to agree about some things. Grant did not make an impressive first impression. At 5'8" tall and 135 pounds,[16] he was smaller than expected.[17] He wore only a rumpled part of his military uniform, so many did not recognize him as General Grant.[18] Lieutenant Horace Porter described his first view of Grant:

> In an arm-chair facing the fireplace was seated a general officer, slight in figure and of medium stature, whose face bore an expression of weariness. He was carelessly dressed, and his uniform coat was unbuttoned and thrown back from his chest. He held a lighted cigar in his mouth, and sat in a stooping posture, with his head bent slightly forward. His clothes were wet, and his trousers and top-boots were spattered with mud.[19]

---

13. *See* McFeely, *supra* note 7, at xii ("There are historians who, when asked to contemplate Grant, insist that he must have had some secret greatness.... I leave to others the problem of accounting for a Mozart or a Marx, but I am convinced that Ulysses Grant had no organic, artistic, or intellectual specialness."). Michael Korda believes Grant had, at least to some degree a "quick glance of genius ... the ability to see at once on the battlefield where the enemy's weakness lay and how to exploit it with one unexpected blow."). Korda, *supra* note 8, at 152.

14. *See* Jean Edward Smith, *Grant* 15 (2001) (noting that academic historians have attributed Grant's victories to a "willingness to sacrifice [Union soldiers] in battle ... despite the fact that Grant's casualty ratio was considerably lower than Lee's.").

15. It is difficult to fit Grant into a box labeled either "success" or "failure." Korda noted, "[Grant], who had failed at almost everything he tried, succeeded quite suddenly as a general, infused with unmistakable self-confidence and unshaken by the noise, carnage, and confusion of battle." Korda, *supra* note 8, at 11.

16. General Horace Porter, *Campaigning with Grant* 14 (1897).

17. *Id.* (popular press at the time depicted Grant as a "swash-buckler," but he was instead a slight, gentle man).

18. *See e.g.* Jean Edward Smith, *supra* note 14, at 233 (Even new recruits would not recognize him as the general because he dressed so plainly.).

19. Porter, *supra* note 16, at 1–2.

President Lincoln described Grant as "the quietest little fellow you ever saw."[20] He was a devoted family man.[21] He was a spectacular horseman and seemed more comfortable riding than walking.[22] He smoked cigars, almost continuously.[23] He did not use profanity.[24] He remained calm in all circumstances.[25] He had the moral courage to lead.[26] His troops admired and respected him.[27] Lincoln recognized that, in Grant, he had finally found his military leader: "Grant is the first general I've had. He's a general."[28] In his time, Grant was the most popular living American.[29]

One other Grant trait is not seriously debated—his writing was a model of clarity. Josiah Bunting suggested that Grant was "one of the most talented writers to occupy the White House."[30] His military strategy, including his orders,

---

20. *Id.* at 307 (referencing a conversation between Lincoln and his third secretary William O. Stoddard, who was ill when Grant arrived in Washington, so he did not have a chance to meet Grant personally).

21. Ulysses and Julia Dent Grant had a very successful marriage. *See* Korda, *supra* note 8, at 32 ("[C]ertainly the Grants would have one of the great marriages of the nineteenth century). Grant was also a devoted parent. McFeely, *supra* note 7, at 63 (Grant had a "deep love for and confidence in his children.").

22. *See* Charles Bracelen Flood, *Grant's Final Victory: Ulysses S. Grant's Heroic Last Year* 108 (2011).

23. Jean Edward Smith, *supra* note 14, at 302. Grant's nearly constant cigar smoking began only after the Fort Donelson capture. Newspapers reported that Grant continued to hold the stump of a cigar throughout the battle, and Northern well-wishers sent as many as 10,000 cigars to Grant, "thinking, no doubt, that tobacco was [Grant's] chief solace." Porter, *supra* note 16, at 381.

24. Ulysses S. Grant, *Personal Memoirs of Ulysses S. Grant* 66 (1992) [hereinafter *Personal Memoirs*] ("I am not aware of ever having used a profane expletive in my life; but I would have the charity to excuse those who may have done so, if they were in charge of a train of Mexican pack mules at the time.").

25. *See e.g.* Jean Edward Smith, *supra* note 14, at 295, 329; Bunting, *supra* note 2, at 61 (Grant had a "calm, clear mind"); Edmund Wilson, *Patriotic Gore: Studies in the Literature of the American Civil War* 134 (1962).

26. Grant took charge; he did not expect or want Lincoln to be involved in his military strategy. Jean Edward Smith, *supra* note 14, at 307.

27. The enlisted men in the Union Army instantly liked Grant. "They liked Grant's reticence, his disregard for pomp and ceremony, his eye for the essential." *Id.* at 306.

28. *Id.* at 307 (Lincoln's response when Stoddard asked about Grant's military ability).

29. Bunting comments, "From the end of the Civil War and the assassination of Abraham Lincoln five days later, and until his own death in 1885, Ulysses S. Grant was first in the hearts of his countrymen. They saluted him as a savior of the Union. He was the most famous and most carefully scrutinized American." Bunting, *supra* note 2, at 1.

30. *Id.* at 117.

is still studied in military schools.[31] Thousands of Americans proudly displayed his two-volume *Personal Memoirs* in their homes.[32] Even the critics lauded *Personal Memoirs*. Mark Twain and Gertrude Stein were vocal admirers of Grant's writing.[33] Twain admired Grant's "clarity of statement, directness, simplicity, manifest truthfulness, fairness and justice toward friend and foe alike and avoidance of flowery speech."[34] All agreed that Grant's clarity is what made him such an astonishingly effective writer.

This chapter reviews Grant's life as a writer, including his writing habits that helped him achieve clarity. Like the other subjects in this book, Grant was an American President.[35] The writings selected as examples of Grant's clarity, however, do not come from his presidential years, in large part because his presidential writings are not known for their clarity. Instead, Grant's military dispatches and *Personal Memoirs* provide the best examples of Grant's clarity. Grant wrote all his own military orders and the *Personal Memoirs*, but he did not write all his presidential communications.[36]

Readers who are not familiar with Grant's dramatic race against a deadline—his own imminent death—to complete his *Personal Memoirs* will be impressed with Grant's fortitude and courage. Clarity is the defining feature of Grant's *Personal Memoirs*. Many passages "read so simply that we hardly realize how every paragraph was drenched in pain."[37] For all Americans, Grant provided a book classifiable as great American literature.[38] For lawyers, Grant provided writing classifiable as a great example of clarity. Grant was resolute, straightforward, disciplined, calm, and determined. These characteristics influenced his writing style, so that when he was at his very best as an author he wrote with clarity.

---

31. *See* Korda, *supra* note 8, at 153.

32. McFeely, *supra* note 7, at 501 ("The result was an astonishing number of two-volume sets sitting proudly on parlor tables in America in the 1880's."). Over 300,000 copies of the two-volume set were sold. Waugh, *supra* note 1, at 209.

33. Wilson, *supra* note 25, at 139–40.

34. Flood, *supra* note 22, at 130–31.

35. Grant is rated as 32 out of 39 presidents reviewed, which puts him in the "below average" category. Taranto & Leo, *supra* note 3, at 12, 94. Even an official White House website about all the presidents reports that Grant, as president, "provided neither vigor nor reform. Looking to Congress for direction, he seemed bewildered." U.S. Govt., *About the White House, Presidents, 18. Ulysses S. Grant*, whitehouse.gov, http://www.whitehouse.gov/about/presidents/ulyssessgrant (last visited Sept. 2, 2016). Several scholars believe that Grant's presidency was not quite as bad as historians suggest. *See* Bunting, *supra* note 2, at 2.

36. McPherson, *supra* note 2, at xiii.

37. Louis A. Coolidge, *Ulysses S. Grant* 564 (1922).

38. Korda calls *Personal Memoirs* "the most successful book in American literature." Korda, *supra* note 8, at 151.

Grant's Biography

The most significant influence on Grant's writing occurred during his service in the United States Army, but several other experiences in Grant's life helped shape his devotion to clarity. Grant noted, "[C]ircumstances always did shape my course differently from my plans."[39]

Before telling Grant's story, one of his defining features should be mentioned. Ulysses S. Grant simply was Ulysses S. Grant, and he made no apologies for that fact. He did not gaze at himself and wonder if he made the most of his talents. A reader of Grant's writings will not learn the answers to any of these questions: Did he ever doubt himself? What did he consider as his weaknesses? Did he have regrets?[40] How does he explain the huge number of Union casualties? How could he have had so little business sense?[41] Grant was a doer, not an explainer.[42] "He addressed his problems, discharged his mission, and moved on." Further, Grant believed that his destiny was not in his own hands.[43] Of course Grant did not believe that there was anything unique about him. He often noted "how little men control their own destiny."[44]

Despite Grant's preference for forward movement instead of backward introspection, he gives readers glimpses into his feelings, his values, and his heroes. He was sad when Lee finally surrendered.[45] He intensely disliked being humiliated; he could not stand to see anyone else humiliated either. He knew fear. Grant loved and adored his family.[46] He supported the preservation of the Union.[47] He believed that slavery had caused the Civil War.[48]

---

39. *Personal Memoirs*, *supra* note 24, at 28.

40. The exception to this is that Grant does write briefly about his regrets at Vicksburg and Cold Harbor. Waugh, *supra* note 1, at 205–06; *see also* McFeely, *supra* note 7, at 511 ("He apologized only for one hideously bloody day outside Vicksburg and for Cold Harbor....").

41. Waugh argues that an audience in the late 19th century would not have expected an autobiography to contain personal revelations or apologies. Waugh, *supra* note 1, at 205. But Bunting argues that Grant's reluctance to explain or justify made him "a profound puzzle to his own generation." Bunting, *supra* note 2, at 2.

42. Waugh, *supra* note 1, at 205.

43. *Personal Memoirs*, *supra* note 24, at 65.

44. *Id.*

45. *Id.* at 629–30.

46. Grant was always faithful to his wife Julia. He also wept openly and nearly constantly through his daughter's wedding at the White House. *See* McFeely, *supra* note 7, at 402; *see also* Waugh, *supra* note 1, at 147. Korda believes Grant "found in his family life a happiness that eluded him in his public life." Korda, *supra* note 8, at 134.

47. Waugh, *supra* note 1, at 1 (Grant had a "resolute determination to defeat those who would split the Union.").

48. Personal Memoirs, supra note 24, at 659.

He admired and respected many men — particularly Zachary Taylor and Abraham Lincoln.

Grant's famous traits of tenacity, honesty, fairness, discipline, and practicality contributed to his great success in writing with clarity. Grant was not one to give up, and this persistence and tenacity when writing translated to a product that was clear and precise. He knew what his goal was, and he wanted his readers to understand and accomplish those goals. Grant was also honest, fair and straightforward, so his writing never masked reality. Instead, Grant got right to the point.[49] Grant was disciplined both physically and mentally,[50] and he wrote with such concentration that he was not aware of his surroundings. Finally, Grant was practical. He had a tendency to treat dramatic matters in a very matter-of-fact way.[51] As a result, his writing did not exaggerate, obfuscate, or confuse his readers.

Grant's *Personal Memoirs* are devoted primarily to the Civil War, but he does tell the story of his childhood and years at West Point. In these early pages of *Personal Memoirs* Grant reveals several features of his personality: his resolve, his courage, his sensitivity to embarrassment and humiliation — both his own and that of others, and his belief that he was equal to others.[52] Some historians wish Grant had devoted more pages to his early years,[53] but even in these scant pages Grant shares what he himself considered the truly defining events.[54]

Ulysses S. Grant was born on April 27, 1822, in Ohio and lived there until he entered West Point at age seventeen.[55] Grant thought of himself as a westerner.[56] He described his childhood as idyllic. He preferred farming to his father's tan-

---

49. Flood, *supra* note 22, at 102.

50. *Id.* at 112.

51. *Id.* at 194.

52. Korda believes that "Grant's virtues — his reserve, his quiet determination, his courage in the face of adversity — were all present in the shy, awkward, withdrawn child who seemed unable to please his father and toward whom his mother showed an indifference that was remarked on even at the very beginning of his life." Korda, *supra* note 8, at 13.

53. *See id.* at 16–17 (Korda counts only seven pages out of 1200 devoted to Grant's childhood).

54. Charles Bracelon Flood notes,

By deciding to give his work the full title, *Personal Memoirs of Ulysses S. Grant*, he did himself a great favor. He could write about the things he wished to put before the reader, and omit those he did not. At one stroke, he relieved himself of the obligation to include everything he might know about a battle or a person, while reserving the right to dwell on a smaller matter of fleeting perception.

Flood, *supra* note 22, at 71.

55. *Personal Memoirs*, *supra* note 24, at 19.

56. Bunting, supra note 2, at 7.

ning business, so he was allowed to complete his chores on the family land and then spend the remainder of his time fishing, swimming, and riding horses.[57]

Perhaps the most defining feature of Grant's personality was his resolve. When Grant, a horse lover for his entire life, was about eight years old, he saw a colt and wanted to buy him. Grant's father offered the colt's owner, Mr. Ralston, $20, but Ralston wanted $25. Grant wanted the colt so desperately that he "begged to be allowed to take him at the price demanded." His father relented and told Grant that he should start by offering $20, increase the offer to $22.50, and offer $25 if Ralston did not accept the earlier offers. Grant rode to Ralston's house and announced, "Papa says I may offer you twenty dollars for the colt, but if you won't take that, I am to offer twenty-two and a half, and if you won't take that, to give you twenty-five." Grant concludes, "It would not take a Connecticut man to guess the price finally agreed upon."[58] Some suggest that this story foreshadows Grant's later business failures.[59] But another view of the story is that it shows Grant's determination and resolve. He likely had a fair idea of the value of the colt.[60] He knew he wanted this horse, he was willing to do what it took to get it, and he was ultimately successful.[61]

Another horse story from Grant's childhood shows his courage, common sense, and ability to solve problems. When he was fifteen, Grant acquired a new saddle horse that had evidently never before worn a collar or a harness. Having traded one of his two carriage horses for the new one, Grant nonetheless hitched the horse to the carriage and started toward home. At one point a "ferocious dog" frightened the horses, and they bolted. Though Grant stopped and calmed them, the new horse soon began to kick and run again. Grant managed to stop them at the very edge of a twenty-foot precipice. The new horse, "frightened and trembl[ing] like an aspen," refused to move on. Finally, Grant calmed the agitated horse logically and humanely by blindfolding it with his bandana.[62]

Grant could not bear humiliation, whether it be his own or that of any other person. Grant shared three stories—more than on any other topic—about his dislike of feeling embarrassed. Grant's sensitivity to embarrassment was part of the reason he was reluctant to write his memoirs.[63] He recalled how the Ralston transaction "caused me great heartburning" when the hometown boys

---

57. *Personal Memoirs, supra* note 24, at 20–21.
58. *Id.* at 22.
59. Bunting, *supra* note 2, at 12.
60. *Id.*
61. *See* Waugh, *supra* note 1, at 17 (Grant was honest and honorable in the exchange).
62. *Personal Memoirs, supra* note 24, at 21–22.
63. *See infra* note 225 and accompanying text.

teased him after learning the story.[64] Grant wryly noted, "Boys enjoy the misery of their companions, at least village boys in that day did, and in later life I have found that all adults are not free from the peculiarity."[65] Grant was next embarrassed after he proudly wore his new infantry uniform, wanting "my old school-mates, particularly the girls, to see me in it."[66] He said he had the "conceit ... knocked out of me" by two incidents.[67] He was riding on a horse in Cincinnati "imagining that every one was looking at me [with great admiration]," but a street urchin teased him.[68] Grant was still feeling the sting from that humiliation when a stable hand in Grant's hometown wore "a pair of sky-blue nankeen pantaloons — just the color of my uniform trousers — with a strip of white cotton sheeting sewed down the outside seams in imitation of mine."[69] Grant admitted that the mocking of his uniform also "gave me a distaste for military uniform that I never recovered from."[70]

These stories about Grant's personal humiliations show another Grant personality trait — he believed in human equality. Grant opens his *Memoirs* with the following sentence: "My family is American, and has been for generations, in all its branches, direct and collateral."[71] Grant's pride in his American lineage supported his belief that he was equal to other men. Michael Korda elaborates, "The Grants may not have thought themselves *better* than anyone, but they certainly thought themselves as *good* as anyone — a very American attitude."[72] Grant claims that he watched his personal hero General Winfield Scott review the West Point cadets and thought, "I could never resemble him in appearance, but I believe I did have a presentiment for a moment that some day I should occupy his place on review...."[73] Again, he recalled the Ralston horse trade and explained that he did not share this presentiment with even his closest friends, fearing that he might again be the subject of ridicule.[74]

Grant gives some insight into his intellectual habits by contrasting his own casual study habits to his father's disciplined study habits. Grant admired his

---

64. *Personal Memoirs, supra* note 24, at 23.

65. *Id.*

66. *Id.* at 30.

67. *Id.*

68. *Id.*

69. *Id.* at 31.

70. *Id.* at 30.

71. *Id.* at 15. Grant provides evidence supporting this statement by tracing his family history on both his maternal and paternal sides. *Id.* at 15–19.

72. Korda, *supra* note 8, at 16.

73. *Personal Memoirs, supra* note 24, at 29.

74. *Id.*

father Jesse's "thirst for education" despite Jesse's formal schooling of only six months.[75] Grant recalled that his father "learned rapidly" and "read every book he could borrow."[76] Because books were scarce, Jesse was a studious reader, "so that when he got through with a book, he knew everything in it."[77] Grant himself attended school from age six until he left for West Point at age seventeen, but he admitted, "I was not studious in habit, and probably did not make progress enough to compensate for the outlay for board and tuition."[78]

Grant's lackadaisical attitude toward studying continued at West Point: "I did not take hold of my studies with avidity, in fact I rarely ever read over a lesson the second time during my entire cadetship."[79] But, importantly, Grant did read voraciously. He explained that cadets could check out books; he used those borrowing privileges to read popular fiction. He may have considered it a waste of his time, but these novels influenced Grant's writing style in a positive way.[80] Grant's reading improved his style more than any time he could have spent on Jomini's text on tactics.[81] It was at this time that Grant recognized the value of clarity[82] and when he began his lifelong habit of writing with clarity: "[Grant's] prose is direct, clear, and never ambiguous, as it was to be for the rest of his life...."[83] At age seventeen Grant was "already a writer of confident, limber English prose."[84]

After West Point, Grant was sent to the Mexican War, where he served under both Generals Taylor and Scott.[85] Grant respected Taylor and adopted several

---

75. *Id.* at 17.

76. *Id.*

77. *Id.*

78. *Id.* at 19 (The "board and tuition" Grant referred to was the cost of his attendance at two boarding schools during the winters of 1836–37 and 1838–39.).

79. *Id.* at 27. Grant never wanted to be at West Point, and in fact hoped that Congress would approve the 1839 bill proposed to abolish West Point so that he could honorably leave the Military Academy. *Id.* at 28. It was Jesse's wish, not Ulysses's, to have Ulysses attend West Point. *Id.* at 23–24. Grant admitted that his time at West Point dragged, recalling that his years there "seemed about five times as long as Ohio years." *Id.* at 29.

80. *See* Stephen King, *On Writing: A Memoir of the Craft* 145 (2000).

81. Korda, *supra* note 8, at 38.

82. *See id.* ("Like the young Winston Churchill, also a failure at school and military college, Grant learned how to master the English sentence.").

83. *Id.* at 38.

84. Bunting, *supra* note 2, at 16.

85. Grant fought valiantly in that war; he also was a quartermaster. Bunting, *supra* note 2, at 24–25. Even though he was not guilty of a theft of $1,000 while he was a quartermaster in Mexico, Grant was held responsible for the missing money and had to repay the sum. Korda, *supra* note 8, at 49.

of Taylor's personality traits, including Taylor's preference for plain military dress,[86] calm demeanor,[87] obedience,[88] and taciturn nature.[89] Grant followed Taylor's lead in not "troubl[ing] the administration much with his demands, but ... [doing] the best he could with the means given him."[90] In fact, this was the quality that Lincoln admired in Grant. Lincoln noted that all his previous Union commanders would complain that they could not win battles without additional resources, generally cavalry, but "[Grant] doesn't ask me to do impossibilities for him, and he's the first general I've had that didn't."[91]

Grant embraced Taylor's habit of writing orders with clarity. Grant could have been describing his own writing style when he recalled that Taylor "could put his meaning so plainly that there could be no mistaking it."[92] Significantly, Grant recognized how Taylor worked to make his military orders clear, a practice that Grant admired, embraced, and emulated.

Grant also served under Scott; his admiration for Scott began during his West Point days. Grant believed both generals were "great and successful soldiers; both were true, patriotic and upright."[93] But Grant preferred Taylor. "Scott saw more through the eyes of his staff officers" where "Taylor saw for himself."[94] In addition to his hands-on approach, Grant respected Taylor's sense of camaraderie with his soldiers: "Both [Scott and Taylor] were pleasant to serve under— Taylor was pleasant to serve with."[95] Taylor and Grant were both known and respected by their soldiers.[96] Grant evoked "familiar reverence" from his soldiers.[97]

---

86. Grant wrote, "General Taylor never made any great show or parade, either of uniform or retinue. In dress he was possibly too plain, rarely wearing anything in the field to indicate his rank, or even that he was an officer...." *Personal Memoirs, supra* note 24, at 63.

87. Grant wrote, "No soldier could face either danger or responsibility more calmly than he. These are qualities more rarely found than genius or physical courage." *Id.*

88. Grant explained that if Taylor "thought that he was sent to perform an impossibility with the means given," he would tell the authorities, let them decide what to do, and "[i]f the judgment was against him he would have gone on and done the best he could with the means at hand." *Id.*

89. Grant noted that Taylor would not "parad[e] his grievance before the public." *Id.*

90. *Id.*

91. Jean Edward Smith, *supra* note 14, at 307 (referencing a conversation between Lincoln and Stoddard).

92. *Personal Memoirs, supra* note 24, at 85; McPherson, *supra* note 2, at xvii.

93. *Personal Memoirs, supra* note 24, at 85.

94. *Id.*

95. *Id.*

96. *Id.*; McPherson, *supra* note 2, at xvii.

97. Keegan, *supra* note 11, at 234 (Keegan labeled Grant an "unhero," but meant this as a compliment).

When recalling this time of his life, Grant reveals one of his superstitions: "[W]hen I started to go any where, or to do anything, not to turn back, or stop until the thing intended was accomplished."[98] Many claim that this trait was the secret to his success as a general—he moved forward, he pressed on, he pursued the enemy, he would find an alternative so that he could continue making progress.[99] Lincoln admired this tenacity and reportedly commented, "When Grant once gets possession of a place, he holds on to it as if he had inherited it."[100]

After the Mexican War, Grant served an additional six years "in a succession of dreary posts."[101] Ultimately, Grant resigned from the Army, likely due to his drinking, which was always exacerbated by his separation from his family.[102]

During the next seven years, before Grant reenlisted during the Civil War, he tried several occupations including farming, selling wood, and selling real estate.[103] He was not successful in any of these endeavors. At one point, people were rumored to cross the street when they saw Grant because they feared he would ask them for a loan.[104] He eventually settled in Galena, Illinois to work for his two younger brothers in their leather goods store.[105]

Grant's recollections of the Civil War years constitute the bulk of his *Personal Memoirs*.[106] Naturally, Grant writes about only those battles in which he was involved.[107] These Civil War years were the time when Grant both realized the value of clear directions and practiced his clear writing.

---

98. *Personal Memoirs, supra* note 24, at 35.

99. *See* Bunting, *supra* note 2, at 35 ("Grant was willing to make decisions and live with their consequences" because of his "constant faith in victory."); Jean Edward Smith, *supra* note 14, at 357 (Grant had a "head-on style.").

100. Porter, *supra* note 16, at 223 (quoting Lincoln).

101. Wilson, *supra* note 25, at 134.

102. Korda, *supra* note 8, at 51.

103. *Personal Memoirs, supra* note 24, at 125–26.

104. Wilson, *supra* note 25, at 134.

105. *Personal Memoirs, supra* note 24, at 126; McFeely, *supra* note 7, at 64–66. Grant did not mind leaving that business, "I never went into our leather store after that meeting, to put up a package or do other business." *Personal Memoirs, supra* note 24, at 138.

106. Even when discussing the Mexican War, Grant often foreshadows events from the Civil War. *See e.g. id* at 59 ("As I looked down that long line of about three thousand armed men, advancing towards a larger force also armed, I thought what a fearful responsibility General Taylor must feel, commanding such a host and so far away from friends."); *id.* at 73 ("My pity was aroused by the sight of the Mexican garrison of Monterey marching out of town as prisoners, and no doubt the same feeling was experienced by most of our army who witnessed it."); *id.* at 93 ("It is always, however, in order to follow a retreating foe, unless stopped or otherwise directed.").

107. Wilson, supra note 25, at 152 (The Union victory is made "to seem a great deal easier than it actually was" because Grant writes only about "those operations in which he himself figured.").

Grant was a superb military leader and particularly suited for a war like the Civil War. He did not believe much in theory; he instead preferred action.[108] He recognized that his army needed no permanent base and that the soldiers could survive on the military supplies provided by river and railroad and the produce of the land through which the army passed.[109] Victory would then come with the three things Grant could provide: "drill, discipline, and belief in [the Union cause]."[110]

Grant knew fear, but that did not stop his progress. Grant, in an oft-quoted passage, explains how he learned the important lesson that his enemy was just as fearful as he was:

> I would have given anything then [before a battle] to have been back in Illinois, but I had not the moral courage to halt and consider what to do; I kept right on.... It occurred to me at once that Harris had been as much afraid of me as I had been of him. This was a view of the question I had never taken before; but it was one I never forgot afterwards.[111]

There was one man whom most Union soldiers feared above all others— Robert E. Lee. Grant recognized that many people would attribute "almost superhuman abilities" to military commanders.[112] Lee had that heroic status for most, but not for Grant, who said, "I had known him personally, and knew that he was mortal; and it was just as well that I felt this."[113]

Almost every account of Grant's temperament suggests that he was calm in all circumstances. The following story is the exception. During The Wilderness campaign Grant heard about Lee's prowess one too many times. A Union brigadier told Grant that the Union was in crisis, he knew "Lee's methods well by past experience," and Lee would send his whole army to cut off Union communications.[114] Porter recalled Grant's response:

> The general rose to his feet, took his cigar out of his mouth, turned to the officer, and replied, with a degree of animation which he sel-

---

108. *Personal Memoirs, supra* note 24, at 151 (Grant admitted he had not studied tactics, but he looked at one lesson and then led his regiment in the Mexican War, determining that tactics "was nothing more than common sense.").

109. Keegan, *supra* note 11, at 192.

110. *Id.*

111. *Personal Memoirs, supra* note 24, at 149.

112. *Id.,* at 116.

113. *Id.* Grant thus likely tired of those who diminished his victories by saying, "Wait until you meet Bobby Lee." Thomas E. Griess, *The American Civil War* 194 (2002).

114. Porter, *supra* note 16, at 69.

dom manifested: "Oh, I am heartily tired of hearing about what Lee is going to do. Some of you always seem to think he is suddenly going to turn a double somersault and land in our rear and on both flanks at the same time. Go back to your command, and try to think what we are going to do ourselves, instead of what Lee is going to do."[115]

Some of Grant's military leadership qualities helped him write with clarity. He had common sense.[116] He was self-confident.[117] He was modest.[118] Grant's approach to writing seemed to mirror his direct and simple approach to military strategy, "The art of war is simple enough. Find out where your enemy is. Get him as soon as you can. Strike at him as hard as you can, and keep moving on."[119]

After Appomattox, Grant became a four-star general.[120] Grant remained as head of the Army until his election in 1868 to the first of his two terms as president.[121] His campaign slogan in 1868 was identical to one of the final sentences in his *Personal Memoirs*, "Let us have peace."[122] Grant's record as a politician is a subject of some controversy with some historians arguing that he is underrated as a president,[123] but many others pointing out that his "political career proved troublesome."[124] No one believed that Grant himself was

---

115. *Id.* at 70.

116. McFeely, *supra* note 7, at xiii (McFeely notes that Grant did not have patience for theory, but he did have "ruthlessly realistic common sense").

117. *Personal Memoirs, supra* note 24, at 116.

118. Keegan, *supra* note 11, at 234. Grant did occasionally drink during the Civil War, and his muddled writing was one clue that he was drinking. Colonel John Rawlins wrote to Grant, "[The] lack of your usual promptness of decision and clearness in expressing yourself in writing tend to confirm my suspicions [that Grant had been drinking]." Jean Edward Smith, *supra* note 14, at 232 (quoting 8 *Grant Papers* 322–23 note). Rawlins's diligence prevented Grant from backsliding into drinking. *Id.*

119. Coolidge, *supra* note 37, at 54 (Coolidge references a conversation Grant had with a "young officer.").

120. Waugh, *supra* note 1, at 2.

121. *Id.*

122. *Personal Memoirs, supra* note 24, at 665.

123. *See* Bunting, *supra* note 2, at 2 ("Grant was the only American president to serve two complete and consecutive terms between Andrew Jackson and Woodrow Wilson, and as president he was bequeathed heavier and less tractable burdens than any other president in our history, save only two."); *see also* David Herbert Donald, *Overrated and Underrated Americans*, 39 Am. Heritage 52 (1988) (listing Grant as the most underrated public figure in American History).

124. Waugh, *supra* note 1, at 2.

corrupt; instead, he was honest and well-meaning.[125] Still, his presidential years were not the most successful years of his life. Grant's lasting legacy is as a general.[126]

After leaving the presidency, the Grants took a two-year world tour. Grant was an international celebrity.[127] The working people adored him.[128] They thought of Grant as a fellow workingman.[129] Grant was a "man of few words," and he did not make long speeches.[130] Following the tour, the Grants returned to live in New York City, where Grant eventually lost all his savings. He then wrote his *Personal Memoirs* during the last year of his life.[131]

Grant's Writing Habits

Grant approached his writing calmly, with diligence and concentration. Two first-hand accounts of Grant physically writing show how Grant approached the task. Porter vividly recalled watching Grant write,

> My attention was soon attracted to the manner in which he went to work at his correspondence. At this time, as throughout his later career, he wrote nearly all his documents with his own hand, and seldom dictated to any one even the most unimportant despatch. His work was performed swiftly and uninterruptedly, but without any marked display of nervous energy. His thoughts flowed as freely from his mind as his ink from his pen; he was never at a loss for an expression and seldom interlined a word or made a material correction.[132]

Adam Badeau, Grant's military secretary, confirmed that Grant wrote with the same calm detachment, even when writing in the field. Badeau reported that even when "[a] shell burst immediately over him," Grant's hand did not shake; instead he "continued the dispatch as calmly as if he had been in

---

125. *Id.*

126. Grant is still remembered "as a general, not as a president." Bunting, *supra* note 2, at 5.

127. Korda, *supra* note 8, at 138.

128. *Id.* at 139.

129. *Id.*

130. *Id.*; Grant disliked public speaking. McFeely, *supra* note 7, at 154. Grant "frequently blushed when applauded and always kept his remarks brief." Flood, *supra* note 22, at 51.

131. Waugh, *supra* note 1, at 2.

132. Porter, *supra* note 16, at 6–7 (describing how Grant and Porter had returned from a day of inspection and Grant had then sat at his desk to write).

camp."[133] Grant's chief goal was clarity.[134] But he knew that to achieve clarity he had to consider his audience, use a simple and direct style, and write with precision and accuracy.

Consider Audience

When I put my pen to the paper I did not know the first word that I should make use of in writing the terms. I only knew what was in my mind, and I wished to express it clearly, so that there could be no mistaking it.

Ulysses S. Grant[135]

Amazingly, Grant used the identical goal of clarity—*"there could be no mistaking it"*[136]—in both his description of Taylor's writing and that of his own goals at Appomattox. This goal of clarity is written with the reader in mind. The writer is envisioning the reader and is writing so that any reader will know exactly what the writer means. Grant envisioned one very specific audience member when he wrote his military orders—the addressee on the dispatch. That reader was always Grant's primary audience. He knew that others, including the public, would read his dispatches. But Grant did not let these shadow audiences dictate his objective of making sure that the addressee knew his precise meaning. In contrasting Scott with Taylor, Grant focused in part on whom each envisioned as his primary audience. Scott prepared his orders "with great care and evidently with the view that they should be a history of what followed";[137] Taylor "gave orders to meet the emergency without reference to how they would read in history."[138]

The audience for Grant's *Personal Memoirs* was the American public, who loved and revered Grant.[139] During his courageous effort to complete the book, he "was serving up to his future readers a masterful overview of his campaigns and battles,"[140] so that all Americans could benefit from his experience and

---

133. Wilson, *supra* note 25, at 135 (quoting Adam Badeau).

134. *Personal Memoirs, supra* note 24, at 631.

135. *Id.* (recalling the events of April 9, 1865, at the Appomattox Court House, Virginia, when General Robert E. Lee surrendered the Army of Northern Virginia).

136. *Id.* at 85, 631.

137. *Id.* at 85.

138. *Id.*

139. Even young Americans, not born until long after the Civil War ended, appreciated Grant's role in preserving the Union and flooded him with letters during his last year of life. Flood, *supra* note 22, at 165–66.

140. *Id.* at 127.

wisdom.[141] There is no doubt that Grant also envisioned his beloved soldiers and sailors as he was writing his *Personal Memoirs*. He completed his dedication on May 23: "These volumes are dedicated to the American soldier and sailor."[142] Grant's son suggested that his father revise his dedication to specify only the Northern soldiers and sailors, but Grant made no change because he wanted to include all those who fought in the Civil War.[143] He hoped his dedication would help restore harmony in America.[144]

Grant's presidential writings, as opposed to his wartime writing and memoirs, are not the best examples of clarity, primarily a result of Grant's discomfort with his audiences during the period of his presidency. Josiah Bunting III explains,

> Ulysses Grant, one of the most talented writers to occupy the White House, labored in writing his inaugural addresses and annual messages to Congress not to disappoint the expectations of his audiences. He imagined that such lofty occasions require a certain kind of language. It is extraordinary, the difference in tone and syntax between these set pieces, on the one hand, and the headlong clarity of his military orders and correspondence, not to mention the limber prose of his *Memoirs*.[145]

Adopt a Simple and Direct Style

> *[General Taylor] knew how to express what he wanted to say in the fewest well-chosen words, but would not sacrifice meaning to the construction of high-sounding sentences.*
>
> Ulysses S. Grant[146]

When the goal is clarity—to have the reader understand exactly what you mean in your writing—a writer will write with simplicity and directness. General Meade's chief-of-staff recognized that "[Grant's] style inclined to be epigrammatic without his being aware of it."[147] Grant's simple and direct style may be more common in our modern times, but Grant was writing "[i]n an age of

---

141. *Id.* at 129.
142. *Personal Memoirs, supra* note 24, at dedication.
143. Flood, *supra* note 22, at 182.
144. *Id.*
145. Bunting, *supra* note 2, at 117.
146. *Personal Memoirs, supra* note 24, at 85.
147. Wilson, *supra* note 25, at 143.

eloquent oratory and chivalrous circumlocution."[148] Grant's style contrasted dramatically with this flamboyant style; he used "plain and unmistakably clear words." Like Lincoln, Grant preferred words of Saxon derivation, so his words were shorter than those derived from Latin and had more punch.[149]

Grant's writing was crisp, forceful, and clear.[150] He used the active voice, which made his sentences shorter and more direct.[151] In the same way that Grant ran his army, he wrote by going directly from a starting point to an end point without being distracted.[152]

Grant noted that his war writings and official Presidential documents had been published and thus "[t]he public has become accustomed to my style of writing. They know that it is not even an attempt to imitate either a literary or classical style; that it is just what it is and nothing else."[153] His goal was to tell his story "so that others can see as I do what I attempt to show...."[154]

Write with Precision and Accuracy

> I would like to see truthful history written. Such history will do full credit to the courage, endurance and soldierly ability of the American citizen, no matter what section of the country he hailed from, or in what ranks he fought.
>
>   Ulysses S. Grant[155]

Grant believed that he should always be precise and scrupulously accurate. He had an excellent memory for both events and topography,[156] but he double-checked all dates and facts.[157] Grant "used the English language as precisely as any military commander before or since."[158] Further, Grant was

---

148. Taranto & Leo, *supra* note 3, at 95.

149. Flood, *supra* note 22, at 68.

150. Keegan, *supra* note 11, at 200.

151. Mark Adler, *Clarity for Lawyers* 98 (2d. ed. 2007).

152. McPherson, *supra* note 2, at xv–xvi, xviii.

153. *See* Bruce Catton, *U.S. Grant: Man of Letters*, 109 Am. Heritage 97, 98 (1968) [hereinafter Catton, *U.S. Grant: Man of Letters*] (Grant considered it a matter of honor to be honest).

154. *Id.*

155. *Personal Memoirs*, *supra* note 24, at 103.

156. *McPherson, supra* note 2, at xviii.

157. Jean Edward Smith, *supra* note 14, at 625–26 (relating Mark Twain's recollection of the "constant and painstaking search of the records" conducted while Grant wrote *Personal Memoirs*).

158. Id. at 226.

honest.[159] He wrote his *Personal Memoirs* objectively and honestly, which set the book apart from other self-serving accounts of the Civil War. Edmund Wilson noted, "Perhaps never has a book so objective in form seemed so personal in every line."[160]

Precision and accuracy are essential qualities for legal writers. Readers trust writers who are precise.[161] Lawyers have an ethical obligation to be truthful.[162] Even without Grant's memory, modern lawyers have an ability to retrieve the law. Grant enjoyed a tactical benefit because of his thorough knowledge of terrain, troop movements, and the traits of the opposing commanders.[163] Lawyers gain a tactical benefit by precision and honesty, too. A distinction or analogy to a prior precedent depends on our careful analysis and comparisons. Further, other lawyers and judges will trust lawyers who thoroughly research and analyze the law, and then accurately report that law.[164]

Grant's Clarity at Work

Grant's War Dispatches—Union Army

Grant knew the importance of clarity in his orders—active warfare is no place for confusion. Unfortunately, "[t]he Civil War had many instances of vague, ambiguous, or confusing orders that affected the outcome of a campaign or battle."[165] In contrast, Grant provided plain, clear, and concise orders.[166] He preferred to write out his instructions, rather than give oral instructions.[167]

---

159. *See* Catton, *U.S. Grant: Man of Letters, supra* note 153, at 98.

160. Wilson, *supra* note 25, at 143.

161. Michael R. Smith, *Advanced Legal Writing* 186 (3d ed. 2013).

162. Model Rules of Prof'l Conduct R. 4.1 (2004).

163. *See, e.g.* Bunting, *supra* note 2, at 35 (Grant had faith in victory and could deal with chaos with calm objectivity and a consideration of all relevant factors); Jean Edward Smith, *supra* note 14, at 343 (Grant knew topography, could remember maps, and was a "master" at maneuvering troops).

164. *See* Stephen D. Easton, *My Last Lecture: Unsolicited Advice for Future and Current Lawyers*, 56 S.C. L. Rev. 229, 248 (2004) (honesty will help your reputation).

165. McPherson, *supra* note 2, at xvii.

166. *Id.*

167. Waugh, *supra* note 1, at 88.

Clarity was such a defining feature of Grant's writing that virtually any of his Civil War orders could exemplify his clear writing.[168] A few orders, selected from his *Personal Memoirs,* show that clarity.

Grant wrote the following to General George Gordon Meade on April 9, 1864:

> *In Field, Culpeper C. H., Va.*
> *Maj.-General Geo. G. Meade,*
> *Com'd'g Army of the Potomac*
>
> ...
>
> *Lee's army will be your objective point. Wherever Lee goes, there you will go also.*
>
> U.S. GRANT,
> *Lieutenant-General*[169]

Meade knew exactly what Grant meant, and so do we: do not be distracted, you must follow Lee. Grant's objective was always to destroy the Confederate army; he did not care about capturing the Confederate capital.[170] Grant knew that Meade was capable and that his reluctance to lead the Army of the Potomac to launch an offensive in northern Virginia resulted not from Meade's shortcomings, but from Meade's obedience in following Major-General Halleck's cautious lead.[171] Meade would excel under "a more audacious general in chief."[172] Grant provided just the direction and encouragement that Meade needed.[173]

The Meade dispatch is simple and direct. But the dispatch is also lyrical. Grant's language has a Biblical counterpart in the *Book of Ruth* when Ruth tells her mother-in-law, Naomi, "Where you go, I will go."[174] Except for the words "wherever" and "also," every other word in the second sentence is only one syllable long. The sentence is compact, yet packed with meaning.

Several other dispatches show Grant's clarity:

---

168. *See* Keegan, *supra* note 11, at 200 (explaining that Porter was amazed that the dispatches he saw Grant writing were "both models of lucidity and of the highest importance," and further noting, "But all Grant's despatches were of that quality").

169. *Personal Memoirs, supra* note 24, at 415–16.

170. Jean Edward Smith, *supra* note 14, at 303.

171. *Id.* at 291–92.

172. *Id.* at 292.

173. *Id.* at 293.

174. *Book of Ruth* 1:16.

Perkins' Plantation, La.,
April 27, 1863
Major-General J. A. McClernand,
Commanding 13th A. C.

   Commence immediately the embarkation of your corps, or so much of it as there is transportation for. Have put aboard the artillery and every article authorized in orders limiting baggage, except the men, and hold them in readiness, with their places assigned, to be moved at a moment's warning.[175]

* * *

May 14, 1863
To: Blair

   Their design is evidently to cross the Big Black.... We must beat them. Turn your troops immediately to Bolton; take all the trains with you.[176]

* * *

City Point, Va. December 6, 1864—4 p.m.
Major-General Thomas,
Nashville, Tenn.

   Attack Hood at once and wait no longer for a remnant of your cavalry. There is great danger of delay resulting in a campaign back to the Ohio River.[177]

* * *

Near Spottsylvania C. H.
May 11, 1864—8:30 a.m.
Major-General Halleck, Chief of Staff of the Army
Washington, D.C.

   We have now ended the 6th day of very hard fighting.... [I] purpose to fight it out on this line if it takes all summer.[178]

---

175. *Personal Memoirs, supra* note 24, at 280–81.
176. *Id.* at 299.
177. *Id.* at 567.
178. *Id.* at 473. Grant removed the word "me" after "takes" to improve the sentence. Catton, *U.S. Grant: Man of Letters, supra* note 153, at 99.

Grant's military orders "bristle with verbs of action."[179] Grant used adjectives and adverbs sparingly, and "only those necessary to enforce his meaning."[180] All of Grant's dispatches to his Army "perfectly illustrate the clarity and force of his writing style."[181]

Not all Union officers gave such clear orders. General Rosencrans issued an order to Brigadier-General Wood to "close up on Reynolds as fast as possible, and support him."[182] But the order was confusing and could not be followed. "Close up on Reynolds" suggested a lateral move, but that was an impossible direction to follow because there was no gap in the line. Further, the order to "support him" would mean pulling out of the line and coming up in the rear of Reynolds which would then create a gap in the line.[183] Wood, who had been humiliated by Rosencrans when he asked for clarification of an order earlier in the day, refused to again ask for clarification, and pulled his three brigades out of the line even though "the order made no sense and appeared disastrous."[184] The confusing order, and Wood's insistence on following it, created "a gap in the Federal line at its weakest and most seriously threatened point."[185] Grant's orders did not cause such confusion or result in such disastrous consequences.

Meade's Chief-of-Staff complimented Grant: "There is one striking thing about Grant's orders: no matter how hurriedly he may write them on the field, no one ever had the slightest doubt as to their meaning, or ever had to read them over a second time to understand them."[186] This is the ultimate praise for an author striving to write "so that there could be no mistaking it."[187]

Grant's War Dispatches — Confederate Army

Grant's clarity was not limited to his correspondence with his own army. He knew that the value of clarity extended to his correspondence with the

---

179. McPherson, *supra* note 2, at xix (McPherson used other examples of Grant's dispatches with the following verbs: move, engage, disencumber, select, feel, move, start).

180. *Id.*

181. Keegan, *supra* note 11, at 200–02 (Keegan uses Grant's dispatches written on May 16, 1863, as examples of this clarity and force).

182. Steven E. Woodworth, *Six Armies in Tennessee* 114 (1998) (Rosencrans gave the task of drawing up this order to a staff officer because future president James Garfield was busy writing other orders).

183. *Id.* at 115.

184. *Id.*

185. *Id.* at 116.

186. Wilson, *supra* note 25, at 143 (quoting General Meade's chief of staff).

187. *Personal Memoirs, supra* note 24, at 631.

enemy. After the Union Army's victory at Donelson, Simon Bolivar Buckner formally requested a truce.[188] Grant replied with "one of the most famous dispatches in the history of warfare."[189]

Feb. 16, 1862
General S. B. Buckner,
Confederate Army

SIR: Yours of this date, proposing armistice and appointment of Commissioners to settle terms of capitulation, is just received. No terms except an unconditional and immediate surrender can be accepted. I propose to move immediately upon your works.

I am, sir, very respectfully,
Your ob't se'v't,
U.S. Grant,
Brig. Gen.

Buckner had hiked in Mexico with Grant,[190] loaned Grant money,[191] and expected some leniency.[192] Grant's dispatch dashed Buckner's hopes and gave the Civil War a "new, grim, and determined character."[193]

Buckner was Grant's primary audience, but Grant's larger audience included Americans and Europeans because Donelson was the first significant Union victory. Grant was informing this broader audience that he was changing the rules; he would make the South suffer the consequences of rebellion.[194] The South was devastated; the North was ecstatic. Europeans now saw the Civil War as a domestic affair.[195]

Grant's dispatch was simple, direct, and precise. It was perhaps not as direct as the response suggested by Brigadier General Charles Ferguson Smith, whose bayonet charge was largely responsible for the Donelson victory.[196] Grant asked Smith how he should reply to Buckner, and Smith replied, "No terms

---

188. Jean Edward Smith, *supra* note 14, at 162.
189. *Id.*
190. *Personal Memoirs, supra* note 24, at 109.
191. Bunting, *supra* note 2, at 32. (Buckner loaned Grant money in 1854 after Grant resigned from the Army and needed money to pay for his hotel and return to Missouri.)
192. McFeely, *supra* note 7, at 101.
193. *Id.*
194. Jean Edward Smith, *supra* note 14, at 163.
195. *Id.* at 165.
196. *Id.* at 159–60.

with the damned rebels."[197] Smith heard Grant read his dispatch out loud and said, "It's the same thing in smoother words."[198] James McPherson focused on the last two sentences and observed, "Not an excess word here; the three adjectives [unconditional, immediate, your] and single adverb [immediately] strengthen and clarify the message; the words produce action—they become action."[199]

The victory at Donelson made Grant famous. The dispatch to Buckner earned Grant the moniker "Unconditional Surrender" Grant.[200] Perhaps the strongest testament to Grant's clarity in the dispatch to Buckner is that it was so clear, simple, and direct that Northern schoolchildren memorized it.[201]

Grant's clearly written military orders can be directly contrasted with Confederate General Robert E. Lee's vague verbal orders. Historian J.F.C. Fuller suggests that Lee had two "cardinal defects" as a commander—he did not guide his subordinates once a battle started, and he relied on verbal orders.[202] Lee, unlike Grant, did not write his orders himself.[203] Lee's orders were vague and confusing.[204] On several occasions, Lee's orders created grave problems for the Confederate army. For example, Lee's orders at Gettysburg instructed his subordinates to carry out several different operations and, further, left the details to them.[205]

Lee himself was sometimes dismayed that his orders were not understood. The Battle of Malvern Hill was one such time. Lee's chief of staff Colonel Robert H. Chilton drafted Lee's orders, but the orders were poorly drawn, and "Lee cannot have intended to turn over direction of the Battle of Malvern Hill to a brigade commander." Further, Lee may have intended to leave some discretion about when to attack, but Captain A. G. Dickinson translated Lee's verbal order and wrote, "General Lee expects you to advance rapidly. He says it is reported the enemy is getting off. Press forward your whole line...." On its face, this was an order to attack immediately with no room for discretion. It was also evidence that General Lee should have written "his own orders instead of relying on staff officers to interpret them for him."[206]

---

197. *Id.* at 162.

198. *Id.*

199. McPherson, *supra* note 2, at xix.

200. Jean Edward Smith, *supra* note 14, at 165–66.

201. *Id.* at 166.

202. J.F.C. Fuller, *Grant & Lee: A Study in Personality and Generalship* 162 (1933).

203. Stephen W. Sears, *To the Gates of Richmond: The Peninsula Campaign* 323 (1992).

204. Fuller, *supra* note 202, at 244 (the orders often left much to the discretion of Lee's subordinates).

205. *Id.*

206. Sears, *supra* note 203, at 317, 322–23.

One final example of Grant's clarity is his message to Lee. Grant's first attempt to secure surrender is "surely one of the most dignified in the history of war."[207]

Headquarters Armies of the U.S.,
5 p.m., April 7, 1865
General R. E. Lee,
Commanding C. S. A.

The results of the last week must convince you of the hopelessness of further resistance on the part of the Army of Northern Virginia in this struggle. I feel that it is so, and regard it as my duty to shift from myself the responsibility of any further effusion of blood, by asking of you the surrender of that portion of the Confederate States army known as the Army of Northern Virginia.

U.S. GRANT,
Lieut.-General[208]

Lee replied the same day, noting that he did not entertain "the opinion you express on the hopelessness of further resistance," reciprocating Grant's desire to "avoid useless effusion of blood," and asking Grant for "the terms you will offer on condition of its surrender."[209] Grant wrote back to Lee with "but one condition I would insist upon, namely: that the men and officers surrendered shall be disqualified for taking up arms again against the Government of the United States until properly exchanged."[210]

The final terms of surrender, written by Grant on a table at Appomattox, were "[c]haracteristically direct and simple:"[211]

Appomattox C. H., Va., Ap'l 9th, 1865.
Gen. R. E. Lee,
Comd'g C. S. A.

Gen.: In accordance with the substance of my letter to you of the 8th inst., I propose to receive the surrender of the Army of N. Va. on the following terms, to wit: Rolls of all the officers and men to be made in duplicate. One copy to be given to an officer designated by me, the other

---

207. Korda, *supra* note 8, at 105.

208. *Personal Memoirs, supra* note 24, at 623.

209. *Id.*

210. *Id.* at 624.

211. Waugh, *supra* note 1, at 99 (the terms also reflected Lincoln's desire not to humiliate or punish the Confederates).

to be retained by such officer or officers as you may designate. The
officers to give their individual paroles not to take up arms against the
Government of the United States until properly exchanged, and each
company or regimental commander sign a like parole for the men of their
commands. The arms, artillery and public property to be parked and
stacked, and turned over to the officer appointed by me to receive them.
This will not embrace the side-arms of the officers, nor their
private horses or baggage. This done, each officer and man will be
allowed to return to their homes, not to be disturbed by United States
authority so long as they observe their paroles and the laws in force where
they may reside.

Very respectfully,
U.S. Grant,
Lt. Gen.[212]

Grant packed much meaning into those final terms of surrender. He used
"less than 200 well-chosen words"[213] to end the Civil War. Those few words
are very clear: Grant's terms granted the South amnesty and were designed to
begin a charitable post-war healing process.[214] Grant did not allow any firing
of victory salutes.[215] He instructed his staff officers to stop the Union soldiers
who had begun firing salutes,[216] saying, "The war is over; the rebels are our
countrymen again...."[217]

While riding away from Appomattox, Grant forgot that he had not yet informed the government of the surrender, so he "dismounted by the roadside,
sat down on a large stone, and called for pencil and paper."[218] He then wrote
"perhaps the least self-congratulatory or exultant message of victory in the
history of warfare."[219] The message was classic Grant: short, simple, direct,
and clear:

212. *Personal Memoirs, supra* note 24, at 630–31.
213. Jean Edward Smith, *supra* note 14, at 405.
214. *See id.*
215. Bruce Catton, *Grant Takes Command* 468 (1968).
216. *Personal Memoirs, supra* note 24, at 633.
217. Porter, *supra* note 16, at 486.
218. *Id.* at 488.
219. Korda, *supra* note 8, at 109.

Headquarters Appomattox C. H., Va.,
April 9th, 1865, 4:30 p.m.
Hon. E. M. Stanton, Secretary of War,
Washington.

    General Lee surrendered the Army of Northern Virginia this afternoon
on terms proposed by myself. The accompanying additional correspondence
will show the conditions fully.

U.S. GRANT,
Lieut.-General[220]

Grant's Personal Memoirs

The story of how Grant finally came to write his *Personal Memoirs* is almost as compelling as the end product.[221] Grant said in his Preface to the *Personal Memoirs*, "Although frequently urged by friends to write my memoirs I had determined never to do so, nor to write anything for publication."[222] Mark Twain was one of those encouraging Grant to write his memoirs, but Grant "wouldn't listen to the suggestion. He had no confidence in his ability to write well; whereas we all know now that he possessed an admirable literary gift and style."[223] Grant's continuous fear of being humiliated contributed to his reluctance. He confided to his doctor, "If anyone had suggested the idea of my becoming an author, as they frequently did, I was not sure whether they were making sport of me or not."[224] But then Grant was financially ruined by "the rascality of a business partner."[225] He needed money; he could no longer refuse to write his memoirs.[226]

---

220. *Personal Memoirs, supra* note 24, at 633.

221. For a fascinating account of Grant's last year of life, see generally Flood, *supra* note 22.

222. *Personal Memoirs, supra* note 24, at 7.

223. Wilson, *supra* note 25, at 131 (referencing a quotation from Mark Twain who met Grant in 1881; Twain said that Grant also feared that the book would not sell).

224. *Id.* at 139 (referencing one of Grant's letters written to his doctor shortly before his death). Grant also told his doctor that he had noticed that others were saving his notes, and thought that his English would be criticized. Horace Green, *General Grant's Last Stand* 319 (1936) (Green collected Grant's writings to his physician).

225. *Personal Memoirs, supra* note 24, at 7. Grant lost his money to Ferdinand Ward in what we would today label a Ponzi scheme. Korda, *supra* note 8, at 143. Wilson wryly notes, "It was the age of the audacious confidence man, and Grant was the incurable sucker." Wilson, *supra* note 25, at 167.

226. Grant begins his Preface by acknowledging that men do not often have a choice in their lives. "'Man proposes and God disposes.' There are but few important events in the affairs of men brought about by their own choice." *Personal Memoirs, supra* note 24, at 7.

Grant started by writing articles about Civil War battles for *Century Magazine*.[227] He "found [the work] congenial, and ... determined to continue it."[228] Grant also made the important discovery that he was a good writer, "He wrote an article on Shiloh and was astonished at himself to find that he could make a story full of human interest as easily as he had once indited orders and reports."[229] Grant also discovered that he enjoyed writing. His *Century* editor gave Grant some suggestions and reported that he had never had "an apter pupil" who was even willing to work on his writing every day of the week.[230]

Then Grant learned that he had terminal throat cancer.[231] He was now penniless and dying. He couldn't bear the thought of leaving his beloved family destitute.[232] He dictated the first part of his *Personal Memoirs*, but eventually he could not speak without extreme pain, so he handwrote the final chapters.[233] Grant's granddaughter recalled that whenever someone suggested that Grant's book was "killing him" another adult would reply, "No, the book is keeping him alive; without it he would already be dead."[234] The nation watched as Grant made his final stand against the formidable foe of cancer.[235] At times, it seemed

---

227. *Id.* Grant admitted, "I consented for the money it gave me; for at that moment I was living upon borrowed money." *Id.*

228. *Id.* Grant wrote articles about Shiloh, Vicksburg, Chattanooga and the Wilderness. Coolidge, *supra* note 37, at 561.

229. Coolidge, *supra* note 37, at 561. Coolidge continues, "He had the faculty of narrative in an unusual degree, as he had often shown among his intimates; for all his life he was an entertaining talker, at times monopolizing conversation in choice groups of friends. His stillness fell upon him only in public or with those he slightly knew." *Id.*

230. Flood, *supra* note 22, at 60.

231. Bunting, *supra* note 2, at 153 (Grant had noticed a pain in his throat after swallowing a peach in midsummer 1884, and his throat cancer was confirmed in October 1884).

232. *See Personal Memoirs, supra* note 24, at 7.

233. *See* Coolidge, *supra* note 37, at 564; McFeely, *supra* note 7, at 509 ("Grant with pencil and pad wrote his strong, quiet prose.").

234. Flood, *supra* note 22, at 164.

235. The American public read almost daily newspaper updates about Grant's illness. James T. Patterson, *The Dread Disease: Cancer and Modern American Culture* 2–4 (1987) ("Until President Ronald Reagan developed a malignancy in his colon a century later, no case of cancer received more thorough coverage in the press."); *see also* McFeely, *supra* note 7, at 509. Grant and his family moved to a cottage in the Adirondacks in July 1885, where a "flood of visitors ... eagerly made the pilgrimage to gaze at the dying general." *Id.* at 508. Old friends from both the North and South came to visit and pay their respects. Jean Edward Smith, *supra* note 14, at 626. Grant remains the only American president to die from cancer. Oral Cancer Found., *People, Political Figures,* oralcancerfoundation.org, http://oral-cancerfoundation.org/people/political_figures.htm (last visited Sept. 2, 2016).

that Grant would not win this last battle.[236] But in the end, he finished his *Personal Memoirs* days before he died.[237] He "wrote 275,000 words in less than a year."[238]

Even in Grant's lifetime a rumor was started, and has since persisted, that Mark Twain or Adam Badeau ghostwrote Grant's *Personal Memoirs*.[239] Grant himself responded to the Badeau rumor by stating, "The composition is entirely my own."[240] Grant's uniform writing style in his military dispatches, letters, and the *Personal Memoirs* showed "[t]hat no one can have tampered much with the original text...."[241]

Clarity is the defining feature of Grant's *Personal Memoirs*. Most everyone who has read and studied the book praises its clarity. William S. McFeely said, "[I]t is wonderfully clear."[242] Edmund Wilson noted, "[I]in general, the writing of the *Memoirs* is perfect in concision and clearness, in its propriety and purity of language."[243] John Keegan was even more effusive, calling the book "a literary phenomenon."[244] Gertrude Stein admired the book, and in particular its "taut prose."[245] Mark Twain pronounced it a "literary masterpiece"[246] and further announced that "[t]here is no higher literature than these mod-

---

236. In March 1885, Grant nearly died. McFeely, *supra* note 7, at 503.

237. Flood explains the poignancy of Grant's final days:

On July 10, Grant had told Douglas that if he could have two more weeks, "I will then feel my work is done." After ten days of those two weeks elapsed, on July 20 he had put away his pencil; now, on Thursday, July 23, with thirteen days of the two weeks he had wished for gone, he lay there, his work done.

Flood, *supra* note 22, at 227–28.

238. Jean Edward Smith, *supra* note 14, at 627. During this same time Congress restored Grant to his rank in the Army, which gave him the pay of a retired officer. Hesseltine, *supra* note 6, at 450–51.

239. Wilson, *supra* note 25, at 142–43 (Adam Badeau falsely claimed that he had written Grant's *Personal Memoirs*.).

240. Flood, *supra* note 22, at 171.

241. Wilson, *supra* note 25, at 142–43.

242. *McFeely, supra* note 7, at 511. McFeely complimented Grant's Civil War story for its clarity even though it "does not have the flashes of fire of Sherman's *Memoirs*, or the novelist's details of Lew Wallace's *Autobiography*." *Id.* at 510. But McFeely noted that Grant's clarity does not permeate every single section of the *Personal Memoirs*. Grant was taking cocaine during the day and morphine at night during the final months of his life, so the latter parts of *Personal Memoirs* are sometimes bland and repetitive. *Id.* at 509–10.

243. Wilson, *supra* note 25, at 142.

244. Keegan, *supra* note 11, at 202.

245. McFeely, *supra* note 7, at 501.

246. Waugh, *supra* note 1, at 209.

est, simple *Memoirs*. Their style is at least flawless, and no man can improve upon it."[247]

Personal Memoirs was criticized by a few. Some Southerners believed it contained grave errors.[248] Matthew Arnold, an English poet, critic, and Confederate sympathizer, categorized Grant's style as "English without charm and without high breeding."[249] Arnold's comment is not considered a criticism to modern American readers who recognize the value of simple, direct writing. And even Arnold admitted that Grant wrote clearly: "I found a language straightforward, nervous, firm, possessing in general the high merit of saying clearly in the fewest possible words what had to be said, and saying it, frequently, with shrewd and unexpected turns of expression."[250]

Grant's writing habits are present throughout his *Personal Memoirs*. He thought about his audience and its need for an accurate account of his role in the Civil War. He used a simple and direct writing style, with his characteristically active verbs.[251] "Action verbs predominate: 'move ... engage ... start ... attack.'"[252] It is as though Grant was back in his Civil War days, writing his famously clear dispatches.[253] Jean Edward Smith comments, "The prose is lean and elegant."[254] Grant was determined to be absolutely precise and correct.[255] He wanted his readers to know that he worked hard to be accurate and precise. He wrote, "I have used my best efforts, with the aid of my eldest son, F.D. Grant, assisted by his brothers, to verify from the records every statement of fact given."[256]

Just days before he died Grant wrote the following note to his physician, "I think I am a verb instead of a personal pronoun. A verb is anything that signifies to be; to do; or to suffer. I signify all three. Ulysses S. Grant."[257]

---

247. *Ulysses S. Grant Homepage*, http://www.granthomepage.com/grantauthor.htm (last visited Sept. 2, 2016).

248. Waugh, *supra* note 1, at 209–10.

249. *Id.* at 210 (citing Matthew Arnold, *General Grant*, 49).

250. Wilson, *supra* note 25, at 140.

251. McPherson, *supra* note 2, at xix (McPherson points out that Grant reverts to passive voice in some of the later chapters).

252. Jean Edward Smith, *supra* note 14, at 627.

253. *See* Hesseltine, *supra* note 6, at 450 ("Its style is simple yet dramatic; it shows a complete absence of personal bitterness.").

254. Jean Edward Smith, *supra* note 14, at 627.

255. *Id.* at 625.

256. *Personal Memoirs*, *supra* note 24, at 8.

257. McFeely, *supra* note 7, at 516 (Grant wrote this note, days before his death, to his physician).

When Grant died, a record one and a half million spectators lined his funeral route through New York City.[258] "At Grant's request, the pallbearers included an equal number of Southern and Union Generals."[259] Grant's popularity peaked at the time of his death.[260] Grant did not have confidence in his writing, but his elegant simplicity, direct style, and "crystal-clear"[261] prose prove that he was too modest. Grant believed that his accurate recording of history memorialized in his *Personal Memoirs* was his only legacy.[262] For lawyers trying to write persuasively, Grant's writings themselves are a legacy of clarity.

---

258. Jean Edward Smith, *supra* note 14, at 18 (citing the *N.Y. Times*).

259. *Id.* at 19.

260. *See Waugh, supra* note 1, at 2.

261. Jean Edward Smith, *supra* note 14, at 622.

262. *See Green, supra* note 224, at 323. Korda commented, "[Grant's] memoirs, which, along with the victory that he won, are his greatest and most lasting legacy to us." Korda, *supra* note 8, at 158.

Chapter 6

The Power of Zeal: Teddy Roosevelt

(October 27, 1858–January 6, 1919)
Presidency 1901–1909

If ever there was a man who could not be captured in just one word, it is Teddy Roosevelt.[1] The potential descriptors are endless: enthusiastic, courageous, smart, strong, powerful, loyal, adventurous, disciplined, confident, charismatic, resolute, patriotic, determined, and energetic. Yet the best single word to describe Roosevelt's personality and his persuasive writings is "zeal." With Roosevelt, there is simply no way to extract his personality from anything he did, including his writing. Thus the main influence on Roosevelt's writing style was simply Roosevelt himself. As he lived his life with zeal, so he wrote with zeal.

In virtually every way, Roosevelt was almost superhuman. He had multiple and varied careers: he was a historian, a rancher, an ornithologist, a military leader, a civil servant, Governor of New York, President of the United States, and a writer. The days of his life were packed with work, adventure, and joy. Roosevelt was a curious man who had numerous interests.[2] He had a passionate enthusiasm for all animals, but he had a special fondness for birds,[3] which he could identify by sight or sound. "When Roosevelt claimed to have

---

1. Roosevelt's pet name as a boy was "Teedie." Henry F. Pringle, *Theodore Roosevelt: A Biography* 5 (1931). Roosevelt was resigned to the public knowing him as "Teddy," but he was not fond of the nickname. Edmund Morris, *The Rise of Theodore Roosevelt* xxii (1979).
2. Louis Auchincloss, *Theodore Roosevelt* 35 (2001).
3. *Id.* at 95.

been the last person to spot a passenger pigeon in the wild, the ornithologists believed him."[4] He is remembered for many accomplishments: his conservation efforts, his devotion to Progressive Republican politics, his fearlessness in tackling big business, and his contributions to natural history.

The focus here is on Roosevelt's achievement as a persuasive writer and speaker. At his literary best, Roosevelt combined his energy with his conviction to create zeal, which he used to persuade. Roosevelt's writing habits were closely tied to his personal values: his belief in the vigor of life motivated him to work hard as a writer, his moral certainty and belief in action led him to write with conviction, and his appreciation for stories inspired him to use vivid language. Three of Roosevelt's writings show his zeal at work: a speech honoring Ulysses S. Grant, passages from his autobiography, and several of his one-liners.

Though the word "zeal" best captures the strengths of Roosevelt's personality and persuasive writing, Roosevelt certainly had other writing strengths. His writing was scrupulously accurate,[5] simple,[6] complete,[7] and full of joy.[8] These strengths also permeated his presidential speeches where Roosevelt "was careful to make his ideas clear, his language direct, and his message striking."[9] But Roosevelt's zeal was the primary quality that made him so persuasive. He was absolutely committed to his message;[10] he combined that conviction with energy to both live his life with zeal and write with zeal.

Roosevelt was the first author to become President of the United States, and he remains the only American president whose most identifiable occupation outside of politics was, or is, writing. Roosevelt produced the greatest volume of written work among all the presidents.[11] Some historians believe that Roo-

---

4. *Id.*

5. Morris, *The Rise of Theodore Roosevelt, supra* note 1, at 24 (Roosevelt was "scrupulously accurate in his diaries and writings.").

6. *Id.* at 66.

7. *Id.* at 136.

8. *Id.* at 35. His writings about American birds were "lyrical, sometimes even song-like." Douglas Brinkley, *The Wilderness Warrior: Theodore Roosevelt and the Crusade for America* 19 (2009) ("His sparkling writings are often good enough to put him in the company of ... first-rate naturalist writers....").

9. Lewis L. Gould, *The Presidency of Theodore Roosevelt* 8 (2d ed. 2011). Some claim that Roosevelt was so attached to his message that he did not always pay attention to the way he said it, but he did not leave his audience confused. Jacob August Riis, *Theodore Roosevelt The Citizen* 413–14 (1903).

10. After Roosevelt spoke his audience left knowing exactly what he meant because he was so committed to his message. Riis, *supra* note 9, at 413–14.

11. Morris, *The Rise of Theodore Roosevelt, supra* note 1, at 20 (Roosevelt authored 38 books).

sevelt, because he read voraciously and wrote prolifically, was the most literary of all our presidents.[12]

Roosevelt's Biography

Roosevelt's life story is difficult to summarize, not only because he had so many different careers,[13] but also because he had so much energy, enthusiasm, and stamina that his sixty years are the equivalent of three times as many years in virtually any other human life. Historian Edmund Morris, who received the Pulitzer Prize for his Roosevelt biography,[14] noted that Roosevelt was the "fastest moving human being I've ever studied," adding that Roosevelt was "lightning quick" in his deliberative qualities yet he was not impulsive.[15]

Roosevelt was born on October 27, 1858, in New York City to a wealthy family.[16] He was plagued by asthma,[17] so he studied at home. Even as a child,

---

12. *The Wisdom of Theodore Roosevelt* xi (Donald J. Davidson ed., 2003) (After listing all of Roosevelt's accomplishments, Davidson concludes, "Finally, and not least, he was a literary man, undoubtedly the best among our presidents, not excluding Jefferson, Adams, Madison, Lincoln, and Wilson.").

13. Roosevelt noted, "A man should have some other occupation—I had several other occupations—to which he can resort if at any time he is thrown out of office...."). *The Autobiography of Theodore Roosevelt* 37 (Wayne Andrews ed., 1975).

14. Morris, *The Rise of Theodore Roosevelt, supra* note 1 (covering the time from Roosevelt's birth in 1858 through his vice-presidency in 1901) (winner of the Pulitzer Prize); Edmund Morris, *Theodore Rex* (2001) (covering Roosevelt's presidency from 1901–1909); Edmund Morris, *Colonel Roosevelt* (2010) (covering Roosevelt's post-presidency years until the time of his death in 1919). Morris's work is highly regarded and admired, and many consider his three-volume biography to be the quintessential work on Roosevelt. *See* Janet Maslin, *Final Scenes from a Life of Bully Adventure*, N.Y. Times (Nov. 18, 2010), at C1 (Morris's three biography series described as "the magnum opus ... [that] deserves to stand as the definitive study of its restless, mutable, ever-boyish, erudite and tirelessly energetic subject.").

15. *Morning Edition: Interview with Edmund Morris* (Nat'l. Pub. Radio broadcast Nov. 27, 2001), http://www.npr.org/programs/morning/features/2001/nov/morris/011127.edmund.morris.html. Morris noted elsewhere that "[t]he President was obviously an adroit politician. Speed was his most astonishing characteristic, combined improbably with thoroughness." Morris, *Theodore Rex, supra* note 14, at 8. Morris emphasized as well that Roosevelt was a jokester who wrote comic pieces. Morris admitted that if Roosevelt "hadn't been such a funny man" he could not have devoted so many years to writing about him. *Interview with Edmund Morris. See also The Autobiography of Theodore Roosevelt, supra* note 13, at x (Andrews notes, "[Roosevelt] had a sense of humor, even if, like many of us, he occasionally misplaced it.").

16. *The Autobiography of Theodore Roosevelt, supra* note 13, at 5.

17. *Id.* at 11.

he was fascinated with nature, and he collected specimens of animals and birds. As a seven-year-old boy, he opened the Roosevelt Museum of Natural History in his home,[18] and he contributed specimens to New York's American Museum of Natural History at the age of 14.[19] He later studied biology and natural history at Harvard University.[20] He attended one year of law school at Columbia, but dropped out when he discovered that his normally passionate nature did not include interest in legal study.[21] Instead, politics and nature were Roosevelt's lasting passions.[22]

His political career started at the age of 23, when he was elected as a New York State Assemblyman.[23] Only two years later, on February 14, 1884, Roosevelt's beloved mother Mittie and his adored wife Alice died on the same day.[24] Alice died of Bright's disease shortly after delivering Roosevelt's first child, also named Alice.[25] Grief stricken, Roosevelt left his daughter Alice in the care of his sister and moved to the frontier.[26] On his way to North Dakota, Roosevelt stopped in Chicago and served as a delegate to the Republican convention. In the "great and deciding moment" of his life, he stuck with his party by backing a candidate he personally opposed.[27] He then became a rancher in western North Dakota, where he also hunted and studied wildlife.[28]

After returning from the West, Roosevelt wrote several books[29] and worked for the Civil Service Commission in Washington, D.C.[30] He left the Civil Service to become President of New York City's Board of Police Commissioners,

---

18. *Id.* at 13 (At the same age he began his habit of recording his findings "in simplified spelling, wholly unpremeditated and unscientific."); *see also* Morris, *The Rise of Theodore Roosevelt, supra* note 1, at 17–18.

19. Candice Millard, *The River of Doubt: Theodore Roosevelt's Darkest Journey* 23 (2005).

20. Morris, *The Rise of Theodore Roosevelt, supra* note 1, at 54–79.

21. *See* Pringle, *supra* note 1, at 32–34.

22. Millard, *supra* note 19, at 24 (Politics was Roosevelt's vocation, but "he never lost his passion for natural history."); *see also* Morris, *The Rise of Theodore Roosevelt, supra* note 1, at 147 ("Theodore Roosevelt was addicted to politics from the moment he won his first election until long after he had lost his last.").

23. Morris, *The Rise of Theodore Roosevelt, supra* note 1, at 140.

24. *Id.* at 229–30.

25. *Id.* at 228–32.

26. *See id.* at 270.

27. Auchincloss, *supra* note 2, at 19.

28. *See id.* at 17.

29. Morris, *The Rise of Theodore Roosevelt, supra* note 1, at 373–99. The topics of these books ranged widely.

30. *Id.* at 404.

where he cleaned up the notoriously corrupt New York City Police Force.[31] He worked hard to make the police force more honest, even traipsing through the city at night to ferret out and fire police officers who were abandoning their patrols or drinking while on duty.[32] Roosevelt later served as Assistant Secretary of the Navy.[33]

Adventure and challenge were constant enticements for Roosevelt. He led the Rough Riders, a volunteer group of cavalry, up San Juan Hill in Cuba during the Spanish-American War in 1898.[34] After his glorious return from Cuba, he was elected Governor of New York. Then in 1900, Roosevelt reluctantly accepted his nomination as the vice president on the Republican ticket with William McKinley.[35]

When President McKinley was assassinated, Roosevelt was 42. He remains the youngest man to hold the office of the president,[36] which he held, as the 26th President of the United States, from 1901–1909.[37] Roosevelt is credited with numerous achievements during his presidency. He won the Nobel Peace Prize for negotiating an end to the Russo-Japanese War.[38] He was the driving force behind the construction of the Panama Canal.[39] He intervened to end a coal miners' strike.[40]

---

31. For a recent book recounting Roosevelt's work on the Police Commission, see Richard Zacks, *Island of Vice: Theodore Roosevelt's Doomed Quest to Clean Up Sin-Loving New York* (2012).

32. Brinkley, *supra* note 8, at 287.

33. Auchincloss, *supra* note 2, at 26.

34. *See* Pringle, *supra* note 1, at 182.

35. Roosevelt did not want to be vice president both because he had a "personal dislike" for the role of the vice president and because he did not want to leave his position as governor of New York to face accusations that he was leaving because of difficult politics. G. Wallace Chessman, *Theodore Roosevelt's Campaign Against the Vice-Presidency*, 14 The Historian 173, 186 (1952).

36. Morris, *Theodore Rex*, *supra* note 14, at 8–9 ("At age 42 he was the youngest man ever called upon to preside over the United States...."); U.S. Govt., *About the White House, Presidents, 26. Theodore Roosevelt*, whitehouse.gov, http://www.whitehouse.gov/about/presidents/theodoreroosevelt (last visited Sept. 2, 2016) (Roosevelt is still "the youngest President in the Nation's history.").

37. Historians note that he was qualified to be president because of the "breadth of his intellect and the strength of his character." Morris, *Theodore Rex*, *supra* note 14, at 10.

38. Auchincloss, *supra* note 2, at 67–69.

39. David McCullough, *The Path Between the Seas: The Creation of the Panama Canal 1870–1914*, at 245–69 (1977).

40. Auchincloss, *supra* note 2, at 45–47. He was never afraid to confront big business, even while he was president. *Id.* at 49.

Historians believe that Roosevelt's most lasting legacy as president was his effort on behalf of conservation.[41] During his presidency, "Roosevelt ... increased our national forests from 42 million acres to 172 million and created 51 national wildlife refuges."[42] Roosevelt believed that wildlife protection and forest conservation were moral imperatives.[43]

After his presidency, Roosevelt made a lengthy big-game hunting trip to Africa.[44] He also embarked on a successful tour of Europe.[45] Unhappy with his Republican successors, but unable to secure a Republican nomination for President, he ran for president as the progressive Bull Moose candidate in 1912,[46] losing to Woodrow Wilson.[47] Then, at the age of 56, he embarked on a journey to descend and map the unexplored River of Doubt through the Amazon jungle, and his harrowing journey was ultimately successful.[48] The River of Doubt is now known as the Rio Roosevelt (The Roosevelt River).[49] Roosevelt died at Sagamore Hill [Roosevelt's home on Long Island] at age 60.[50]

As for his physical appearance, Roosevelt is remembered for a few defining features: his glasses, his prominent teeth, and his steely eyes. He began wearing glasses at age 13, which he remembered "opened an entirely new world to me. I had no idea how beautiful the world was until I got those spectacles."[51] Woe to the man who mocked Roosevelt's glasses because he would find himself on the receiving end of Roosevelt's right-left-right punching sequence.[52] Roosevelt's teeth were large and "extremely white."[53] His voice was high and reedy, and his laugh was infectious, "rising gradually to falsetto chuckles."[54]

---

41. Brinkley, *supra* note 8, at 20–21.

42. Auchincloss, *supra* note 2, at 97.

43. Brinkley, *supra* note 8, at 20. Brinkley calls Roosevelt's conservation efforts "the high-water mark of his entire tenure at the White House." *Id.*

44. Morris, *Colonel Roosevelt, supra* note 14, at 3–26.

45. *Id.* at 40.

46. Auchincloss, *supra* note 2, at 117–20.

47. *Id.* at 122.

48. *See* Millard, *supra* note 19, at 330–35.

49. *Id.* at 240.

50. Morris, *Colonel Roosevelt, supra* note 14, at 549–52.

51. *The Autobiography of Theodore Roosevelt, supra* note 13, at 14.

52. *Id.* at 79–80 (Roosevelt details an event that started with a cowboy in North Dakota calling him "four-eyes.").

53. David McCullough, *Mornings on Horseback* 160 (1981) [hereinafter McCullough, *Mornings on Horseback*]. McCullough notes, "The teeth and glasses were the outstanding features, though he preferred his ears...." *Id.* at 161.

54. Morris, *The Rise of Theodore Roosevelt, supra* note 1, at xxi.

Several features of Roosevelt's personality are defining. He was a magnetic person, and he charmed both women and men.[55] He had a photographic memory, not just for words but also for names and faces.[56] He retained a childlike enthusiasm for the world throughout his life; his friend British Ambassador Cecil Spring Rice famously remarked, "You must always remember ... that the President is about six."[57] He was nonetheless a devoted husband and father.[58]

Roosevelt loved publicity and used the power of the press to his advantage, particularly when he was president.[59] For example, shortly after he became president, Roosevelt told the publisher of the Chicago *Times-Herald* that he intended to replace two Cabinet members, even though he had no such intention, because he knew the publisher would attempt to convince him to retain them. Believing he had great influence, the publisher made a personal appeal to one of those very two Cabinet members, whom Roosevelt feared would resign.[60]

Manipulating the power of the press in this way was perhaps related to Roosevelt's actor's flair for drama, including the drama of a well-timed entrance.[61] On the night his nomination as Mayor of New York was ratified, he waited to enter until every seat in Cooper Union was filled, allowing every eye to follow him as he entered.[62]

Woven into everything Roosevelt did was a seemingly inexhaustible supply of sheer joy. He had an absolute zest for life.[63] Roosevelt used two words constantly—"dee-lighted"[64] and "bully,"[65] by which he meant "wonderful."

---

55. *Id.* at xxvii, xxix.

56. *Id.* at xxx.

57. *Id.* at xxii.

58. *The Wisdom of Theodore Roosevelt, supra* note 12, at xiv. Roosevelt had one child with Alice Lee, and after her death he married Edith Carow and had five more children. *Id.*

59. Morris, *Theodore Rex, supra* note 14, at 18–19.

60. *Id.*

61. Morris, *The Rise of Theodore Roosevelt, supra* note 1, at 143–44.

62. *Id.* at 346.

63. Roosevelt never lost his "boyish good cheer." Morris, *Theodore Rex, supra* note 14, at 15. McCullough believes that "[b]lack care ... clung to him more than he let on," but that the world knew Roosevelt for his "brave and cheerful front." McCullough, *Mornings on Horseback, supra* note 53, at 366.

64. Morris, *The Rise of Theodore Roosevelt, supra* note 1, at xx–xxi. "Phonetically, the word is made for him, with its grinding vowels and snapped-off consonants." *Id.* at xxvi.

65. Roosevelt's constant use of the word "bully" was memorialized in the play *Arsenic and Old Lace. See* McCullough, *Mornings on Horseback, supra* note 53, at 9 (McCullough dates his interest in Roosevelt to watching his older brother play the role of Teddy Brewster in that play).

Hunting in the pouring rain for four days was "bully." On a trip with John Muir to Yosemite, Roosevelt yelled, "This is bully," while enjoying an outdoor fire, only to proclaim, "This is bullier" when he awoke under four inches of snow.[66] At age 56, after a jaguar hunt in Brazil that exhausted every other hunter, a concerned reporter asked Roosevelt if he was all right; Roosevelt responded, "I'm bully."[67]

People were not neutral about Roosevelt; his admirers were absolutely devoted, but "those who hated Roosevelt did so with passion[.]"[68] He has been criticized for being egotistical,[69] an imperialist,[70] and a war romanticizer.[71] Some found it hard to forgive him for breaking with the Republican party, running for the presidency on the Bull Moose ticket, and facilitating Woodrow Wilson's election as president.[72] Louis Auchincloss pointed out, "What he may have done to his party may still affect it to this day. Has the Republican Party ever really recovered the liberal wing which abandoned it to follow TR in 1912?"[73] But the men in Roosevelt's regiment remembered that he knew each of them by name, spent his own money to give them better food, and courageously led them in battle.[74]

---

66. Morris, *Theodore Rex*, *supra* note 14, at 231.

67. Millard, *supra* note 19, at 84. Roosevelt was often known to declare that something was "bully" when everyone else thought that same something was a complete disaster. Morris, *The Rise of Theodore Roosevelt*, *supra* note 1, at 59 (describing a college incident when Roosevelt skated in an icy wind for three hours while all his freezing companions marveled at his attitude).

68. Morris, *The Rise of Theodore Roosevelt*, *supra* note 1, at 118.

69. *Id.* Other critics have found Roosevelt "selfish, vindictive, melodramatic ... dishonest, [and] shallow." *See* Auchincloss, *supra* note 2, at 6 (quoting Nathan Miller).

70. Auchincloss, *supra* note 2, at 72.

71. *See* Brinkley, *supra* note 8, at 310.

72. Auchincloss, *supra* note 2, at 122.

73. *Id.* at 122–23.

74. Murat Halstead, *The Life of Theodore Roosevelt: Twenty-fifth President of the United States* 145 (1903). One cowboy lieutenant said Roosevelt did the bravest thing he ever saw. The Spaniards appeared at the top of the hill, but then the anxious men "saw Colonel Roosevelt walking calmly along the top of the entrenchment with a faded blue handkerchief flapping from the back of his hat, wholly unmindful of the bullets which hummed around him like a hive of bees. A cheer went up and calls for the colonel to come down, and that was the end of the [anxiety]." *Id.* George Cherrie, an ornithologist and explorer who accompanied Roosevelt on the River of Doubt expedition, eulogized Roosevelt shortly after his death, "I have always thought it strange ... since I had the opportunity to know him intimately—because I feel that I did know him very intimately—how any man could be brought in close personal contact with Colonel Roosevelt without loving the man." Millard, *supra* note 19, at 352.

Roosevelt's Literary Life:
Intertwined Personal Traits and Writing Habits

Roosevelt was so completely comfortable with himself that his personality governed all aspects of his life. This was true of his writing; his personality, more than anything else, was the main influence on his writing. In short, he wrote as he lived—with zeal.

Roosevelt's characteristic zeal translated into voracious reading and daily writing. David McCullough noted that a study of even part of Roosevelt's life is "almost overwhelming" because so much has been written about Roosevelt, plus "he wrote and published so much himself *and* read so much that had a direct bearing on his life."[75]

Roosevelt was a writer throughout his life. He began a daily journal at age 10[76] and continued it until his death. He published his first book, *The Naval War of 1812*, at the age of 18. The book was widely acclaimed and helped him become established as both a historian and writer. Roosevelt ultimately published 38 books.[77] These books, like his reading, were wide ranging and included topics such as natural history, hunting, the frontier, the outdoors, and politics. He even wrote several biographies in addition to his autobiography. Roosevelt also wrote his own speeches, and sometimes he spoke several times a day without ever giving the same speech twice.[78] He wrote 150,000 letters during his lifetime.[79] He wrote daily, even when the conditions for writing were challenging.[80] He was a fast writer, once writing a 92,000-word manuscript in just over three months.[81] Roosevelt had a "compulsion to write," and his "habit, in moments of joy or sorrow, had always been to reach for a pen, as others might reach for a rosary or a bottle."[82]

---

75. McCullough, *Mornings on Horseback*, *supra* note 53, at 11 (1981).
76. Morris, *The Rise of Theodore Roosevelt*, *supra* note 1, at 20.
77. *Id.* at 135–36.
78. *See id.* at 718, 768–69.
79. Auchincloss, *supra* note 2, at 6.
80. *See* Millard, *supra* note 19, at 108. Roosevelt often wrote at the beginning of the day on the River of Doubt expedition. *Id.* His co-commander marveled that Roosevelt did so, even when he was sick with fever. *Id.* at 253.
81. Morris, *The Rise of Theodore Roosevelt*, *supra* note 1, at 385 (Roosevelt wrote this quickly for his biography entitled *Gouverneur Morris*).
82. *Id.* at 120. Even as early as his teenage years, Roosevelt had also begun to write to an audience. *Id.*

It is impossible to separate Roosevelt's personality traits from the habits he developed to attack life, including his life as a writer. First, his belief in a vigorous life made him work hard at everything, including his writing. Second, his moral certainty and compulsion to take action influenced his habit of writing with conviction. Third, his love of stories led him to use vivid language. It is the combination of these personality traits and writing habits that made Roosevelt's writing persuasive.

Roosevelt's Belief in "The Vigor of Life" Motivated Him to Work Hard as a Writer [83]

Despite his sickly nature, Roosevelt loved the outdoors and exercise, even as a child. In a famous father-son encounter, Theodore Sr. decided to present a challenge to Theodore Jr., then almost twelve years old: "Theodore, you have the mind but you have not the body, and without the help of the body the mind cannot go as far as it should. You must make your body. It is hard drudgery to make one's body, but I know you will do it."[84] Teddy agreed, and spent the rest of his life fulfilling his boyhood promise to "make my body."[85]

He achieved this vigorous life through legendary hard work. With unending persistence, he worked diligently to make his body strong.[86] He made daily visits to a gym, exercised at home, swam in icy rivers, and hiked up mountains.[87] The result of this rigorous life was that Roosevelt had "unbounded energy and vitality[,] [which] impressed one like the perennial forces of nature."[88] He found such healing in rigorous physical activity that he engaged in intense physical challenges throughout his life, particularly when faced with sorrow or setbacks.[89] The most notable example was his

---

83. Roosevelt himself preferred that his life be described as "vigorous," instead of "strenuous." His speech entitled "The Strenuous Life" was translated in Italian to "The Vigor of Life" and Roosevelt noted, "I thought this translation a great improvement on the original, and have always wished that I had myself used 'The Vigor of Life' as a heading to indicate what I was trying to preach, instead of the heading I did use." Theodore Roosevelt, *An Autobiography* 50–51 (1920). He did use "The Vigor of Life" as a chapter heading in his autobiography. *The Autobiography of Theodore Roosevelt, supra* note 13, at 26.

84. Morris, *The Rise of Theodore Roosevelt, supra* note 1, at 32.

85. *Id.*

86. Pringle, *supra* note 1, at 4.

87. Morris, *The Rise of Theodore Roosevelt, supra* note 1, at 32–33.

88. Millard, *supra* note 19, at 178a (quoting naturalist John Burroughs).

89. *Id.* at 15. "When confronted with sadness or setbacks that were beyond his power to overcome, Roosevelt instinctively sought out still greater tests, losing himself in pun-

heading out to North Dakota to ranch and spend days alone in the wilderness after his wife and mother died on the same day.[90] "The impulse to defy hardship became a fundamental part of Roosevelt's character, honed from early childhood."[91]

Roosevelt applied this belief in the vigorous life to his writing. He admitted that "[w]riting is horribly hard work to me; and I make slow progress. My style is very rough and I do not like a certain lack of sequitur that I do not seem to be able to get out of it."[92] In his autobiography, Roosevelt proposed that two separate kinds of human ability resulted in success: genius or hard work, and he attributed his success to hard work.[93] When Roosevelt's hopes for a political appointment failed, he would turn again to his other occupation—writing.[94] He was so disciplined that he would position his desk to face a wall, so that he would not be distracted by a beautiful view out a window.[95]

It is encouraging to know that even Roosevelt suffered from doubt in his early days as an author. While on his honeymoon in Europe with Alice, he admitted that work on his first book had suffered. We can sympathize with his lament to his sister: "I have plenty of information, but I can't get it into words; I wonder if I won't find everything in life too big for my abilities."[96] Still, he harbors that common hope that we can also understand, "Well, time will tell."[97]

Hard work never stopped Roosevelt, and it would not stop him from what he considered his essential duties as the president. He knew that he could lead the nation only if he was able to "vividly portray the path down which he wished to take [Americans]."[98] Writing was very hard work for Roosevelt, but it was absolutely essential to his ability to lead the United States, so he persisted.

---

ishing physical hardship and danger—experiences that came to shape his personality and inform his most impressive achievements." *Id.*

90. *See* Morris, *The Rise of Theodore Roosevelt, supra* note 1, at 261–65.

91. *Id.*

92. George Grant, *Carry a Big Stick: The Uncommon Heroism of Theodore Roosevelt* 109 (1996) (quoting James Austin Wills, *The Letters and Speeches of Theodore Roosevelt* 94 (1937)); *see also* Morris, *The Rise of Theodore Roosevelt, supra* note 1, at 319.

93. Roosevelt, *An Autobiography, supra* note 83, at 51–52.

94. Morris, *The Rise of Theodore Roosevelt, supra* note 1, at 378–79.

95. *Id.* at 382.

96. *Id.* at 130 (quoting *The Letters of Theodore Roosevelt* 50 (John Blum & Elting E. Morison eds., 1951–54)); Carleton Putnam, 1 *Theodore Roosevelt: The Formative Years, 1858–1886,* at 221 (1958).

97. *Id.*

98. Grant, *supra* note 92, at 109.

Roosevelt's Moral Certainty and Belief in Action
Led Him to Write with Conviction

Moral certainty contributed to Roosevelt's zeal. Roosevelt was obsessed with virtue, something he attributed to his Victorian upbringing.[99] Roosevelt's father taught him a strong sense of right and wrong, and strengthened Roosevelt's own intolerance of injustice.[100] This moral certainty meant that Roosevelt did not spend time second-guessing himself.[101] Although he did not sleep much, his sleep was not troubled by thoughts of indecision or regret.[102] He did not reflect on his actions, but instead believed in the "rightness of his own decisions."[103] Invariably, Roosevelt's moral certainty drove him to act. Henry Adams, an intellectual man of thought, said that his friend Roosevelt was "pure act."[104]

A perfect example of Roosevelt's practical approach and decisive action was his response to the news that President McKinley had been assassinated, making him the new president. "It is a dreadful thing to come into the Presidency this way," he wrote [to his friend] Henry Cabot Lodge, "But it would be a far worse thing to be morbid about it. Here is the task, and I have got to do it to the best of my ability; and that is all there is about it."[105]

At least part of Roosevelt's moral certainty stemmed from his self-confidence and strong ego. He did not hesitate to talk about himself, and his sentences often started with the word "I."[106] In fact, Roosevelt used "I" so often in his book *The Rough Riders* that "[r]eviewers poked fun at Roosevelt's egotism. Rumor claimed that the publisher had run out of the uppercase letter *I* in set-

---

99. James R. Holmes, *Theodore Roosevelt and World Order: Police Power in International Relations* 10 (2006).

100. *Id.*

101. Morris, *Theodore Rex, supra* note 14, at 302.

102. H.W. Brands described this as "the sound Roosevelt sleep of moral self-assurance and physical exhaustion." H. W. Brands, *American Colossus: The Triumph of Capitalism 1865–1900*, at 550 (2010) (referring specifically to the night following Booker T. Washington's dinner visit to the White House when President Roosevelt "awoke the next morning to the self-righteous rage of the white South.").

103. *Id.*

104. *Theodore Roosevelt: An Autobiography* vi (Elting E. Morison ed., 1985) (quoting Henry Adams).

105. Brands, *supra* note 102, at 546 (quoting H.W. Brands, *TR: The Last Romantic* 415–-18 (1997)).

106. Morris, *The Rise of Theodore Roosevelt, supra* note 1, at xxvi.

ting the type."[107] Roosevelt believed that he was fully capable of performing difficult tasks, and this belief often extended even further to a conviction that he was usually the best man for a difficult job. Roosevelt was fiercely devoted to his principles and passionately put those beliefs into action.[108]

Roosevelt's Appreciation for Stories Inspired Him to Use Vivid Language

Stories held a special place for Roosevelt—he loved hearing stories, reading stories, and telling stories. Beginning in his childhood, stories were an essential part of his life. His mother Mittie was a wonderful storyteller with a "gift for mimicry."[109] She told stories with "marvelous detail."[110] She also had a wonderful sense of humor.[111] Mittie's sister Annie Bulloch, who lived with the Roosevelts and taught the children, was also an excellent storyteller.[112] Even before he could read, Roosevelt would carry a book around with him and ask adults to tell him the stories that fit with the illustrations.[113] These early experiences with the power of story stuck with Roosevelt; in his writing he became a storyteller who strove to make his narrative active, vivid, and educational.[114] Here Roosevelt tells the story of the decline of the American bison:

> Gone forever are the mighty herds of the lordly buffalo. A few solitary individuals and small bands are still to be found scattered here and there in the wilder parts of the plains ... but the great herds ... have vanished forever. The extermination of the buffalo has been a veritable tragedy of the animal world.... The most striking characteristics of the buffalo, and those which had been found most useful in maintaining the species until the white man entered upon the scene, were its phenomenal gregariousness ... its massive bulk, and unwieldy strength.[115]

---

107. Brands, *supra* note 102, at 521. Still, Roosevelt was equally proud of his men. "The book swelled to bursting with Roosevelt's pride in himself and his men. 'Is it any wonder I loved my regiment?' he asked after recounting one gallant deed of many." *Id.*

108. Millard, *supra* note 19, at 81.

109. McCullough, *Mornings on Horseback*, *supra* note 53, at 43.

110. *Id.* at 45.

111. Morris, *The Rise of Theodore Roosevelt*, *supra* note 1, at 6.

112. *Id.* at 14.

113. *Id.* at 15.

114. *See id.* at 15.

115. Theodore Roosevelt, *The Adventures of Theodore Roosevelt* 27–29 (Anthony Brandt ed., 2005) (Roosevelt also describes, in great detail, hunting buffalo.).

Oral storytelling was as natural to Roosevelt as breathing. He loved to re-gale his audience with stories of his adventures.[116] His co-commander on the River of Doubt expedition was stunned by just how much Roosevelt could talk: "He talked endlessly"—while swimming, during meals, traveling in the canoe, and around the camp fire—"and on all conceivable subjects."[117]

Roosevelt believed that good writing should be interesting. He lamented that many scientific books rarely had "literary value," but added, "Of course a really good scientific book should be as interesting to read as any other good book...."[118] He was not afraid to criticize himself for failing to make writing in-teresting. He admitted the following about his initial work on *The Naval War of 1812*: "Those chapters were so dry that they would have made a dictionary seem light reading by comparison."[119] He recognized that a writer must take an interest in the subject to achieve success;[120] it was his interest in politics and nat-ural history that ultimately made his writing on those subjects so persuasive.

Roosevelt's Zeal at Work

Many, indeed most, of Roosevelt's writings and speeches show his zeal. The challenge in choosing which of his works to analyze is a common problem with Roosevelt because there is an astonishing amount of material to choose from. I selected the following three examples because they demonstrate how Roo-sevelt's zeal made him persuasive and how Roosevelt's zeal permeated his speeches and his written work.

Roosevelt's Speech Delivered at Galena, Illinois in 1900[121]

Roosevelt made a speech on April 27, 1900, in Galena, Illinois, to com-memorate Ulysses S. Grant.[122] Roosevelt's zeal was the tool he used as he

---

116. *See* Millard, *supra* note 19, at 155.

117. *Id.* (quoting Cândido Mariano da Silva Rondon).

118. *The Autobiography of Theodore Roosevelt, supra* note 13, at 307.

119. *Id.* at 19.

120. *Id.*

121. Theodore Roosevelt, *Grant Speech Delivered at Galena, Illinois* (Apr. 27, 1900) *in* Theodore Roosevelt, *The Strenuous Life: Essays and Addresses* 205–25 (1902) [hereinafter *Grant speech*].

122. Halstead, *supra* note 74, at 139.

urged his "Fellow Citizens" to be brave people of action, to be determined, and to value personal character.[123] All of Roosevelt's habits are at work in this speech—his hard work, his conviction, and his vivid language. His hard work is evident in the simple fact that he wrote this speech himself. Roosevelt was a prolific public speaker, and he wrote individualized speeches for every event.[124] His diligence in preparing the Galena speech is reflected in his in-depth study of Grant as contrasted with a boilerplate, laudatory speech. Roosevelt praised Grant for his "tenacity" and "stubborn fixity of purpose."[125] He admitted, "In the Union armies there were generals as brilliant as Grant, but none with his iron determination."[126] Roosevelt goes even further and suggests that without this determination neither man nor nation can succeed: "A nation that has not the power of endurance, the power of dogged insistence on a determined policy, come weal or woe, has lost one chief element of greatness."[127] Roosevelt also made it clear that he had considered the alternatives to Grant's strong qualities, then he systematically showed how these alternatives produced unsuccessful men, and in turn, unsuccessful nations.[128]

The Galena Address exemplifies how Roosevelt translated his lifelong personal convictions into rhetorical themes. His policy of "speaking softly and carrying a big stick"[129] is reflected in his statement that "our three leaders [Washington, Lincoln, and Grant] were men who, while they did not shrink from war, were nevertheless heartily men of peace."[130] Grant "was slow to strike, but he never struck softly."[131] Roosevelt's belief that the true credit belongs to the "man in the arena"[132] is reflected in his admonition that "in the long run our gratitude was due primarily, not to the critics, not to the fault-finders, but

---

123. Although the speech is an example of Roosevelt's zeal, it is also an example of some of his common flaws. He is sometimes a bit overdramatic and repetitive. *See* Morris, *The Rise of Theodore Roosevelt, supra* note 1, at 291 (noting that Roosevelt's book *Hunting Trips of a Ranchman* was "lyrical, lush, and cheerfully rambling," but Roosevelt sometimes repeated his anecdotes). He used the Grant celebration to support his own expansionist views—in this case, the United States' involvement in the Philippines.

124. *See id.* at 718, 768–69.

125. *Grant speech, supra* note 121, at 212.

126. *Id.*

127. *Id.* at 214.

128. *Id.* at 213.

129. Holmes, *supra* note 99, at 19.

130. *Grant speech, supra* note 121, at 209.

131. *Id.* at 217.

132. *The Wisdom of Theodore Roosevelt, supra* note 12, at 48.

to the men who actually did the work: not to the men of negative policy, but to those who struggled towards the given goal."[133] Roosevelt praised Grant as a man of action: "His promise squared with his performance. His deeds made good his words."[134] Roosevelt further admired Grant because he "faced facts as they were and not as he wished they might be."[135] Roosevelt not only admired this quality of Grant's realism, but he also adopted the same approach to the issues he faced.

Roosevelt's extensive explanation of Grant's character drives home his point that Americans should value personal character above all other virtues. "[Grant's] greatness was not so much greatness of intellect as greatness of character, including in the word 'character' all the strong, virile virtues."[136] Like Roosevelt, Grant also believed in mercy, and Roosevelt commends this virtue with the example of Grant allowing the Confederate soldiers to take their horses back to "their little homes because they would need them to work on their farms."[137]

To support his arguments, Roosevelt used vivid language and he gave specific examples. He noted that the Romans had been successful because they "had character as well as masterful genius, and when pitted against peoples either of less genius [barbarians] or less character [Greeks and Carthagenians], these peoples went down."[138] Here is his imagery: "If the great silent soldier, the Hammer of the North, had struck the hackles off the slave only, as so many conquerors in civil strife before him had done, to rivet them around the wrists of the freemen, then the war would have been fought in vain."[139] Even describing Grant's determination, his "supreme virtue as a soldier," as "doggedness"[140] evokes a visual, vivid image of a dog who will not release a bone.

At the end of his speech Roosevelt urged Americans to honor our mightiest heroes by emulating their qualities of bravery, action, determination, and strong character:

> To do our duty; that is the sum and substance of the whole matter.
> We are not trying to win glory. We are not trying to do anything es-

---

133. *Grant speech, supra* note 121, at 216.

134. *Id.* at 217–18.

135. *Id.* at 224.

136. *Id.* at 219. Roosevelt then lists several specific qualities, "sobriety, steadfastness, the sense of obligation towards one's neighbor and one's God, hard common sense, and combined with it, the lift of generous enthusiasm toward whatever is right." *Id.*

137. *Id.* at 218.

138. *Id.* at 221.

139. *Id.* at 210.

140. *Id.* at 216.

pecially brilliant or unusual. We are setting ourselves vigorously at each task as the task arises, and we are trying to face each difficulty as Grant faced innumerable and infinitely greater difficulties.[141]

There was no mistaking Roosevelt's zeal for his values, his heroes, and his call to action in this speech honoring Grant.

Roosevelt's Autobiography

Of the twenty-five American presidents to hold office before Roosevelt, only Grant had published an autobiography before 1913, when Roosevelt published his own.[142] Roosevelt's habits of hard work, writing with conviction, and vivid language are evident throughout the work, which many consider to be his best book.[143] Roosevelt wrote virtually all of the lengthy work, and he extensively revised and corrected the manuscript.[144] The autobiography is praised for its complete coverage of Roosevelt's life as president, but also for his lively and engaging stories about his life as an ornithologist, rancher, big-game hunter, and soldier.[145] The joy and enthusiasm with which Roosevelt embraced life permeates the work.[146] His delight with life shines through in this sentence: "At Sagamore Hill we love a great many things—birds and trees and books, and all things beautiful, and horses and rifles and children and hard work and the joy of life."[147]

In his autobiography, Roosevelt omitted some important events from his life—notably he failed to even mention his first wife Alice.[148] But with the ex-

---

141. *Id.* at 225.

142. *See* Carolyn Vega, *Theodore Roosevelt on His Presidency: "In the End the Boldness of the Action Fully Justified Itself,"* The Morgan Library & Museum Blog (May 17, 2011, 11:30 AM), http://www.themorgan.org/blog/theodore-roosevelt-his-presidency-end-boldness-action-fully-justified-itself.

143. Roosevelt's autobiography may be his "finest book" because it "re-creates this strong man in strong prose so vivid that it has a value transcending its historical accuracy." Auchincloss, *supra* note 2, at 21. Others believe that Roosevelt's best work was *Winning of the West. Id.* at 20.

144. Vega, *supra* note 142.

145. *Theodore Roosevelt: An Autobiography, supra* note 104, at v.

146. *See id.* ("[Roosevelt] believed in what one of his favorite poets called the joy of life, "the mere living of it," and the pages that follow may be taken as a celebration of that belief.").

147. *The Autobiography of Theodore Roosevelt, supra* note 13, at 171.

148. Morris, *The Rise of Theodore Roosevelt, supra* note 1, at 233. Nor did Roosevelt mention his father's lack of service in the Civil War in his autobiography. *Id.* at 10. Mc-

ception of events that he found too painful to revisit,[149] his autobiography is full of anecdotes about his life, explanations of his beliefs, and observations about his intellectual interests. His vivid description of one White House jaunt bubbles with mischief:

> While in the White House I always tried to get a couple of hours' exercise in the afternoons—sometimes tennis, more often riding, or else a rough cross-country walk.... Most of the men who were oftenest with me on these trips ... were better men physically than I was; but I could ride and walk well enough for us all thoroughly to enjoy it. Often, especially in the winters and early springs, we would arrange for a point-to-point walk, not turning aside for anything—for instance, swimming Rock Creek or even the Potomac if it came in our way. Of course in such circumstances we had to arrange that our return to Washington should be when it was dark, so that our appearance might scandalize no one. On several occasions we thus swam Rock Creek in the early spring when the ice was floating thick on it. If we swam the Potomac, we usually took off our clothes. I remember one such occasion when the French ambassador, Jusserand ... was along; and just as we were about to get in to swim, somebody said, "Mr. Ambassador, Mr. Ambassador, you haven't taken off your gloves," to which he promptly responded: "I think I will leave them on; we might meet ladies!"[150]

Roosevelt was so certain that hard work was important in every aspect of life that he confidently shared a story to make his point:

> As with all other forms of work, so on the round-up, a man of ordinary power, who nevertheless does not shirk things merely because

Cullough notes that Roosevelt also says nothing of his defeat in his race for the mayor of New York City or of his brother Elliott's tragic life. McCullough, *Mornings on Horseback*, *supra* note 53, at 366. Roosevelt also fails to mention an incident when he discharged "without honor" the entirety of an all-black military regiment after a riot in Brownsville, Texas. Auchincloss, *supra* note 2, at 89.

149. Roosevelt had a lifelong habit of not writing about anything tragic or disgraceful. "Triumph was worth the ink; tragedy was not." Morris, *The Rise of Theodore Roosevelt*, *supra* note 1, at 93.

150. *The Autobiography of Theodore Roosevelt, supra* note 13, at 32–33. His life is "presented in splendid prose with the aid of engaging and often funny anecdotes and with—at least from time to time—a recognition that opinions and conclusions alternative to those here given do exist. But you do know at all times exactly where [Roosevelt] stands." *Theodore Roosevelt: An Autobiography, supra* note 104, at vi–vii.

they are disagreeable or irksome, soon earns his place. There were crack riders and ropers who, just because they felt such overwhelming pride in their own prowess, were not really very valuable men.... [In contrast], the man [who] steadily persists in doing the unattractive thing [such as chasing a cow for two hours out of the bullberry bushes] ... [is] an asset of worth in the round-up, even though neither a fancy roper nor a fancy rider.[151]

Roosevelt admired other men, particularly men of action. Even as a boy, he admired both real men and fictional characters and admitted, "I felt a great admiration for men who were fearless and who could hold their own in the world, and I had a great desire to be like them."[152] Roosevelt believed that private virtue should transfer to an improvement of public welfare for the common good of all humanity.[153]

We are never left to wonder what Roosevelt really meant: "I have always had a horror of words that are not translated into deed, of speech that does not result in action—in other words, I believe in realizable ideals and in realizing them, in preaching what can be practised and then in practising it."[154]

Roosevelt wrote his autobiography with his usual writing habits. He worked hard when drafting and editing. He was honest and crystal-clear as he shared the convictions he held most dear. Finally, he told his story with vivid language, especially when telling specific stories from his life.

Roosevelt's One-Liners

Roosevelt was not always a concise writer or speaker, but he had a talent for capturing his thoughts in now-famous one-liners. In these "golden sentences" Roosevelt shares his thoughts and "vividly sketches his ideals[.]"[155] In fact, many of Roosevelt's one-liners can be furthered reduced to short phrases such

---

151. *The Autobiography of Theodore Roosevelt, supra* note 13, at 74–75. Here are Roosevelt's thoughts about basic equality: "The only kinds of courage and honesty which are permanently useful to good institutions anywhere are those shown by men who decide all cases with impartial justice on grounds of conduct and not on grounds of class." *Id.* at 51.

152. *Id.* at 26.

153. Holmes, *supra* note 99, at 13.

154. *The Autobiography of Theodore Roosevelt, supra* note 13, at 101. Roosevelt was a man of "violent likes and dislikes," and he was never afraid to reveal exactly what fit into each of those categories. *Id.* at x (Andrews Introduction).

155. Halstead, *supra* note 74, at 143.

as "big stick," "bully pulpit," "strenuous life,"[156] and "man in the arena" that have become part of our American lexicon.[157]

Roosevelt's one-liners are akin to the "theme" of the case lawyers use when writing persuasive briefs. A theme summarizes the essence of the case — the real heart of the controversy.[158] A good theme will capture the litigant's persuasive argument in a sentence.[159] When expressed to a judge, who has no time for "leisurely, detached meditation," Ruggero Aldisert advises, "You'd better sell the sizzle as soon as possible, the steak can wait."[160]

The following examples of Roosevelt's one-liners sizzle with all the best qualities of zeal — conviction, confidence, passion, and vivid language:

- In reference to Justice Oliver Wendell Holmes Jr., who had dissented from a United States Supreme Court decision upholding the breakup of the Northern Securities monopoly: "I could carve out of a banana a judge with more backbone than that."[161]
- "I have about the same desire to annex it [the Dominican Republic] as a gorged boa constrictor might have to swallow a porcupine wrong end to."[162]

---

156. Roosevelt gave a speech entitled "The Strenuous Life" in Chicago on April 10, 1899, and later included the speech in his book *The Strenuous Life*. Theodore Roosevelt, *The Strenuous Life: Essays and Addresses* 1–21 (1902). Here is the first line of his speech:

> In speaking to you, men of the greatest city of the West, men of the State which gave to the country Lincoln and Grant, men who preeminently and distinctly embody all that is most American in the American character, I wish to preach, not the doctrine of ignoble ease, but the doctrine of the strenuous life, the life of toil and effort, of labor and strife; to preach that highest form of success which comes, not to the man who desires mere easy peace, but to the man who does not shrink from danger, from hardship, or from bitter toil, and who out of these wins the splendid ultimate triumph.

Id. at 1.

157. *The Wisdom of Theodore Roosevelt, supra* note 12, at xiii; *see also* Gould, *supra* note 9, at 8 (noting that Roosevelt's phrases "captured national attention").

158. *See* Ross Guberman, *Point Made: How to Write like the Nation's Top Advocates* 1–2 (2d ed. 2014).

159. *See* Richard K. Neumann, Jr., J. Lyn Entrikin & Sheila Simon, *Legal Writing* 177 (3d ed. 2015) ("A *theme* is a sentence or two or even just a phrase that summarize the theory ... a way of looking at the controversy that makes your client the winner.").

160. Guberman, *supra* note 158, at 1 (quoting Ruggero J. Aldisert, *Winning on Appeal: Better Briefs and Oral Argument* 142 (2d. ed. 2003)).

161. Morris, *Theodore Rex, supra* note 14, at 316.

162. *Id.* at 319.

- In response to attacks about his River of Doubt expedition: "I want to call your attention to the fact that I am using my term to scientific precision, and when I say 'put it on the map,' I mean what I say."[163]
- "I have always been fond of the West African proverb: 'Speak softly and carry a big stick; you will go far.'"[164]
- "I suppose my critics will call that preaching, but I have got such a bully pulpit!"[165]
- "I have only a second-rate brain, but I think I have a capacity for action."[166]
- "A man who is good enough to shed his blood for his country is good enough to be given a square deal afterwards."[167]

The following is perhaps Roosevelt's best known single-sentence statement.[168] It is a very long sentence, but what a sentence!

The credit belongs to the man who is actually in the arena, whose face is marred by dust and sweat and blood; who strives valiantly; who errs and comes up short again and again because there is no effort without error or shortcoming; but who does actually strive to do the deeds; who knows the great enthusiasms, the great devotions; who spends himself in a worthy cause; who at the best knows in the end the triumph of high achievement, and who at the worst, if he fails, at least

---

163. Millard, *supra* note 19, at 340. Roosevelt added, "I mean that … [the River of Doubt] is not on any map, and that we have put it on the map." *Id.*

164. Holmes, *supra* note 99, at 19; *see also The Wisdom of Theodore Roosevelt, supra* note 12, at 9 (quoting a January 26, 1900 letter from Roosevelt to Henry L. Sprague). Roosevelt first used this phrase when he was Governor of New York to remove an influential but corrupt Republican. Roosevelt explained that the African maxim meant "being absolutely inflexible on matters of principle while remaining flexible in less critical areas—all leavened with the utmost in tact and good humor." Holmes, *supra* note 99, at 19. Roosevelt's Big Stick philosophy, which he extended to apply to international affairs, meant that the United States should have strong diplomacy backed by a strong navy. *Id.* at 121.

165. Lyman Abbott, *A Review of President Roosevelt's Administration* 430, Outlook (Feb. 27, 1909).

166. *The Wisdom of Theodore Roosevelt, supra* note 12, at 70 (quoting Owen Wister, *Theodore Roosevelt: The Story of a Friendship* 65 (1930)).

167. *Id.* at 74.

168. Admittedly, the sentence before this one is often included in the quotation. That sentence reads, "It is not the critic who counts; not the man who points out how the strong man stumbles, or where the doer of deeds could have done them better." *Id.* at 48 (quoting Teddy Roosevelt, Speech, Citizenship in a Republic (April 23, 1910), *available at* http://design.caltech.edu/erik/Misc/Citizenship_in_a_Republic.pdf.

fails while daring greatly, so that his place shall never be with those cold timid souls who know neither victory nor defeat.[169]

The sentence works because, despite its superfluities, it expresses Roosevelt's theme that striving is both arduous and continuous. Roosevelt is describing a man he knows very well—himself. But he is not describing only himself; he met many men in North Dakota, New York, Washington, D.C., and Cuba who fit this description just as easily as he did. His use of the word "arena" evokes a boxing ring, but it also evokes the larger arena of the world itself. We can see the man "whose face is marred by dust and sweat and blood" because those vivid words paint a picture of that struggling man. Roosevelt describes a man of action devoted to "a worthy cause"—precisely the way he viewed his own life. And that man, though he may fail, will not be a "cold timid soul."

Again, Roosevelt's hard work, conviction, and vivid language are what persuade his audience. Many of his one-liners capture themes that he worked on and refined throughout his life. His confidence and conviction are also at work here. He was blunt because he believed wholeheartedly in his message. He was transparent because he had no doubt that he was correct. He used vivid language because he wanted his message to be memorable.

As advocates, one of our roles is to educate others about both the law and the facts. Elihu Root, who served in several cabinet positions under Roosevelt, said that "a President was first and foremost an educator ... and that Teddy Roosevelt was the greatest educator [I] ever knew."[170] As advocates, however, our role is not only to educate but also to persuade others that our client's position is correct. Advocacy is an art, not a science, but we do know some things about how to persuade others.[171] People are more likely to be persuaded by someone who has zeal—a combination of conviction, confidence, and belief in the message being delivered. There is no better model for zeal than Roosevelt. Certainly, it may have been easier for Roosevelt to have "fervor for a person, cause, or object; eager desire or endeavor; enthusiastic diligence; ardor"[172] because he was speaking on behalf of himself instead of representing and speaking on behalf of another. Still, our clients deserve lawyers who can support their causes with zeal. When writing for our clients, we can adopt

---

169. *Id.*

170. *Theodore Roosevelt: An Autobiography, supra* note 104, at ix.

171. Kathryn M. Stanchi, *Moving Beyond Instinct: Persuasion in the Era of Professional Legal Writing*, 9 Lewis & Clark L. Rev. 935, 950 (2005). Stanchi also points out that there is something "mysterious and unknowable" about persuasion. *Id.*

172. *Webster's American Dictionary* 915 (2000).

Roosevelt's habits of working hard, writing with conviction, and using vivid language. Those habits will help us convey to our readers that we have been thorough, we are committed to our clients, and we have confidence in the client's position. The result will reflect zeal, which will help as we strive to increase our persuasiveness.

Chapter 7

The Presidents' Reading Habits and Favorite Books

Good writers read—a lot. This is true for all professional writers: novelists, nonfiction writers, journalists, essayists, poets, columnists, academics, playwrights, and lawyers. Stephen King advised, "If you want to be a writer, you must do two things above all others: read a lot and write a lot."[1] The ancillary benefit of reading for writers is that it is instructive. Bad writing teaches what not to do; good writing teaches us what we can and should do. Good writing is inspirational. "We read in order to measure ourselves against the good and the great, to get a sense of all that can be done."[2]

But the primary reason good writers read is simply because they like to read, they want to read, they even need to read. A voracious reader needs air and books in equal measure. Jefferson perfectly summed it up when he wrote to John Adams, "I cannot live without books."[3]

Jefferson, Madison, Lincoln, Grant, and Roosevelt didn't just love to read—they were addicted to reading. They kept books close at hand in case they had even a few minutes to read. Jefferson stashed books in every room in his home in Monticello, so that he could read if he had a spare minute while waiting for dinner guests to arrive.[4] Madison was an "omnivorous reader."[5] As a child, Lin-

---

1. Stephen King, *On Writing: A Memoir of the Craft* 145 (2000).

2. *Id.* at 147.

3. Letter from Thomas Jefferson to John Adams (June 10, 1815), *in* 8 *The Papers of Thomas Jefferson: Retirement Series* 523 (J. Jefferson Looney et al. eds., 2004) [hereinafter *The Papers of Thomas Jefferson: Retirement Series*].

4. *A Day in the Life: Sanctum Sanctorum, Dig-Deeper Books*, Th. Jefferson Monticello, https://www.monticello.org/site/jefferson/dig-deeper-books (last visited Sept. 1, 2016).

5. Garrett Ward Sheldon, *The Political Philosophy of James Madison* 53 (2001).

coln carried a book when "he went out to work anywhere" so that he could "always read while resting."[6] Even while he was president, Lincoln used what little time he had at the end of the day—sometimes just a minute, but sometimes an hour—to read.[7] Grant plowed through the latest popular novels in his West Point room after he learned, to his delight, that he could borrow the books from the college library.[8] Roosevelt's vivid picture of when he found time to read speaks for itself:

> I almost always read a good deal in the evening; and if the rest of the evening is occupied I can at least get half an hour before going to bed. But all kinds of odd moments turn up during even a busy day, in which it is possible to enjoy a book; and then there are rainy afternoons in the country in autumn, and stormy days in winter, when one's work outdoors is finished and after wet clothes have been changed for dry, the rocking-chair in front of the open wood-fire simply demands an accompanying book.
>
> Railway and steamboat journeys were, of course, predestined through the ages as aids to the enjoyment of reading. I have always taken books with me when on hunting and exploring trips.[9]

All five presidents had an almost primal need to read. Any avid reader will relate to Jefferson's refusal to find himself unoccupied without a book or Roosevelt's near panic at the thought that he might run out of reading material before his expeditions ended.

The presidents' interest in books extended beyond simply reading. They talked about books, shared books, and recommended books. Some are famous for their extensive personal libraries. Jefferson had a vast and complete library. He sold his personal collection of about 6,500 volumes to replace the much-smaller collection destroyed when the British burned the Capitol, including the Library of Congress, in the War of 1812.[10] Madison kept some of his 4,000 pamphlets and books at his Montpelier library.[11] Roosevelt's home was filled

---

6. Fred Kaplan, *Lincoln: The Biography of a Writer* 19 (2008).

7. *Id.* at 347.

8. Ulysses S. Grant, *Personal Memoirs of Ulysses S. Grant* 27 (1992) [hereinafter *Personal Memoirs*].

9. Theodore Roosevelt, *A Book-Lover's Holiday[s] in the Open* 264–65 (1916) [hereinafter Roosevelt, *A Book-Lover's Holiday*].

10. *Sale of Books to the Library of Congress,* Th. Jefferson Monticello, https://www.monticello.org/site/research-and-collections/sale-books-library-congress-1815 (last visited Sept. 1, 2016).

11. Lynne Cheney, *James Madison: A Life Reconsidered* 9 (2014).

with books.[12] Roosevelt even helped advance the careers of several aspiring authors. While serving as president, he wrote a laudatory review of Edwin Arlington Robinson's poetry, and later provided Robinson with a position at the New York Customs House to help him with his finances.[13]

The presidents were often asked to provide recommended reading lists. They often complied, but they also recognized the limitations of such lists. Roosevelt was hesitant to provide any lists because he did not think it was possible to create a generic reading list, particularly without knowing much about the reader. As the reader of 20,000 books, the task of listing his favorite books must have been daunting. He noted, "It would be hopeless to try to enumerate all the books I read, or even all the kinds.... [I provide] a very imperfect answer to a question [about what books one should read] which admits of only such an answer."[14]

With Roosevelt's admonition in mind, I recognize that any reading list purporting to collect the presidents' favorite books will be incomplete and imperfect. Yet we are just as curious as the young acquaintances and strangers who asked the presidents for reading advice. The following analysis of the presidents' reading is designed not as a complete list of everything each president read, but as a glimpse into some of the books each president read, enjoyed, or recommended.

Thomas Jefferson— "I cannot live without books."

Jefferson's granddaughter Ellen Wayles Randolph Coolidge noted, "Books were at all times his chosen companions...."[15] He looked forward to his retirement from public life at least in part because it would give him more time to read.[16] His tastes were eclectic—he read about science, farming, philosophy, history, and language. His extensive reading, along with his habit of corresponding with knowledgeable men, helped Jefferson become proficient in "subjects as diverse in nature as Anglo-Saxon and architecture or politics and plows."[17]

---

12. *See* Theodore Roosevelt, *The Autobiography of Theodore Roosevelt* 171 (Wayne Andrews ed., 1975).

13. Scott Donaldson, *Edwin Arlington Robinson* 16 (2007).

14. Roosevelt, *A Book-Lover's Holiday*, *supra* note 9, at 273.

15. Letter from Ellen Wayles Randolph Coolidge to Henry Randall (185–), *in* Henry S. Randall, 3 *The Life of Thomas Jefferson* 346 (1858).

16. *Id.*

17. Roy J. Honeywell, *The Educational Work of Thomas Jefferson* 4 (1931).

Jefferson kept three separate journals of information (called commonplace books): a literary commonplace book, a legal commonplace book, and an equity commonplace book.[18] Like all readers, Jefferson's style was influenced by the books he read. Jefferson copied lines from John Milton's work into one of his personal notebooks. Charles Miller surmises, "In contrast to most seventeenth and eighteenth century literature, which was so unlike his own practice, Jefferson must have been relieved to find the classically controlled nautical imagery of Milton, where he could see his own future style."[19]

·Jefferson believed so much in the educational power of books that he once advised a young man seeking an education that he need not look for an instructor, writing, "We have now such excellent elementary books in every branch of science as to make every subject as plain as a teacher can make it."[20]

Jefferson often wrote to young men with advice about reading and education.[21] He often replied with long lists of books, by topic. For example, in his letter to Peter Carr on August 10, 1787, he listed books in the following categories: Ancient History, Modern History (English, American, and Foreign), Poetry, Mathematics, Astronomy, Natural Philosophy, Botany, Chemistry, Agriculture, Anatomy, Morality, Religion, and Politics & Law.[22]

In response to one young man who planned to study law, Jefferson began by noting, "Before you enter on the study of law a sufficient ground-work must be laid."[23] That foundation consisted of Latin, French, mathematics, natural philosophy, and mathematical reasoning and deductions. He advised that after the foundation was laid, the student should study law and its "kindred sciences ... Physics, Ethics, Religion, Natural law, Belles lettres, Criticism, Rhetoric, and Oratory."[24] Not willing to leave anything to chance, Jefferson prepared a detailed daily schedule with suggested authors and books for every part of the day:

> Early morning–8 a.m.: Read Physical studies, Ethics, Religion (natural and sectarian), and Natural law.

---

18. David Mayer, *The Constitutional Thought of Thomas Jefferson* 6 (1994).

19. Charles A. Miller, *Ship of State: The Nautical Metaphors of Thomas Jefferson* 29 (2003).

20. Letter from Thomas Jefferson to Joseph Echols (May 23, 1822), Founders Online, National Archives, http://founders.archives.gov/documents/Jefferson/98-01-02-2825.

21. Morris L. Cohen, *Thomas Jefferson Recommends a Course of Law Study*, 119 U. Pa. L. Rev. 823, 826 (1970).

22. Letter from Thomas Jefferson to Peter Carr (Aug. 10, 1787), *in Thomas Jefferson Writings* 900–06 (Merrill D. Peterson ed., 1984).

23. Letter from Thomas Jefferson to John Minor (Aug. 20, 1814) including Letter from Thomas Jefferson to Bernard Moore, [ca. 1773?], *in 7 The Papers of Thomas Jefferson: Retirement Series* 625.

24. *Id.* at 625–26.

8 a.m.–noon: Read law
Noon–1 p.m.: Read politics
Afternoon: Read history
From dark to bedtime: Read Belles letters, Criticisms, Rhetoric, Oratory.[25]

Jefferson acknowledged that his suggested readings "by no means constitute the whole of what might be usefully read in each of these branches of science."[26] But these books would "give him a respectable, an [sic] useful, & satisfactory degree of knolege [sic] in these branches, and will themselves form a valuable and sufficient library for a lawyer, who is at the same time a lover of science."[27]

In an earlier letter to Peter Carr, Jefferson also pointed out the value of taking a break from the books with physical activity:

> Give about two of them [hours] every day to exercise; for health must not be sacrificed to learning. A strong body makes the mind strong ... Never think of taking a book with you [on walks]. The object of walking is to relax the mind. You should therefore not permit yourself even to think while you walk. But divert your attention by the objects surrounding you.[28]

It seems a break from books may have been needed based on Jefferson's suggested plan for reading each day. Those two hours were virtually the only free hours on his recommended schedule.

The following list is distilled from several letters Jefferson wrote recommending authors and books.[29] Jefferson was careful to list his recommended reading according to topic, but this is an alphabetical list of authors to maintain consistency with the lists for the other eloquent presidents.

Addison, Joseph
Aeschylus

---

25. *Id.* at 626–30.
26. *Id.* at 630.
27. *Id.*
28. Letter from Thomas Jefferson to Peter Carr (Aug. 19, 1785), *in Thomas Jefferson Writings, supra* note 22, at 816.
29. Letter from Thomas Jefferson to John Minor (Aug. 20, 1814), *supra* note 23; Letter from Thomas Jefferson to Peter Carr (Aug. 19, 1785), *supra* note 28; Letter from Thomas Jefferson to Peter Carr (Aug. 10, 1787), *supra* note 22; Letter from Thomas Jefferson to Nathaniel Burwell (Mar. 14, 1818) *in* 7 *The Writings of Thomas Jefferson* 101–03 (H.A. Washington ed., 1854); Letter from Thomas Jefferson to Robert Skipwith (Aug. 3, 1771), *in Thomas Jefferson Writings, supra* note 22, at 740–45.

Antoninus
Aristotle
The Bible
Blackstone, William
Burke, Edmund
Caesar, Julius
Cervantes
Chaucer
Cicero
Congreve
Demosthenes
Dryden
Epictetus
Euclid
Euripides
Gibbon, Edward
Gordon
Gray, Thomas
Herodotus
Homer, *Odyssey* (Jefferson chose two lines from *The Iliad* for his wife's
    epitaph: "Nay if even in the house of Hades the dead forget their
    dead, yet will I even there be mindful of my dear comrade")[30]
Horace
Hume, David
Hutchinson, Thomas
Justinian
Livy
Locke, John
Lord Kames (Henry Home)
Milton, John
Moliére
Newton
Ossian
Otway
Plato
Plutarch

---

30. *Martha Wayles Skelton Jefferson*, Th. Jefferson Monticello, https://www.monticello.org/site/jefferson/martha-wayles-skelton-jefferson (last visited Sept. 1, 2016).

Polybius
Pope, Alexander
Quintus Curtius Rufus
Robertson, William
Sallust
Seneca
Shakespeare, William
Socrates
Sophocles
Sterne, Laurence
Swift, Jonathan
Tacitus
Terence
Theocritus
Thompson
Thucydides
Virgil
Voltaire
Xenophon
Young

James Madison—
"Since I have been at home I have had the leisure to review the literary cargo for which I am so much indebted to your friendship. The collection is perfectly to my mind."[31]

Madison read throughout his life, often as part of his preparation for political issues. Ralph Ketcham, a celebrated biographer of James Madison, thoroughly analyzed Madison's reading habits and book preferences.[32] The following review of Madison's reading habits is based on Ketcham's thorough analysis. Madison, like Jefferson, had an extensive personal library. The cura-

---

31. Letter from James Madison to Thomas Jefferson (Mar. 18, 1786), *in* 2 *The Writings of James Madison: Comprising his Public Papers and His Private Correspondence* 224, 226 (Gallard Hunt ed., 1910).

32. Ralph Ketcham, *James Madison's Books and Reading*, https://www.montpelier.org/blog/james-madisons-books (last visited Sept. 1, 2016).

tors of Montpelier have identified over 1,500 books and pamphlets that were once part of Madison's personal library containing over 4,000 volumes.[33]

As a young child, Madison had books around him. His grandfather owned 28 books. His father could read and ordered several books two years before Madison was born. Madison's mother and paternal grandmother could also read; they were "each capable of educating children in the basics."[34]

From age eleven to sixteen, Madison went to Rev. Donald Robertson's boarding school where he learned about the Scottish Enlightenment. He studied both Latin and Greek, and borrowed books from his teachers. Robertson's books included many of the best books about modern European learning.[35]

Madison continued his education at the College of New Jersey (now Princeton). He studied science, geography, rhetoric, logic, mathematics, moral philosophy, Latin, Greek, and Hebrew. His favorite ancient authors were Cicero, Demosthenes, and Livy. His favorite modern English writers were Shakespeare, Milton, and Addison.[36]

Princeton was an ideal place for Madison as he developed his habit of rigor. The Princeton students "took part in and listened to debates, orations, and forensic contests in the chapel, all 'critically examined with respect to the correctness of the language.'"[37]

Books, always a part of Madison's life, also surrounded him at Princeton. Governor Jonathan Belcher donated many volumes to the college library; Princeton President John Witherspoon also brought 800 volumes from Scotland. Witherspoon believed that ideas should not be suppressed, but that bad ideas should be criticized. Thus, he attacked Hume, Mandeville, and Johnson. Madison "had in Witherspoon a teacher who could not only introduce him to the 'great books' of the day, but also schooled the pupil in open-minded yet deeply critical ways of dealing with them."[38]

Madison's reading continued after college when he shared and discussed books with his college friend William Bradford, whose family owned a Philadelphia printing and book shop. He later lived with his second cousin, another James Madison, who was the president of the College of William and Mary.[39]

---

33. *James Madison's Reading List,* James Madison's Montpelier, https://www.montpelier.org/james-and-dolley-madison/james-madison/james-madison-reading-list (last visited Sept. 1, 2016).

34. Ketcham, *supra* note 32.

35. *Id.*

36. *Id.*

37. *Id.*

38. *Id.*

39. *Id.*

Madison asked Jefferson what he should read as he prepared to draft the American Constitution. Jefferson, then in Paris, sent books on "almost every historical experiment with federated and confederated governments, from ancient Greece to the medieval Holy Roman Empire to modern Swiss, Dutch, and German regimes."[40] Madison was thrilled. He thanked Jefferson in a letter, writing, "Since I have been at home I have had the leisure to review the literary cargo for which I am so much indebted to your friendship. The collection is perfectly to my mind."[41]

The following list of books Madison read is based on Ketcham's work compiling the authors and books Madison read during various stages of his life:

Addison
Aristotle
Bacon
Barbeyrac
Bayle
Bible (The New Testament)
Blackstone
Bunyan
Butler, Samuel, *Hudibras*
Cicero
Coke
Defoe
Demosthenes
Dryden
Ferguson
Gibbon
Gordon, *Cato's Letters*
Grotius
Harrington
Homer
Hooker
Horace
Hume
Hutcheson
Johnson, Samuel
Justinian

---

40. Sheldon, *supra* note 5, at 49.
41. Letter from Madison to Jefferson (Mar. 18, 1786), *supra* note 31.

Livy
Locke, John, *Essay Concerning Human Understanding*
Lord Kames
Mably
Milton
Montaigne, *Essays*
Montesquieu, *The Spirit of the Laws*
Newton
Ovid
Plato
Pope, *Essay on Man*
Price
Priestley
Robertson
Sallust
Shakespeare
Smith, Adam
Smollett, *History of England*
Sydney
Terence
Tillotson
Trenchard
Tucker
Voltaire
Watts
Wollaston, *Religion of Nature*
Xenophon

Abraham Lincoln— "He devoured all the books he could get or lay hands on; he was a Constant and voracious reader."[42]

Americans have an iconic image of Lincoln with a book in his hand; several artists have depicted him reading in both his youth and adulthood. This

---

42. Kaplan, *supra* note 6, at 19 (Lincoln's reading habits as reported by his stepsister). She also noted, "Abe was not Energetic Except in one thing ... he was active & persistant in learning—read Everything he Could." *Id.*

American myth is grounded in reality because Lincoln was an avid reader throughout his life. As a child, Lincoln's reading was limited only by the availability of books. His stepmother noted, "He was the best boy I ever saw. He read all the books he could lay his hands on."[43]

Lincoln scholars have studied Lincoln's reading list in great depth. Fred Kaplan reviewed the books Lincoln read throughout his life and concludes that Lincoln most often read Shakespeare, followed by the Bible.[44] Lincoln's son Robert reported that when Lincoln was president he often carried a copy of Shakespeare's plays with him.[45] He attended performances of Shakespeare's plays, but often preferred his own interpretation of the lines, so he read out loud his favorite lines to himself and to others.[46]

Robert W. Bray, a literature professor, compiled a bibliography of the books that Lincoln read, listing all the books that any serious scholar, biographer, or bibliographer asserted that Lincoln read.[47] Bray then assigns a grade to each of these books, based on the likelihood that Lincoln actually read the book. The following is a partial list of these titles:

Addison, Joseph, *Cato: A Tragedy*
Aesop's Fables
Akenside, Mark, "Am I For Peace? Yes!" (poetry)
Bacon, Francis, *Essays*
The Bible (King James)
Blackstone, William, *Commentaries on the Laws of England*
Bulwer-Lytton, Edward, *The Lady of Lyons*
Bunyan, John, *Pilgrim's Progress*
Burns, Robert, *Poems*
Byron, George Gordon, Lord, *Poems*
Chandler, Mary G., *Elements of Character*
Clay, Henry, *Speeches*
Defoe, Daniel, *Robinson Crusoe* and "The Democratic Battle Hymn"
    (poetry)

---

43. *Id.* at 20.
44. *Id.* at 346–47.
45. William Lee Miller, *Lincoln's Virtues* 81 (2003) [hereinafter Miller, *Lincoln's Virtues*].
46. Kaplan, *supra* note 6, at 347.
47. Robert Bray, *What Abraham Lincoln Read—An Evaluative and Annotated List*, 28 J. of the Abraham Lincoln Ass'n 28 (2007) (listing all the books that any serious scholar or historian has claimed that Lincoln read and then adding a category of the likelihood that Lincoln actually read the book). Bray continued his work and wrote a book. Robert Bray, *Reading with Lincoln* 226 (2010).

Elliott, Jonathan, *Journal and Debates of the Federal Constitution* (1836)

Emerson, Ralph Waldo, *Essays*

Euclid, *Geometry*

Ford, Thomas, *History of Illinois*

Gibbon, Edward, *History of the Decline and Fall of the Roman Empire*

Gray, Thomas, "Elegy Written in a Country Churchyard" (poetry)

Halleck, Fitz-Greene (poetry)

Halleck, H.W., *Military Art and Science*

Helper, Hinton Rowan, *The Impending Crisis of the South*

Holmes, Oliver Wendell, *Poems*

Homer, *Iliad* and *Odyssey*

Hood, Thomas, *Poems*

Horace, *Works of Horace*

Hume, David, *Essays* and *History of England*

Jackson, Andrew, *Proclamation Against Nullification*

Jefferson, Thomas, *Works*, vols. 4, 7–9 and "First Inaugural Address"

Kirkland, Charles P., *A Letter to the Honorable Benjamin P. Curtis* (pamphlet)

Knox, William, "Mortality" (poetry)

Lear, Edward, *A Book of Nonsense*

Longfellow, Henry Wadsworth, *Poems*

Macaulay, Thomas B., *History of England from the Accession of James II*

Mill, John Stuart, *On Liberty* and *Principles of Political Economy*

Milton, John, "Lycidas" (poetry)

Murray, Lindley, *The English Grammar* and *The English Reader*

Olmsted, Frederick L., *A Journey in the Seaboard Slave States*

Paine, Thomas, *The Age of Reason*, *Common Sense*, and *Complete Political Works*

Plutarch, *Lives*

Poe, Edgar Allan, *Poems*

Pope, Alexander, *An Essay on Man*

Quin, *Quin's Jests*

Ramsay, David, *Life of George Washington*

Robertson, George, *Scrap Book on Law and Politics, Men and Times*

Scott, Winfield, *Infantry Tactics*

Seward, William H., *Speeches*

Shakespeare, William, *Hamlet, Henry IV, Henry V, Henry VIII, King John, King Lear, Macbeth, Merchant of Venice, Merry Wives of Windsor, Othello, Richard II, Richard III*

Stowe, Harriet Beecher, *The Key to Uncle Tom's Cabin*

Thucydides, *The Peloponnesian War*

Voltaire (Francois-Marie Arouet), *An Important Examination of the Scripture*

Webster, Daniel, "Reply to Hayne" and *Speeches*

Weems, Mason Locke, *Life of General Francis Marion* and *Life of George Washington*

Young, Edward, *The Last Day*

Some of the books Lincoln read can be grouped according to Lincoln's purpose in reading them. He consulted books on English grammar, dictionaries, and thesauri first as part of his efforts to teach himself and then later to improve his writing. Thus, he consulted Nathan Bailey's *Dictionary of English Etymology*; James Barclay's *Dictionary*; Samuel Kirkham's *English Grammar*; John Lempriere's *Classic Dictionary*; Lindley Murray's *The English Grammar* and *The English Reader*; Peter M. Roget's *Thesaurus*; Noah Webster's *An American Dictionary*, *The American Spelling Book*, and *A Dictionary for Primary Schools*; and John Wilson's *Elements of Punctuation*.

As a young adult, Lincoln read to further his self-education for a profession. He read several surveying texts including Charles Davies, *Elements of Surveying*; Abel Flint, *System of Geometry, Trigonometry & Rectangular Surveying*; and Robert Gibson, *Theory & Practice of Surveying*. The legal texts he read included: Joseph Chitty, *A Practical Treatise on Pleading*; Simon Greenleaf, *A Treatise on the Law of Evidence*; James Kent, *Commentaries on American Law* (1826); and Joseph Story, *Commentaries on Equity Jurisprudence* (1836) and *Equity Pleadings* (1805). Lincoln also read Jefferson's First Inaugural Address when he was preparing to take office as president.

He also read contemporary accounts of his own life and speeches including Abraham Lincoln and Stephen A. Douglas' *Political Debates*; John Hill's *Opposing Principles of Henry Clay and Abraham Lincoln*; William Dean Howells' *Lives and Speeches of Abraham Lincoln and Hannibal Hamlin*; and John Locke Scripps' *Life of Lincoln*. He read Edward Everett's *Address at Gettysburg*, which was delivered on the same day as his own *Gettysburg Address*.

As is often true for Lincoln, there is an entertaining story about one book that he added to his reading list. John L. Scripps of the *Chicago Tribune* wrote that Lincoln read Plutarch, but then sheepishly suggested to Lincoln that he should get a copy and read it, so that his report was true. "Lincoln, it is said, much amused, did as he was told—and loved to tell the story."[48]

---

48. Miller, *Lincoln's Virtues*, *supra* note 45, at 274.

Ulysses S. Grant—
"I devoted more time to these (novels), than to the books relating to the course of study."[49]

Grant knew what a voracious, lifelong reader looked like because his father was one. Grant's father had less than a year of formal schooling. With much admiration, Grant explained, "But his thirst for education was intense. He learned rapidly, and was a constant reader up to the day of his death—in his eightieth year."[50] Grant's father was like Lincoln in his thirst for reading material. "Books were scarce in the Western Reserve during his youth, but he read every book he could borrow in the neighborhood where he lived. This scarcity gave him the early habit of studying everything he read, so that when he got through with a book, he knew everything in it."[51]

Grant's father kept a home library of 35 books, which would have been considered a marvel.[52] Even though Grant claimed he was not a book reader as a child, he probably read more than any other boy in town. Historian Geoffrey Perret noted, "It seems a safe bet that he read his way through his father's private library, the biggest collection of serious reading for miles around."[53]

Grant made a point of acknowledging that he was not "studious in habit."[54] Grant preferred spending his time outdoors, preferably horseback riding, but he also may have been more inclined to read during his childhood if he had not been so bored in school. Math was the subject that came most easily to Grant, but in the two years before he left for West Point his time at school was "spent in going over the same old arithmetic which I knew every word of before."[55] His English study was equally monotonous; Grant noted that he spent his time "repeating, 'A noun is the name of a thing,' which I had also heard my Georgetown teachers repeat until I had come to believe it...."[56] How poignant that at the very end of his life he wrote a note to his physician stating, "I think I am a verb instead of a personal pronoun. A verb is any-

---

49. *Personal Memoirs, supra* note 8, at 27.
50. *Id.* at 17.
51. *Id.*
52. Geoffrey Perret, *Ulysses S. Grant: Soldier & President* 15 (1997).
53. *Id.* at 16.
54. *Personal Memoirs, supra* note 8, at 19.
55. *Id.* at 19–20.
56. *Id.* at 20 ("Georgetown" referred to Georgetown, Ohio).

thing that signifies to be; to do; or to suffer. I signify all three. Ulysses S. Grant."[57]

Grant's self-assessment that he was a poor student is probably inaccurate. He would never have passed the rigorous West Point admission test without some intellectual aptitude. He recognized that himself when he noted that he passed the admission examination "without difficulty, very much to my surprise."[58] He may have been surprised because about one out of four candidates failed the exam and was sent home.[59] Grant also knew that he only had the opportunity to attend West Point because another Ohio cadet was failing and due to be dismissed, thus opening up a slot for Grant.[60]

In his *Personal Memoirs*, Grant covered his reading list for only a narrow part of his life—his time at West Point. Grant conceded that he was a casual student at West Point, probably because a military life "held no charms" for him and he never intended to stay in the army even if he graduated which, he said, "I did not expect."[61] He noted, "I did not take hold of my studies with avidity, in fact I rarely ever read over a lesson the second time during my entire cadetship."[62] Obviously, he wasn't spending his reading time on his textbooks.

But, importantly, Grant did read voraciously during this time. He admitted that he "could not sit in my room doing nothing."[63] He was delighted to learn that West Point had a library and he was allowed to borrow books to read in his quarters.[64] Grant revealed, a bit sheepishly, that he preferred to read fiction. "Much of the time, I am sorry to say, was devoted to novels, but not those of a trashy sort."[65] It is likely, given the context, that he was "sorry to say" that he read novels because others might have believed he should have focused on his textbooks, or at least on nonfiction.

In any case, Grant remembered his reading list, "I read all of Bulwer's then published, Cooper's, Marryat's, Scott's, Washington Irving's works, Lever's, and many others that I do not now remember." Grant's list included the most

---

57. William S. McFeely, *Grant* 516 (1981) (Grant wrote this note, days before his death, to his physician).
58. *Id.*
59. Perret, *supra* note 52, at 21.
60. *Id.*
61. *Personal Memoirs, supra* note 8, at 27.
62. *Id.* at 27.
63. *Id.*
64. *Id.*
65. *Id.*

popular fiction in his day, and Grant learned the value of writing for his audience from those novels.

Four of the writers on Grant's reading list were not American authors. Edward Bulwer-Lytton, a bestselling English novelist, was also a poet, playwright, and politician. He was a popular and well-known author in Grant's time; until 1914 "the sales of his books rivalled those of [Charles] Dickens."[66] Some of his books included *The Last Days of Pompeii*, *The Pilgrims of the Rhine*, *The Disowned*, *Pelham: or the Adventures of a Gentleman*, and *Falkland*. If Grant read "all" of the books published by 1839 he would have read 15 of Bulwer-Lytton's books, including his early books about the dandy to his later books about the prisoners in London's Newgate prison. Bulwer-Lytton suggested that the dandy could have moral integrity and the prisoner could be a hero; he was criticized by some for this view.[67] Frederick Marryat was an English naval officer and popular novelist in the first half of the 19th century.[68] His books included *The Three Cutters*, *Mr. Midshipman Easy*, and *The Naval Officer, or Scenes in the Life and Adventures of Frank Mildmay*. He was known for his wit and humor. He was a vivid writer; his heroes did not always fit the mold of virtue and perfection, but were sometimes unpleasant, selfish, and ruthless, but still triumphed.[69] Charles Lever, born in Ireland to English parents, was a physician and novelist known for his rollicking anecdotes.[70] He wrote *The Confessions of Harry Lorrequer*. Sir Walter Scott was a Scottish novelist, poet, and biographer. He is often credited with inventing the historical novel. He died in 1832, so Grant would have had an opportunity to read all of his work including his novels *Rob Roy* and *Ivanhoe* (part of the *Waverley Novels* which were published from 1814–1832) and his poem *The Lady of the Lake*.[71]

Two American authors also make Grant's list. James Fenimore Cooper's *The Last of the Mohicans: A Narrative of 1757*, one of the novels in the *Leatherstocking Tales* series, was one of the most popular novels in the 19th century

---

66. Leslie Mitchell, *Bulwer Lytton: The Rise and Fall of a Victorian Man of Letters* xv (2003).

67. *Id.* at xvii–xviii.

68. Tom Pocock, *Captain Marryat: Seaman, Writer, and Adventurer* 9 (2000).

69. *Id.*

70. Philip V. Allingham, *Charles Lever (1806–1872): Anglo-Irish Novelist, Physician, and Diplomat*, The Victorian Web, http://www.victorianweb.org/authors/lever/bio.html (last visited Sept. 1, 2016).

71. *Sir Walter Scott, 1st Baronet*, Encyclopaedia Britannica, http://www.britannica.com/biography/Sir-Walter-Scott-1st-Baronet (last visited Sept. 1, 2016).

in both America and Europe.[72] Washington Irving, the author of "Rip Van Winkle" and "The Legend of Sleepy Hollow" was the first best-selling American author.[73] Washington Irving wrote for the masses—and the masses loved his work even though the critics often did not.[74]

Grant continued to read after West Point. He wrote to Julia on Feb. 2, 1854, "My Dear Wife, You do not know how forsaken I feel here!"[75] He was miserable and lonely in his station at Fort Humboldt, California. Yet reading provided at least some solace. He wrote, "I do nothing but set in my room and read and occasionally take a short ride on one of the public horses."[76] Eleven years later, as the Civil War was ending, Grant read out loud to Julia in the evenings when she joined him at City Point.[77]

Teddy Roosevelt— "Reading with me is a disease."[78]

Roosevelt read 20,000 books during his lifetime.[79] Roosevelt read constantly, even as a child.[80] During his presidency, Roosevelt found both distraction and comfort in reading.[81] For expeditions he carefully chose the books he would bring, and he even special-ordered lightweight books which allowed him to take more books with him.[82] He became desperate for additional books after he had read and reread his own large stash of books. As just one example, Roosevelt read some of his son Kermit's books on the River of Doubt expedition after he had read and reread his own copies of Thomas More's *Utopia*, the plays

---

72. James Fenimore Cooper, *The Last of the Mohicans* 13 (Paul Gutjar ed., Broadview ed. 2009).

73. Brian Jay Jones, *Washington Irving: An American Original* ix (2008).

74. *Id.*

75. Letter from Ulysses S. Grant to Julia Dent Grant (Feb. 2, 1854), *in* 1 *The Papers of Ulysses S. Grant: 1837–1861* 316 (John Y. Simon ed. 1967).

76. *Id.*

77. Perret, *supra* note 52, at 349 (citing Letter from Julia Dent Grant to Lillian Rogers (Feb. 7, 1865)).

78. Louis Auchincloss, *Theodore Roosevelt* 17 (2001) (quoting Theodore Roosevelt).

79. Edmund Morris, *Theodore Rex* 11 (2001).

80. *See* Henry F. Pringle, *Theodore Roosevelt: A Biography* 4 (1931).

81. Auchincloss, *supra* note 78, at 44.

82. *See* Candice Millard, *The River of Doubt: Theodore Roosevelt's Darkest Journey* 311–12 (2005) (Roosevelt special-ordered lightweight books for his African expedition which allowed him to take more books with him).

of Sophocles, the last two volumes of Edward Gibbon's *Decline and Fall of the Roman Empire*, Marcus Aurelius, Epictetus, and others.[83] He sometimes read two books in one evening,[84] and reading "was about the only thing that could make him sit still."[85]

In typical Roosevelt fashion, he had plenty to say about reading. He was adamant that personal preference influenced the choice of what to read, so that it was impossible to recommend a list of books for all readers. He explained in his autobiography, "I like very many and very different kinds of books, and do not for a moment attempt anything so preposterous as a continual comparison between books which may appeal to totally different sets of emotions."[86] He was hesitant to make any generalizations about books and noted, "There is no such thing as a list of 'the hundred best books' or the 'best five-foot library.'"[87]

Roosevelt's taste in books was eclectic and could vary even with regard to just one author. He liked Sir Walter Scott's *Guy Mannering* and *The Antiquary*, but not *Fortunes of Nigel*. He liked William Makepeace Thackeray's *Vanity Fair* and *The History of Pendennis: His Fortunes and Misfortunes, His Friends and Greatest Enemy*, but not *Esmond*. He liked Charles Dickens's *Our Mutual Friend*, and *Pickwick Papers*, but not *The Old Curiosity Shop*. He liked and often reread Shakespeare's *Macbeth* and *Othello*, but not *King Lear* or *Hamlet*. He liked Henryk Sienkiewicz's *With Fire and Sword*; *Sir Michael*; *The Deluge*; and *The Knights of the Cross*, but not *Quo Vadis*. He liked Leo Tolstoy's *Anna Karenina*, *War and Peace*, *The Sebastopol Sketches*, and *The Cossacks*, but he warned against the morals in *The Kreutzer Sonata*.[88]

His general preferences in reading are not surprising. He was an adventurous, optimistic, happy man so he read adventurous, optimistic, happy books. He liked "hunting books and books of exploration and adventure."[89] He knew critics scorned the happy ending, but observed "there is enough of horror and grimness and sordid squalor in real life," so that when he turned to "the world of literature—of books considered as books, and not instruments of my profession—I do not care to study suffering unless for some sufficient purpose."[90]

---

83. *Id.* at 311–12.
84. Edmund Morris, *The Rise of Theodore Roosevelt* xxxiii (1979).
85. David McCullough, *Mornings on Horseback* 367 (1981).
86. *The Autobiography of Theodore Roosevelt* 309 (Wayne Andrews ed., 1975).
87. Roosevelt, *A Book-Lover's Holiday*, *supra* note 9, at 262.
88. *Id.*
89. *Id.* at 263.
90. *Id.* at 264.

He admits, "It is only a very exceptional novel which I will read if He does not marry Her; and even in exceptional novels I much prefer this consummation. I am not defending my attitude. I am merely stating it."[91] He acknowledged that "[n]ow and then one's soul thirsts for laughter," so he read humor books.[92]

Books comforted and grounded him. If, as president, he was "exasperated over the shortcomings of the legislative body with which he deals," he said he needed only to consult Macaulay's history to learn the poor way William was treated by his Parliament.[93] When he was missing the mountains and plains he could read to remember them; when he was living in "cow camps" he would instead read Swinburne "as a kind of antiseptic" to that rough and dusty world.[94] Books provided an escape from "national conventions," "congressional investigations," or "hard-fought political campaigns" when he would "delight" in reading "some really enthralling book—Tacitus, Thucydides, Herodotus, Polybius, or Goethe, Keats, Gray, or Lowell—and lose all memory of everything grimy."[95]

Despite his insistence that there was no single list of great books, Roosevelt freely shared his own reading list. In his entertaining and informative chapter "Books for Holidays in the Open," included in his book *A Book-Lover's Holidays in the Open*,[96] he mentioned scores of authors from different centuries and various countries who wrote in multiple genres. In following Roosevelt's lead, the list that follows includes only the author's last name unless Roosevelt himself included the author's first name and titles are included if Roosevelt listed specific titles:

Lord Acton
Addison
Aeschylus
Alger, George
Austen, Jane
Aristophanes (a German edition with erudite explanations of the jokes)
Bagehot
Beowulf
Bible (Old Testament)

---

91. *Id.*
92. *Id.* at 270.
93. *Id.* at 272.
94. *Id.* at 269.
95. *Id.* at 265–66.
96. *Id.* at 259–73.

Bordeaux, Henry (morals)
Brieux, Eugene (morals)
Browning (poetry)
Burke
Burroughs
Carlyle, *Frederick the Great*
Coleridge (poetry)
Coulton
Crothers
Dickens, Charles, *Our Mutual Friend*; *Pickwick Papers*; *Martin Chuzzlelewit*
Emerson (poetry)
The Federalist
Ferrero
Gibbon
Goethe
Grahame, Cunningham
Grahame, Kenneth
Gray
Harris, Joel Chandler (humor)
Harte, Bret (poetry)
Hawthorne
Herodotus
Herrick (poetry)
Holmes, Oliver Wendell ("the laughing philosopher")
Horace (poetry)
Hudson, *El Ombú*
Irving
Keats
Kingsley, Mary
Kipling (poetry)
Körner (poetry)
Lamb
Lea, *History of the Inquisition*
Leacock, Stephen (humor)
Lecky
Longfellow (poetry)
Lowell
Macaulay
Mahaffy

Mahan

Malthus

Marbot, *Memoirs*

Milton

Montaigne

Motley

Murray, Gilbert

Napier, *Peninsular War*

Oman, *Seven Roman Statesmen*

Parkman, *Montcalm and Wolfe*

Phoenix, John (humor)

Poe (poetry)

Polybius

Pope (poetry)

Ross

Schiller (poetry)

Scott, Walter, *Guy Mannering*; *The Antiquary* (and poetry)

Shakespeare, William, *Macbeth* and *Othello*

Sheldon, Charles

Shelley (poetry)

Sienkiewicz, Henryk, *With Fire and Sword*; *Sir Michael*; *The Deluge*; *The Knights of the Cross*

Smith, Adam

Smith, Sydney (humor)

Sophocles

Spencer, Herbert

Steele

Stevenson

Swift

Swinburne

Tacitus

Tennyson (poetry)

Thackeray, William Makepeace, *Vanity Fair*; *The History of Pendennis: His Fortunes and Misfortunes, His Friends and Greatest Enemy*

Thucydides

Tolstoy, Leo, *Anna Karenina*, *War and Peace*, *The Sebastopol Sketches*, *The Cossacks*

Trevelyan

Turgot

Twain, Mark (humor)

Waddington, *Guerre de Sept Ans*
Ward, Artemus (humor)
Ward, Herbert, *Voice from the Congo*
White, Stewart Edward
Whitman (poetry)
Wister, Owen

Additionally, he mentioned *The Federalist*, epic tales, "parts of the Old Testament, to the Nibelungenlied, to the Roland Lay and the *chansons de gestes* to Beowulf, and finally to the great Japanese hero-tale, the story of the Forty-Nine Ronins."[97] He also recommended a German study of the Mongols, the histories of Eugene of Savoy and Turenne, old volumes about De Ruyter and "the daring warrior merchants of the Hansa," and study of the "feats of Suffren and Tegethoff."[98]

Combined Reading List of the Eloquent Presidents

Each president's individual reading list is only a partial glimpse into the books the president read. A combined reading list is thus incomplete because of that limitation. There are additional challenges when attempting to produce a combined reading list. We don't know much about what Grant read throughout his lifetime, so he does not have much overlap with the other presidents. Further, some of the authors Lincoln, Grant, and Roosevelt read were not living or writing when Jefferson and Madison were alive. A further caveat is that the presidents read, almost exclusively, books authored by white men. There are a few exceptions: Jefferson read Elizabeth Carter's translation of *Epictetus* and Lady Mary Wortley Montagu's letters;[99] Lincoln read Harriet Beecher Stowe and Mary Chandler; and Roosevelt read Jane Austen and Mary Kingsley. Yet even an imperfect combined reading list tells us something about what books influenced several of our eloquent presidents. The following is a list of the authors and books more than one eloquent president read.

---

97. *Id.* at 267.
98. *Id.*
99. Letter from Thomas Jefferson to Robert Skipwith (Aug. 3, 1771), *in Thomas Jefferson Writings, supra* note 22, at 744–45.

Authors/Books Likely Read by All Five Presidents

1. The Bible (Jefferson, Madison, Lincoln, Roosevelt) (assume Grant)
2. Shakespeare, William (Jefferson, Madison, Lincoln, Roosevelt) (assume Grant)

Authors/Books Likely Read by Four Presidents

1. Addison, Joseph (Jefferson, Madison, Lincoln, Roosevelt)
2. Gibbon, Edward (Jefferson, Madison, Lincoln, Roosevelt)
3. Horace (Jefferson, Madison, Lincoln, Roosevelt)
4. Milton, John (Jefferson, Madison, Lincoln, Roosevelt)
5. Pope, Alexander (Jefferson, Madison, Lincoln, Roosevelt)

Authors/Books Likely Read by Three Presidents

1. Aeschylus (Jefferson and Roosevelt) (assume Madison)
2. Blackstone, William (Madison, Lincoln) (assume Jefferson; probably Roosevelt during his one year of law school)
3. Defoe, Daniel, *Robinson Crusoe* (Madison, Lincoln) (assume Grant and/ or Roosevelt)
4. Gray, Thomas (Jefferson, Lincoln, Roosevelt)
5. Homer, *Iliad* and *Odyssey* (Jefferson and Madison could read in Greek: Lincoln read a translated version)
6. Hume, David (Jefferson, Madison, Lincoln).
7. Robertson, William (Jefferson, Madison, Lincoln)
8. Sophocles (Jefferson, Roosevelt) (assume Madison)
9. Tacitus (Jefferson and Roosevelt) (assume Madison)
10. Thucydides (Jefferson, Lincoln, Roosevelt)
11. Voltaire (Jefferson, Madison, Lincoln)

Note that even though Jefferson, Madison, and Lincoln all read Hume, Jefferson responded to one man's request for advice about how to acquire an education with a caution to avoid Hume, "I omit Hume as too false in his matter, and too seducing in his style to be trusted."[100] Madison's mentor John Witherspoon also "condemned 'the infidel Hume' for his absurd 'natural ethics.'"[101]

---

100. Letter from Thomas Jefferson to Joseph Echols (May 23, 1822), *supra* note 20.
101. *See* Ketcham, *supra* note 32.

Authors/Books Likely Read by Two Presidents

1. Aristotle (Jefferson, Madison)
2. Bacon, Francis (Madison, Lincoln)
3. Bulwer-Lytton, Edward (Lincoln, Grant)
4. Bunyan, John (Madison, Lincoln)
5. Butler, Samuel (Madison, Lincoln)
6. Cicero (Jefferson, Madison)
7. Demosthenes (Jefferson, Madison)
8. Emerson, Ralph Waldo (Lincoln, Roosevelt)
9. Euclid, *Geometry* (Jefferson, Lincoln)
10. Holmes, Oliver Wendell (Lincoln, Roosevelt)
11. Justinian (Jefferson, Madison)
12. Lord Kames (Henry Home) (Jefferson, Madison)
13. Livy (Jefferson, Madison)
14. Locke, John (Jefferson, Madison)
15. Longfellow, Henry Wadsworth (Lincoln, Roosevelt)
16. Macaulay, Thomas B. (Lincoln, Roosevelt)
17. Plato (Jefferson, Madison)
18. Plutarch (Jefferson, Lincoln)
19. Poe, Edgar Allan (Roosevelt, Lincoln)
20. Polybius (Jefferson, Madison)
21. Sallust (Jefferson, Madison)
22. Scott, Sir Walter (Grant, Roosevelt)
23. Scott, Winfield (Lincoln and likely Grant)
24. Swift, Jonathan (Jefferson, Roosevelt)
25. Terence (Jefferson, Madison)
26. Virgil (Jefferson, Madison)
27. Xenophon (Jefferson, Madison)
28. Young, Edward (Jefferson, Lincoln)

Jefferson, Grant, and Roosevelt had strong views about the books a reader should avoid. In one letter Jefferson warned a young man to "avoid wasting time on books of little merit."[102] In his letter responding to a request for his advice about a plan for female education, Jefferson cautioned against reading too many novels or too much poetry due to the "time lost in that reading which should be instructively employed."[103] Grant implied that readers should not

---

102. *Id.*

103. Letter from Thomas Jefferson to Nathaniel Burwell (Mar. 14, 1818), *supra* note 29, at 102.

read novels of "a trashy sort."[104] Roosevelt, even when pointing out that a reader's taste must govern book selection, believed personal preference had a limit. He cautioned, "[T]he reading of vicious books for pleasure should be eliminated. It is no less clear that trivial and vulgar books do more damage than can possibly be offset by any entertainment they yield."[105] Roosevelt's definition of "vicious books" were books without sound moral teachings. He explained by giving one specific example, "Tolstoy is an interesting and stimulating writer, but an exceedingly unsafe moral advisor."[106] He also advised readers who had not read "serious literature" to "try to train himself" to read the classics, suggesting, "Let man or woman, young man or girl, read some good author, say Gibbon or Macaulay, until sustained mental effort brings power to enjoy the books worth enjoying."[107]

Reading Like the Presidents

Anyone who wants to read like the eloquent presidents should read the Bible, Shakespeare, and poetry. These three have long been recognized as Lincoln's favorites—he turned to them again and again. Robert Bray emphasized Lincoln's reading practice, "[p]oetry and Shakespeare for private delight; the Bible and rhetorical studies for public speeches and writings...."[108] Not all the eloquent presidents relied on the Bible, Shakespeare, and poetry to the same degree as Lincoln, but all did read these works. Perhaps this isn't surprising because the Bible, Shakespeare, and poetry were commonly read by the literate and the educated when the eloquent presidents were alive.

Still, it is striking how often the presidents read poetry. In his book *Poetry and the American Presidents*, Professor Paul J. Ferlazzo asks, "What does an appreciation of poetry reveal about a person, even a President?"[109] He lists several generalities about poetry, including its value in requiring the reader to hold opposites in mind and its ability to present a deeper truth about life. But it is his observation about poetry and language that should inspire legal writers to read poetry: "On a basic level an appreciation of poetry reveals the love of language, a respect and admiration for the precise word or phrase that

---

104. *Personal Memoirs, supra* note 8, at 27.
105. Roosevelt, *A Book-Lover's Holiday, supra* note 9, at 262.
106. *Id.*
107. *Id.* at 260.
108. Robert Bray, *Reading with Lincoln* 199 (2010).
109. Paul J. Ferlazzo, *Poetry and the American Presidency* xii (2012).

captures and renders with special clarity and authority a particular thought or expression."[110] Our eloquent presidents knew the value of choosing that precise word or phrase and read poetry, at least in part, because of their love of language.

The classics also make up a significant part of the combined reading list. While they were being educated, Jefferson and Madison studied the classics. Whenever he had to pick a book to read, Jefferson could not resist reading one of the classics. He wrote to a friend, "to read the Latin and Greek authors in their original, is a sublime luxury."[111] His granddaughter Ellen Wayles Randolph Coolidge recalled, "I saw him more frequently with a volume of the classics in his hand than with any other book."[112] He noted this preference in a letter to John Adams when he wrote, "I have given up newspapers in exchange for Tacitus, and Thucydides, for Newton and Euclid, & I find myself much the happier."[113]

For lawyers hoping to strengthen their persuasive writing techniques, the classics are inspiring. Jefferson defended and emulated the style of the classics. He wrote, "I readily sacrifice the niceties of syntax to euphony and strength. It is by boldly neglecting the rigorisms of grammar that Tacitus has made himself the strongest writer in the world.... Some of his sentences are as strong as language can make them."[114] He recommended that a student study "the art of writing & speaking correctly" by "[c]riticiz[ing] the style of any books whatever, committing your criticisms to writing."[115] He advised that writing these critical compositions would require effort, but the student should pay "great attention to the correctness and elegance of your language."[116] He suggested several models of eloquence, including Demosthenes and Cicero.[117]

---

110. *Id.*

111. Letter from Thomas Jefferson to Dr. Joseph Priestley (Jan. 27, 1800), *in* 31 *The Papers of Thomas Jefferson (1 February 1799–31 May 1800)* 339, 339 (Barbara B. Oberg ed., 2004).

112. Letter from Ellen Wayles Randolph Coolidge to Henry Randall (185–), *supra* note 15.

113. Letter from Thomas Jefferson to John Adams (Jan. 12, 1812), *in* 4 *The Papers of Thomas Jefferson, Retirement Series* 428, 429 (J. Jefferson Looney ed. 2007).

114. Thomas Jefferson to Edward Everett (Feb. 24, 1823) *in* 7 *The Writings of Thomas Jefferson* 273 (Henry Augustine Washington ed. 1854). Jefferson gave one example: if the syntax of "Rebellion *to* tyrants is obedience to God" had been correctly changed to "Rebellion *against* tyrants is obedience to God" then the motto would have "lost all the strength and beauty of the antithesis." *Id.*

115. Letter from Thomas Jefferson to John Minor (Aug. 20, 1814) including Letter from Thomas Jefferson to Bernard Moore, [ca. 1773?], *supra* note 23, at 629.

116. *Id.* at 630.

117. *Id.*

Modern lawyers can learn much from the classics as models of both eloquent writing and strong reasoning. Jefferson certainly appreciated the classics for both reasons. He wrote, "I think the Greeks & Romans have left us the purest models which exist of fine composition, whether we examine them as works of reason, or of style & fancy; and to them we probably owe these characteristics of modern composition."[118] Prof. A.E. Dick Howard, a former clerk for United States Supreme Court Justice Hugo L. Black, remembered, "Justice Black insisted that I read the classics — Gibbon and Carlyle, Polybius and Tacitus.... Through these books, I got a glimpse of what made him not only a great legal thinker, but also a consummate master of the English language."[119]

The classics have at least one other benefit, at least according to Roosevelt. Roosevelt acknowledged the literary value of the classics, but also added that books from the past "yield consolation of a non-literary kind."[120] Those consolations encouraged a gratitude "that [the reader's] lot has been cast in the present age, in spite of all its faults."[121]

A reader should not stop at the classics because all the presidents read, and were influenced by, many other books. Roosevelt was particularly critical of "the fetishism of the irrational adoration of things merely because they are old."[122] He believed Lincoln was a stronger writer than Demosthenes and Cicero.[123] Roosevelt encouraged reading current books to help a reader "know something of what especially interests the mass of our fellows, and ... may really set forth something in a genuine fashion which for the moment stirs the hearts of all of us."[124] Even Jefferson's devotion to the classics did not prevent him from acknowledging that fiction could be "useful as well as pleasant."[125] Despite his strong grounding in a classical education, he vehemently disagreed with the "notion that nothing can be useful but the learned lumber of Greek and Roman reading" because "every thing is useful which contributes to fix us

---

118. Letter from Jefferson to Priestley (Jan. 27, 1800), *supra* note 111, at 339.

119. Bryan A. Garner, *Regaining the Joy of Reading*, A.B.A. J., Nov. 24, 2014, at 24, 25 [hereinafter Garner, *Regaining*].

120. Roosevelt, *A Book-Lover's Holiday*, *supra* note 9, at 272.

121. *Id.* at 273.

122. Adriana Maynard, *A Man of Strong Opinions*, Theodore Roosevelt Center blog (July 8, 2011), http://www.theodorerooseveltcenter.org/Blog/2011/July/08-A-Man-of-Strong-Opinions.aspx.

123. *Id.*

124. Roosevelt, *A Book-Lover's Holiday*, *supra* note 9, at 271.

125. Letter from Thomas Jefferson to Robert Skipwith (Aug. 3, 1771), *in Thomas Jefferson Writings*, *supra* note 22, at 741.

in the principles and practice of virtue."[126] Grant's reading of contemporary fiction helped develop his clear, straightforward writing style.

Perhaps even more important than trying to follow a particular reading list, we should focus on emulating the voracious reading habits of our eloquent presidents. Like all writers, we can learn from good writing. Chief Justice John Roberts emphasizes, "[T]he only good way to learn about good writing is to read good writing.... [T]he way to be a good writer is to be a good reader."[127] Judge Kevin Ross noted that he can "pause and appreciate particularly well-crafted sentences in any writing."[128] Lawyer Aimee Furness explained, "You can become a better writer only through reading."[129] The presidents, too, learned how to become better writers through their reading, but the primary reason they read was because they loved to read.

No matter what book the eloquent presidents read, they found joy in their reading. Grant enjoyed reading only once he began to read for pleasure. No reading list, whether it is based on one individual president's recommendations or a combined reading list, will be a perfect fit for any reader. Roosevelt understood. He equated preferences in books to personal taste in eating. He explained, "[W]ithin certain broad limits the matter [of taste in books] is merely one of individual preference, having nothing to do with the quality of the reader's mind."[130] He explained that he liked "apples, pears, oranges, pineapples, and peaches," but disliked "bananas, alligator-pears, and prunes." He wouldn't defend those choices over anyone else's choice in fruit, just like he wouldn't defend his choice in reading material over anyone else's choice, as long as the book was morally sound. He admitted that *Fortunes of Nigel, Esmond,* and *The Old Curiosity Shop* might be "as good as" the books he preferred by the same authors (Sir Walter Scott, William Makepeace Thackeray, Charles Dickens), but "I do not like them any more than I like prunes or bananas."[131]

Roosevelt's honesty is refreshing. He preferred *Macbeth* and *Othello* over *King Lear* and *Hamlet* even though he knew "perfectly well that the latter are as wonderful as the former."[132] He also revealed that he would not admit that

---

126. *Id.*

127. *Chief Justice John Roberts Jr. [Interview by Bryan A. Garner]*, 2010 Scribes J. Legal Writing 6, 39–40.

128. Garner, *Regaining, supra* note 119, at 24 (quoting Judge Kevin Ross, Minnesota Court of Appeals).

129. *Id.* (quoting Dallas lawyer Aimee Furness).

130. Roosevelt, *A Book-Lover's Holiday, supra* note 9, at 260.

131. *Id.* at 261.

132. *Id.*

he did not like some of Shakespeare's plays unless he could "proudly express my appreciation" for some of his other plays. He concluded, "But at my age I might as well own up, at least to myself, to my limitations, and read the books I thoroughly enjoy."[133]

That is one motto we can follow. The reading recommendations from our eloquent presidents can be instructive because we will benefit from reading the authors and books on their reading lists. In the end, though, we too should read the books we enjoy.

---

133. *Id.* at 261–262.

Chapter 8

Presidents Influencing the Writing of Other Presidents: Friendship, Letter Writing, and Admiration

When I was selecting the presidents to include as writing models, I chose each president individually based on his ability to write with a quality that remains essential for persuasion. It was only after I chose all five presidents that I realized I had picked two pairs of friends: Jefferson/Madison and Lincoln/ Grant. Teddy Roosevelt did not have a friend in my group, but he also read and emulated the writings of some other presidents on my list.[1] My goal in this chapter is to look at those friendships and influences, with a special focus on writing. Some presidents consciously studied and analyzed the writings of other presidents and then emulated that writing style. Further, I suggest that even at an unconscious level the presidents' writing styles were influenced by other eloquent presidents.

Chapter 7 included the eloquent presidents' reading lists, but these five presidents also spent a significant amount of time reading letters and speeches written by other eloquent presidents. Jefferson and Madison collaborated on political issues for thirty years, but they wrote letters to each other for nearly fifty years. This amazing friendship developed in large part through their let-

---

1. Teddy Roosevelt did have a friend (and rival) in another president—William Howard Taft—but Taft is not on my list of eloquent presidents. For a fascinating look at the Roosevelt/Taft relationship see Doris Kearns Goodwin, *The Bully Pulpit: Theodore Roosevelt, William Howard Taft, and the Golden Age of Journalism* (2013).

ter writing. Lincoln and Grant respected and admired each other. Their relationship would have become one of the great friendships in American history if Lincoln had not been assassinated. Even in the short time that they knew each other, each was impressed by the writing style of the other. Lincoln's brevity and Grant's clarity were mirrored in the other; each wrote with both brevity and clarity. Even after the presidents' deaths, some eloquent presidents continued to impact the writing styles of other presidents. Lincoln studied Jefferson's writing. Roosevelt admired Lincoln and Grant, and he recognized that part of what made both men great was their ability to communicate effectively.

When the eloquent presidents read what other eloquent presidents wrote, their own writing was affected. Chief Justice John Roberts explained that reading good writing subtly changes the reader:

> You can't do it consciously. You can't say, "This is how you need to structure a sentence." But your mind structures the words and it sees them, and when you try to write them again, they tend to come out better because your mind is thinking of what was a pleasing sentence to read and remembers that when you try to write.[2]

Letter writing can qualify as good writing. Randall Tietjen read hundreds of Clarence Darrow's letters and observed that Darrow's letters showed his writing strengths: "His letters—at least some of them—were beautifully written and interesting to read."[3] Jefferson, Madison, Lincoln, and Grant subtly changed how they wrote based on the letters written during their friendships.

Thomas Jefferson and James Madison

Jefferson and Madison met in 1776, the year of America's independence, when both were members of the Virginia House of Delegates.[4] Jefferson was thirty-three; Madison was twenty-five. "Neither could have foreseen how essential the other would become to his public career and individual legacy."[5] Their friendship grew when Madison became a member of Jefferson's Execu-

---

2. *Chief Justice John Roberts Jr. [Interview by Bryan A. Garner]*, 2010 Scribes J. Legal Writing 6, 40.

3. *In the Clutches of the Law: Clarence Darrow's Letters* xiii (Randall Tietjen ed., 2013).

4. Lee Wilkins, *Madison and Jefferson: The Making of a Friendship*, 12 Pol. Psychol. 593, 594 (No. 4, Dec. 1991).

5. Andrew Burstein & Nancy Isenberg, *Madison and Jefferson* 6 (2010).

tive Council in 1779 when Jefferson was the Governor of Virginia.[6] Historians have long recognized that these two men were more than just good friends. Gordon S. Wood explained, "These two Virginians and Founding Fathers participated in what was probably the greatest political collaboration in American history."[7] It was the friendship between Jefferson and Madison that set the groundwork for their ability to influence each other's writing.

Jefferson and Madison were almost predestined to become friends. Like many good friends, they had many things in common. Both came from similar Virginia gentry backgrounds. Both read the same books. Both shared basic ideas about how to build the nation. Both shared an interest in the natural sciences.[8] "Both needed a political confidant, a man whose intellectual prowess and vision matched his own."[9] They were intellectual equals, but "Jefferson was the more farsighted revolutionary while Madison was the reasoned pragmatist."[10]

In their letters, and in person, Jefferson and Madison often discussed books. Their love of reading and devotion to books was extraordinary. Ralph Ketcham noted, "This began the half-century long, most important and fruitful, and deeply learned conversation about books ever between two American statesmen."[11] Both believed that Congress should have a library. In 1783, Madison proposed a "List of Books to be imported for the use of Congress" which included books on international law, history, world geography, and natural history.[12] Jefferson likely had an influence on Madison's final list of suggested books because Madison's list was an expansion of the 2,640 books that Jefferson had cataloged.[13] The Library of Congress was not established at that time, but instead was started in 1800 during John Adams's presidency.[14] The British burned the Capitol, which included the Library of Congress, in the War of

---

6. *Id.* at 66.

7. Gordon S. Wood, *The Company of Giants*, New Republic, Mar. 6, 2011, at 25, 25 (reviewing Burstein & Isenberg, *supra* note 5).

8. Gaye Wilson, *James Madison*, Th. Jefferson Monticello, (Oct. 24, 1997 rev. by Anna Berkes Aug. 29, 2014), https://www.monticello.org/site/jefferson/james-madison.

9. Wilkins, *supra* note 4, at 596.

10. *Id.* at 597.

11. Ralph Ketcham, *James Madison's Books and Reading*, https://www.montpelier.org/blog/james-madisons-books (last visited Sept. 1, 2016).

12. James Madison, *Report on Books for Congress* (Jan. 23, 1783), *in* 6 *Papers of James Madison* 62–115 (William T. Hutchinson and William M.E. Rachal eds., 1969).

13. Burstein & Isenberg, *supra* note 5, at 98.

14. Library of Congress, *History of the Library*, Libr. of Congress, https://www.loc.gov/about/history-of-the-library/ (last visited Sept. 1, 2016).

1812. Jefferson then sold his personal collection of about 6,500 volumes to create the new Library of Congress, which replaced the much-smaller original collection.[15] The purchase of Jefferson's books was made during Madison's presidency. Jefferson and Madison both built substantial personal libraries; they also shared books, so that "books went regularly the thirty miles between Montpelier and Monticello."[16]

Jefferson and Madison, of course, always kept their own separate styles both in how they approached issues and in how they wrote about those issues. Gordon Wood explains, "Jefferson was high-minded, optimistic, visionary, and often quick to grab hold of new and sometimes bizarre ideas.... This was not how Madison thought. He was generally more direct, deliberate, and practical."[17] These differing styles and temperaments resulted in some differences in how Jefferson and Madison wrote. Jefferson "reached for beauty as he expressed his ideals" and used both metaphor and hyperbole.[18] In contrast, Madison "shunned all extravagance" which resulted in a "quieter" prose.[19] In one of Jefferson's last letters, he used dramatic language to explain that he feared for the "plundered ploughman and beggared yeomanry" under a consolidated government.[20] Madison cautioned that not too much should be read into Jefferson's dramatic language, "'As in others of great genius,' he explained, Jefferson had the habit 'of expressing in strong and round terms, impressions of the moment.'"[21]

Yet Jefferson and Madison also shared some common writing traits. Both had studied the classics, were interested in the study of eloquence and persuasion, and wrote with elegance.[22] Importantly, both were effective communicators and successful at persuading:

> While Jefferson's pathos was finely balanced, and his rhythmic arrangement of words and phrases was a gift no other political writer of his day could equal, Madison's *control* of language was exemplary, which

---

15. *Sale of Books to the Library of Congress*, Th. Jefferson Monticello, https://www.monticello.org/site/research-and-collections/sale-books-library-congress-1815 (last visited Sept. 1, 2016).

16. Ketcham, *supra* note 11.

17. Wood, *supra* note 7, at 25.

18. Burstein & Isenberg, *supra* note 5, at 623.

19. *Id.*

20. *Id.* (quoting Dec. 26, 1825 letter from Jefferson to William Branch Giles).

21. *Id.* (quoting May 15, 1832 letter from Madison to Nicolas P. Trist).

22. Burstein and Isenberg also note, "From the time they were children, they were steeped in the spectacle of classical oratory and taught to be clever by reading the *Spectator* essays of Oxford-educated Joseph Addison and Richard Steele." *Id.* at 623.

was one of the reasons Jefferson turned over so much of the responsibility for newspaper essay writing to him.[23]

Their mutual respect also helped each recognize the writing strengths of the other. Madison may not have used metaphor, but he appreciated that Jefferson used it effectively to persuade. Likewise, Jefferson did not always write with Madison's precision, but he supported that precise style and knew that it, too, could persuade.

The friendship and mutual admiration between Jefferson and Madison is evident in the numerous letters they wrote to each other. Their surviving written correspondence begins in March 1780[24] and lasts until just months before Jefferson's death in 1826.[25] Both wrote their letters with forthrightness, clarity, and honesty. At least at an unconscious level, each influenced the other as a result of this writing friendship.

Jefferson's faith in Madison was recorded in a letter he wrote to Peter Carr in 1783. He urged Carr to visit Madison and consider him a valuable patron. He ended with this compliment to Madison, "His judgment is so sound and his heart so good that I would wish you to respect every advice he would be so kind as to give you, equally as if it came from me."[26]

In 1784, Jefferson wrote a letter to Madison asking him to join him at Monticello. Jefferson was still lonely after his wife Martha's death.[27] Jefferson used a forthright approach as he attempted to persuade Madison:

> I once hinted to you the project of seating yourself in the neighborhood of Monticello, and my sanguine wishes made me look on your answer as not absolutely excluding the hope. Monroe is decided in settling there and is actually engaged in the endeavor to purchase. Short is the same. Would you but make it a "partie quatre" I should believe that life had still some happiness in store for me. Agreeable society is the first essential in constituting the happiness and of course

---

23. *Id.* (emphasis in original).

24. *Id.* at 73.

25. The correspondence between Jefferson and Madison is collected in *The Republic of Letters: The Correspondence between Thomas Jefferson and James Madison 1776–1826* (James Morton Smith ed., 1995) [hereinafter *The Republic of Letters*].

26. Letter from Thomas Jefferson to Peter Carr (Dec. 11, 1783), *in* 6 *The Papers of Thomas Jefferson: May 21, 1781–March 1, 1784*, at 379–80 (Julian P. Boyd ed., 1952).

27. Burstein & Isenberg, *supra* note 5, at 93. Martha Jefferson died on September 6, 1782. *Id.*

the value of our existence.... You shall find with me a room, bed and plate, if you will do me the favor to become of the family.[28]

Even though Madison did not take Jefferson up on his offer, their friendship was thriving.

The depth of their friendship, and the resulting influence Madison had on Jefferson, is demonstrated by an incident when Madison disagreed with Jefferson. In 1789, Jefferson suggested to Madison his unique and disastrous idea that all personal and national debts, all laws, and all constitutions should expire every nineteen years, so that no generation would be bound by the actions of a predecessor generation.[29] Madison's reply to Jefferson was a "model of tact."[30] Madison wrote on February 4, 1790:

> The idea which the latter evolves is a great one, and suggests many interesting reflections to legislators; particularly when contracting and providing for public debts. Whether it can be received in the extent your reasonings give it, is a question which I ought to turn more in my thoughts than I have yet been able to do, before I should be justified in making up a full opinion on it. My first thoughts though coinciding with many of yours, lead me to view the doctrine as not in *all* respects compatible with the course of human affairs. I will endeavor to sketch the grounds of my skepticism.[31]

Madison gently prods Jefferson with a few questions about tossing out all constitutions and laws every nineteen years, "Would not a Government so often revised become too mutable ...? Would not such periodical revision engender pernicious factions that might not otherwise come into existence?"[32] Madison also pointed out, "Debts may even be incurred principally for the benefit of posterity: such, perhaps, is the present debt of the U. States."[33] He thus reminded Jefferson that the debt resulting from the American Revolution benefited future generations. Instead of frankly telling Jefferson that his idea was terrible, Madison said his concerns were not meant "to impeach either the

---

28. Letter from Thomas Jefferson to James Madison (Dec. 8, 1784), *in* 1 *The Republic of Letters, supra* note 25, at 353–55.

29. Wood, *supra* note 7.

30. *Id.*

31. Letter from James Madison to Thomas Jefferson (Feb. 4, 1790), *in* 1 *The Republic of Letters, supra* note 25, at 650.

32. *Id.* at 650–51.

33. *Id.* at 651.

utility of the principle [as applied] … or the general importance of it in the eye of the philosophical Legislator." He went a step further, "On the contrary, it would give me singular pleasure to see it first announced in the proceedings of the U. States, and always kept in view, as a salutary curb on the living generation from imposing unjust and unnecessary burdens on their successors."[34] His final sentence could only be written by someone who values a friendship. He notes that he viewed Jefferson's idea through "the naked eye of the ordinary Politician," so he may have overlooked the benefits that Jefferson saw "thro' the medium of Philosophy." Madison was truthful, but kind, and Jefferson ultimately abandoned the idea.

The letters Madison and Jefferson exchanged at the end of Jefferson's life are poignant examples of their shared writing quality of honesty as each expressed his sincere admiration for the other. On February 17, 1826, Jefferson wrote to Madison asking him for advice about finding a law professor for the new University of Virginia. He also mentioned his own financial problems. But it is the end of the letter where he reveals just how much Madison's friendship and support meant to him. He wrote, with his traditional practice of not capitalizing the first word in a sentence:

> the friendship which has subsisted between us, now half a century, and the harmony of our political principles and pursuits, have been sources of constant happiness to me thro' that long period. and, if I remove beyond the reach of attentions to the University, or beyond the bourne of life itself, as I soon must, it is a comfort to leave that institution under your care, and an assurance that they will neither be spared, nor ineffectual. it has also been a great solace to me to believe that you are engaged in vindicating to posterity the course we have pursued for preserving to them, *in all their purity*, the blessings of self-government, which we had assisted too in acquiring for them. if ever the earth has beheld a system of administration conducted with a single and steadfast eye, to the general interest and happiness of those committed to it, one which, protected by truth, can never know reproach, it is that to which our lives have been devoted. to myself you have been a pillar of support thro' life. take care of me when dead, and be assured that I shall leave with you my last affections.

Th. Jefferson[35]

---

34. *Id.* at 652–53.

35. Letter from Thomas Jefferson to James Madison (Feb. 17, 1826), http://founders.archives.gov/documents/Jefferson/98-01-02-5912.

Madison quickly replied to Jefferson:

> You cannot look back to the long period of our private friendship and political harmony, with more affecting resolutions than I do.... Wishing and hoping that you may yet live to increase the debt which our Country owes you, and to witness the increasing gratitude, which alone can pay it, I offer you the fullest return of affectionate assurances.[36]

In Jefferson's will, he left Madison a "gold-mounted walking staff of animal horn, taken as a token of the cordial and affectionate friendship which for nearly now an half century, has united us in the same principles and pursuits of what we have deemed for the greatest good of our country."[37] Madison had promised Jefferson that he would take over Jefferson's responsibilities as rector of the University of Virginia. He kept that promise and held that position for eight years until his own declining health prevented him from continuing to serve.[38]

The collaboration between Jefferson and Madison, as they together "work[ed] out a comprehensive ideology of democracy,"[39] resulted in the founding of our American democracy. Their incredible collaboration was made possible because of their friendship. For fifty years, they wrote to each other and read each other's words. As a result, each had an impact on the writing of the other.

Abraham Lincoln and Ulysses S. Grant

Like Jefferson and Madison, it is no surprise that Lincoln and Grant became friends. They both grew up in the West. They both approached the world with common sense. They both had a self-deprecating humor. They were both ambitious, but that ambition was tempered with an overarching goal of serving their country. They both were deeply humble.[40] But Lincoln and Grant's relationship differed in one critical way from Jefferson and Madison's relationship. Jefferson and Madison were friends for nearly fifty years, but Lincoln and

---

36. Letter from James Madison to Thomas Jefferson (Feb. 24, 1826), https://www.loc.gov/resource/mjm.21_0487_0489/?sp=2.

37. Burstein & Isenberg, *supra* note 5, at 599.

38. *Id.*

39. Adrienne Koch, *Jefferson and Madison: The Great Collaboration* vi (1950).

40. Edward H. Bonekemper III noted that Lincoln and Grant shared traits of steadiness, aggressiveness, and purposefulness. He noted, "Sharing those traits and similar origins, Lincoln and Grant both came of age in what was then American's frontier region—where diligence and humility trumped pedigree and pretentiousness." Edward H. Bonekemper, III, *Lincoln and Grant: The Westerners Who Won the Civil War* 11 (2012).

Grant's friendship tragically ended with Lincoln's assassination just over thirteen months after they met. Even in that brief time, each developed tremendous respect, admiration, and warmth for the other.

The war gave both Lincoln and Grant the chance to shine, including the chance to become magnificent writers. During the war, Grant had a "context for using his linguistic skills, especially in writing."[41] Thus, Grant was "one of the most articulate of all American soldiers."[42] Grant's intertwined qualities of clarity and brevity marked his communications. Grant biographer Bruce Catton notes that a reader can recognize Grant's writing even before seeing his signature: "[I]t gets to the point, avoids unnecessary verbiage, and tells the recipient exactly what the recipient needs to know."[43] Catton's assessment that "one of Grant's unlooked-for assets was a simple mastery of the art of composing clear English prose"[44] applies with equal force to Lincoln. The observation that Grant had "an instinctive grasp of the weight and significance of words"[45] also could be said of Lincoln. Admittedly, Lincoln was an accomplished writer and speaker before the war, but it was the circumstances of the war that catapulted Lincoln into distinction as America's most eloquent president. In fact, Lincoln is also one of our best American writers. Grant's writings may not have had the "eloquence and poetry that come out in Lincoln's best papers…,"[46] but their writings do share a common-sense approach and simple, but effective, style.

Lincoln and Grant's own words demonstrate their brevity and clarity, so those words are used whenever possible as examples. They exchanged several letters and telegraphs. Lincoln talked with others about his impressions of Grant. Grant tells multiple stories in his *Personal Memoirs* about his encounters with Lincoln, always calling him either "the President" or "Mr. Lincoln." In their communications with each other, Grant and Lincoln used a "matter-of-fact, common-sense" style which reflected the "mutual respect of the president and the general."[47]

---

41. George R. Goethals, *Imaging Ulysses S. Grant: Sifting Through the Shifting Sands of Conventional Wisdom*, 19 Leadership Q. 488, 499 (2008).

42. Bruce Catton, *Preface, in* 1 *The Papers of Ulysses S. Grant: 1837–1861* xiv (John Y. Simon ed., 1967).

43. *Id.* at xv.

44. *Id.*

45. John Y. Simon, *Introduction, in* 1 *The Papers of Ulysses S. Grant, supra* note 42, at xxxi.

46. Allan Nevins, *Preface, id.* at xviv.

47. Brooks Simpson, *Lincoln and Grant: A Reappraisal of a Relationship in Abraham Lincoln: Sources and Styles of Leadership* 119 (Frank J. Williams, William D. Peterson & Vincent J. Marsala eds., 1994) [hereinafter Simpson, *Lincoln and Grant*].

One early communication from Lincoln to Grant helped to establish the guiding rules for their relationship. Grant had just captured Vicksburg. Ida Tarbell called Lincoln's letter "his first recognition of Grant."[48] The letter is notable because Lincoln congratulated Grant, but also admitted that his own thought about military strategy was wrong:

Washington, July 13, 1863

Major-General Grant

My Dear General: I do not remember that you and I ever met personally. I write this now as a grateful acknowledgement for the almost inestimable service you have done the country. I wish to say a word further. When you first reached the vicinity of Vicksburg, I thought you should do what you finally did — march the troops across the neck, run the batteries with the transports, and thus go below; and I never had any faith, except a general hope that you knew better than I, that the Yazoo Pass expedition and the like could succeed. When you got below and took Port Gibson, Grand Gulf, and vicinity, I thought you should go down the river and join General Banks, and when you turned northward, east of the Big Black, I feared it was a mistake. I now wish to make the personal acknowledgment that you were right and I was wrong.

Yours very truly,
A. Lincoln[49]

Those last words bear repeating: "[Y]ou were right and I was wrong." In one short, clear phrase, Lincoln set the tone for the honesty and humility that would be the bedrock of his relationship with Grant.

One other early telegram from Lincoln to Grant is telling because it identifies three of the characteristics Lincoln admired in Grant from the start — skill, courage, and perseverance:

Washington, D.C.
December 8, 1863, 10.2 a.m.

Maj.-General U.S. Grant:

Understanding that your lodgment at Knoxville and Chattanooga is now secure, I wish to tender you, and all under your command, my

---

48. Ida M. Tarbell, *The Life of Abraham Lincoln* 144 (1900).
49. *Id.* at 144–45.

more than thanks, my profoundest gratitude for the skill, courage, and perseverance with which you and they, over so great difficulties, have effected that important object. God bless you all.

A. Lincoln

President U.S.[50]

Grant included a copy of this telegram in his *Personal Memoirs*, noting, "The President especially was rejoiced that Knoxville had been relieved without further bloodshed."[51] Grant knew that Lincoln had experienced "much anxiety" about the army and "the loyal people of East Tennessee."[52] Grant, as he did many times, wanted to alleviate Lincoln's concerns.

Grant and Lincoln first met in person on March 8, 1864, the night before Lincoln formally presented Grant with his commission as Lieutenant-General. The rank was available only because Congress had passed a law "restoring that grade" and the Senate confirmed Grant's commission.[53] Grant's description of receiving the commission is characteristically understated, "The commission was handed to me on the 9th. It was delivered to me at the Executive Mansion by President Lincoln in the presence of his Cabinet, my eldest son, those of my staff who were with me and a few other visitors."[54] What Grant doesn't say is that George Washington was the only other American who had held that rank while commanding the army. Grant now would be subordinate to only one person—Lincoln as the Commander-in-Chief.[55]

The story of how Grant arrived in Washington, D.C. has been retold multiple times. When Grant and his fourteen-year-old son Fred arrived at the Willard Hotel the hotel clerk did not recognize him and offered him a small room on the top floor. Grant's inconspicuous physical appearance had again masked his identity. Grant, who never stood on ceremony, said that would be fine, but when the clerk saw Grant's signature on the guest register he quickly revised his offer and suggested Parlor 6, the same room where Lincoln had stayed before his inauguration.[56]

---

50. Ulysses S. Grant, *Personal Memoirs of Ulysses S. Grant* 394–95 (1992) [hereinafter *Personal Memoirs*].

51. *Id.* at 394.

52. *Id.* at 395.

53. *Id.* at 403.

54. *Id.*

55. William S. McFeely, *Grant* 154 (1982).

56. Geoffrey Perret, *Ulysses S. Grant: Soldier and President* 294–95 (1997).

Later in the evening, Grant walked to the White House after Lincoln invited him to attend his weekly reception.[57] Grant explains what he knew of Lincoln before that meeting:

> Although hailing from Illinois myself, I never met Lincoln until called to the capital.... I knew him, however, very well and favorably from the accounts given by officers under me at the West who had known him all their lives. I had also read the remarkable series of debates between Lincoln and Douglas a few years before.... I was then a resident of Missouri, and by no means a "Lincoln man" in that contest; but I recognized his great ability.[58]

When Lincoln saw Grant enter the room, he extended his hand and exclaimed, "Why, here is General Grant. Well, this is a great pleasure, I assure you."[59] The two shook hands, listened to the applause from the crowd, and briefly talked with each other. Grant then chatted with Mrs. Lincoln. The eager crowd pressed in on Grant, so Secretary of State William Seward convinced Grant to stand on a crimson sofa in the East Room.[60] The crowd of well-wishers shook his hand for an hour.[61]

Lincoln and Grant had another chance to talk later that night when Seward brought Grant to the Blue Room where both Lincoln and Secretary of War Stanton were waiting. Lincoln explained the ceremony the next day, shared a copy of the remarks he would make, and told Grant that he would be expected to make a brief reply. Lincoln suggested that Grant say something to both prevent jealousy from the other generals and to put Grant on good terms with the Army of the Potomac.[62]

Grant went back to the Willard Hotel, wrote his remarks on a scrap of paper, and delivered his brief speech the following day:

> Mr. President, I accept the commission, with gratitude for the high honor conferred. With the aid of the noble armies that have fought in so many fields for our common country, it will be my earnest endeavor not to disappoint your expectations. I feel the full weight of the responsibilities now devolving on me; and I know that if they are

---

57. Jean Edward Smith, *Grant* 289 (2001).
58. *Personal Memoirs*, *supra* note 50, at 407.
59. Smith, *supra* note 57, at 289.
60. *Id.* at 290.
61. Perret, *supra* note 56, at 296.
62. Smith, *supra* note 57, at 290.

met, it will be due to the armies, and above all, to the favor of that providence which leads both nations and men.[63]

Notably, he did not include the two suggestions that Lincoln had made.[64] Lincoln had wanted an independent leader, and he must have appreciated this demonstration of Grant's independence even as he was accepting his commission.

Grant may have only briefly described the ceremony, but he gave more details about his first meeting alone with Lincoln. Lincoln reassured Grant that "he had never professed to be a military man or to know how campaigns should be conducted," but the procrastination of his former commanders and "the pressure from the people at the North, and Congress, *which was always with him*" forced him to issue military orders.[65] Grant noted that Lincoln admitted that his military orders were sometimes deficient, "He did not know that they were all wrong, and did know that some of them were."[66] Grant remembered:

> All he had ever wanted was someone who would take the responsibility and act, and call on him for all the assistance needed, pledging himself to use all the power of the government in rendering such assistance. Assuring him that I would do the best I could with the means at hand, and avoid as far as possible annoying him or the War Department, our first interview ended.[67]

Lincoln and Grant found their common ground because Lincoln wanted an independent leader and Grant wanted to *be* an independent leader.

Once Lincoln put Grant in charge, he was relieved to discover that Grant was up to the task of actually *leading* the Union army. Lincoln trusted Grant, and Grant gave an example of that trust:

> In one of my early interviews with the President I expressed my dissatisfaction with the little that had been accomplished by the cavalry so far in the war, and the belief that it was capable of accomplishing much more than it had done if under a thorough leader. I said I wanted the very best man in the army for that command. Halleck was present and spoke up, saying: "How would Sheridan do?" I

---

63. *Personal Memoirs*, *supra* note 50, at 403–04.
64. Perret, *supra* note 56, at 298.
65. *Personal Memoirs*, *supra* note 50, at 407 (emphasis in the original).
66. *Id.*
67. *Id.* at 407–08.

replied: "The very man I want." The President said I could have any man I wanted.[68]

At the end of his Personal Memoirs Grant reiterated, "Mr. Lincoln was not timid, and he was willing to trust his generals in making and executing their plans."[69] Grant then compared Lincoln to Stanton. He grudgingly admitted that both had great ability.[70] Then he revealed why he had a special respect for Lincoln:

> Mr. Lincoln gained influence over men by making them feel that it was a pleasure to serve him. He preferred yielding his own wish to gratify others, rather than to insist upon having his own way. It distressed him to disappoint others. In matters of public duty, however, he had what he wished, but in the least offensive way. Mr. Stanton never questioned his own authority to command, unless resisted. He cared nothing for the feelings of others. In fact it seemed to be pleasanter to him to disappoint than to gratify.[71]

Grant wanted to clarify that Lincoln and Stanton were not, as the public at that time thought, a "complement of each other" because "Mr. Lincoln did not require a guardian to aid him in the fulfillment of a public trust."[72] If Lincoln had a complement, it was Grant himself.

Grant's willingness to accept responsibility took another form—he protected Lincoln from the ups and downs of the war. In his first private meeting, Lincoln told Grant that "he did not want to know what I proposed to do."[73] Even with this directive, Lincoln could not resist showing Grant a "plan of campaign of his own which he wanted me to hear and then do as I pleased about."[74] Lincoln pulled out a map of Virginia, marked with the positions of the Confederate and Union armies, and then he noted a spot where two streams emptied into the Potomac. He "suggested that the army might be moved on boats and landed between the mouths of these streams" so the Potomac could be used to bring supplies and "the tributaries would protect our flanks while we moved out."[75] Grant dryly noted, "I listened respectfully, but did not sug-

---

68. *Id.* at 414.
69. *Id.* at 656.
70. *Id.*
71. *Id.*
72. *Id.*
73. *Id.* at 408.
74. *Id.*
75. *Id.*

gest that the same streams would protect Lee's flanks while he was shutting us up."[76] Grant complied with Lincoln's request that Grant keep his plans to himself whenever that was possible.

Grant did, however, communicate with Lincoln when he thought he could alleviate some of Lincoln's anxiety. For example, when writing to Major-General Halleck from Spottsylvania on May 16, 1864, Grant explained, "All offensive operations necessarily cease until we can have twenty-four hours of dry weather." Then, in an effort to reassure Lincoln, he ended with this sentence, "You can assure the President and Secretary of War that the elements alone have suspended hostilities, and it is in no manner due to weakness or exhaustion on our part."[77] Beyond just reassurance, Grant wanted Lincoln to know that he was still a strong, independent, and committed leader.

Lincoln and Grant each recognized the importance of the other to the success of the Union cause. During the summer of 1864 Lincoln was troubled by the rumors that Grant would run against him for President. As Colonel John Eaton explained, "It was distinctly not the personal rivalry with Grant which Mr. Lincoln dreaded, but rather the loss which our cause would suffer if Grant could be induced to go into politics before the military situation was secure."[78] Lincoln "thought it might be risky, — swapping horses in midstream."[79] While Eaton was at the White House, Lincoln said, "Do you know what General Grant thinks of the effort now to nominate him for the presidency? Has he spoken of it to you?"[80] Eaton replied that he knew nothing because he had been away from Grant for some time. Lincoln asked Eaton to go to Grant's headquarters at City Point to talk with him about it.[81] Eaton spent a long evening with Grant, giving him messages from Lincoln and watching Grant open and respond to his mail, but not breaching the "main object of [his] mission."[82] Eaton could not think of a way to raise the sensitive issue, but then he remembered a conversation he had on the train with several men who had asked Eaton about Grant's political bias, and whether Grant could be induced to run.[83] Eaton recalled:

> "The question is," said I "not whether you wish to run, but whether you could be compelled to run in answer to the demand of the peo-

---

76. *Id.*
77. *Id.* at 480.
78. John Eaton, *Grant, Lincoln, and the Freedmen* 186 (1907).
79. *Id.* at 185 (Eaton recording Lincoln's statement).
80. *Id.* at 186 (Eaton recording Lincoln's question).
81. *Id.*
82. *Id.* at 188.
83. *Id.* at 190.

ple for a candidate who should save the Union." We had been talking very quietly, but Grant's reply came in an instant and with a violence for which I was not prepared. He brought his clenched fists down hard on the strap arms of his camp-chair. "They can't do it! They can't compel me to do it!"[84]

Eaton asked if Grant had thought to tell Lincoln this, but Grant replied he had not thought it worthwhile because he considered it "as important for the cause that he should be elected as that the army should be successful in the field."[85] Eaton told Lincoln the next day that he had been right. Eaton reported, "The President fairly glowed with satisfaction. 'I told you,' said he, "they could not get him to run until he had closed out the rebellion.'"[86]

Before Eaton left, Lincoln asked what Grant had said about Lincoln's response to Grant's letter. Eaton had left City Point before Lincoln's message arrived, and thus he could not report on Grant's response. But Eaton recalled Lincoln's next statement:

> Mr. Lincoln repeated to me his famous message of August 17 [1864]: "I have seen your despatch expressing your unwillingness to break your hold where you are. Neither am I willing. Hold on with a bull-dog grip, and chew and choke as much as possible."[87]

Lincoln's language fit with his assessment that Grant had the tenaciousness of a bulldog. Lincoln described what he saw as Grant's strength to artist Francis Carpenter, "The great thing about Grant, I take it, is his perfect coolness and persistency of purpose.... I judge he is not easily excited,—which is a great element in an officer, and he has the *grit* of a bull-dog! Once let him get his 'teeth' *in*, and nothing can shake him off."[88]

Grant sometimes struggled with his two competing concerns—a conviction in his battle plans and a desire to not disappoint or distress Lincoln. Grant explained the situation as it was in early April 1865:

> Mr. Lincoln was at City Point at the time, and had been for some days. I would have let him know what I contemplated doing, only

---

84. *Id.*

85. *Id.* at 190–91.

86. *Id.* at 191.

87. *Id.*; *see also Civil War and Reconstruction* (1850–1877), *Siege of Petersburg*, Nat'l Archives & Records Admin., http://www.archives.gov/exhibits/american_originals/petersbg.html (last visited Sept. 1, 2016).

88. Brooks D. Simpson, *Ulysses S. Grant: Triumph Over Adversity* 461–62 (2000) (emphasis in original).

while I felt a strong conviction that the move was going to be successful, yet it might not prove so; and then I would have only added another to the many disappointments he had been suffering for the past three years. But when we started out he saw that we were moving for a purpose, and bidding us Godspeed, remained there to hear the result.

...

About the first thing Lincoln said to me [following the capture of Petersburg], after warm congratulations for the victory, and thanks both to myself and to the army which had accomplished it was: "Do you know, general, that I have had a sort of sneaking idea for some days that you intended to do something like this."[89]

In this situation, Grant could finally share his objectives with Lincoln.[90] And Lincoln could have the satisfaction of successfully anticipating Grant's plan.

Lincoln sometimes asked Grant directly for reassurance. During Sherman's march, the Southern papers painted Sherman's troops in dire conditions, and those papers had reached the North "causing much distress to all loyal persons—particularly those who had husbands, sons or brothers with Sherman."[91] Lincoln wrote to Grant and asked if Grant could say anything to comfort those distressed people. Grant replied that "there was not the slightest occasion for alarm; that with 60,000 such men as Sherman had with him, such a commanding officer as he was could not be cut off in the open country.... [H]e would get though somewhere ... and even if worst came to worst he could return North."[92] Grant later heard that whenever Lincoln was asked about Sherman's army he replied that Sherman was fine and "Grant says they are safe with such a general, and that if they cannot get out where they want to, they can crawl back by the hole they went in."[93]

Grant and Lincoln also found camaraderie in a shared sense of humor. In late January 1865, Grant hosted the "peace commissioners from the so-called Confederate States" on a Hudson River boat near City Point. Grant did not know any of the men, but he knew of their reputations and "had been a par-

---

89. *Id.* at 612.

90. *Id.*

91. *Personal Memoirs, supra* note 50, at 556.

92. *Id.* at 557.

93. *Id.* Grant commented that Lincoln's later apprehension about Sherman's march "was induced no doubt by his advisers"—and that Grant's own chief of staff had been opposed to the march, so "finding that he could not move me, he appealed to the authorities at Washington to stop it." *Id.* at 562.

ticular admirer of Mr. Stephens."[94] Grant continued, "I had always supposed that he was a very small man, but when I saw him in the dusk of the evening I was very much surprised to find so large a man as he appeared to be."[95] It turns out that Stephens was wearing a thick, long overcoat. Grant remarked that, once the overcoat was removed, "I was struck with the apparent change in size, in the coat and out of it." Lincoln noticed too:

> [Lincoln] asked me if I had seen that overcoat of Stephens's. I replied that I had. "Well," said he, "did you see him take it off?" I said yes. "Well," said he, "didn't you think it was the biggest shuck and the lit- tlest ear that ever you did see?"[96]

Grant included another of Lincoln's anecdotes in his *Personal Memoirs*. Virginia Governor Smith had asked if he could perform the duties of his office and, if not, asked if he could leave the country without interference. Lincoln said the request reminded him of an Irishman from Springfield. Grant recalled Lincoln's story:

> [The Irishman] was very popular with the people, a man of consid- erable promise, and very much liked. Unfortunately he had acquired the habit of drinking, and his friends could see that the habit was growing on him. These friends determined to make an effort to save him, and to do this they drew up a pledge to abstain from all alco- holic drinks. They asked Pat to join them in signing the pledge, and he consented. He had been so long out of the habit of using plain water as a beverage that he resorted to soda-water as a substitute. After a few days this began to grow distasteful to him. So holding the glass behind him, he said: "Doctor, couldn't you drop a bit of brandy in that unbeknownst to myself."[97]

Grant wryly concluded that Governor Smith was not allowed to perform his duties, but that Lincoln would not have prevented anyone from leaving the country.[98]

Grant valued Lincoln's ability to capture a concept with a homespun phrase. While in Washington, Grant explained to Lincoln the idea of a "gen- eral movement ... 'all along the line'" which Lincoln "seemed to think ... a

---

94. *Id.* at 590.
95. *Id.* at 590–91.
96. *Id.*
97. *Id.* at 654.
98. *Id.*

new feature in war."[99] Grant said troops were needed to guard and hold the territory. Grant said to Lincoln, "These troops could perform this service just as well by advancing as by remaining still; and by advancing they would compel the enemy to keep detachments to hold them back, or else lay his own territory open to invasion."[100] Grant reports, "His answer was: 'Oh, yes! I see that. As we say out West, if a man can't skin he must hold a leg while somebody else does.'"[101] This provides just one example of how Lincoln's writing influenced Grant because Grant liked the skinning analogy so much that he used it himself.[102]

Lincoln and Grant shared another essential quality—they were loyal and committed to the Union cause. Grant described what Lincoln said to him:

> He spoke of his having met the commissions [Confederate representatives at City Point in February 1865], and said he had told them that there would be no use in entering into any negotiations unless they would recognize, first: that the Union as a whole must be forever preserved, and second: that slavery must be abolished.[103]

Lincoln's two conditions could not be stated more clearly or briefly. Grant said Lincoln would have been willing to accept almost any specific terms "[i]f they were willing to concede these two points...."[104]

Perhaps the most difficult communication Lincoln sent to Grant was his request that Grant find a place for his son Robert away from combat. The Lincolns had already lost two sons, and Mary Todd Lincoln was hysterical at the thought that Robert "may never come back to us."[105] Lincoln knew that every single family in America felt the same, but fearing for his wife's emotional stability, he wrote to Grant:

Jan. 19, 1865

> Please read and answer this letter as though I was not President, but only a friend. My son, now in his twenty second year, having graduated at Harvard, wishes to see something of the war before it ends.

---

99. *Id.* at 420.

100. *Id.*

101. *Id.*

102. Perret, *supra* note 56, at 343 (citing Ulysses S. Grant, *Preparing for the Campaigns of 1864*, in 4 *Battles and Leaders of the Civil War* 112 (1887)).

103. *Personal Memoirs, supra* note 50, at 591.

104. *Id.*

105. David Herbert Donald, *Lincoln* 571 (1995).

I do not wish to put him in the ranks, nor yet to give him a commission, to which those who have already served long, are better entitled, and better qualified to hold. Could he, without embarrassment to you, or detriment to the service, go into your Military family with some nominal rank, I, and not the public, furnishing his necessary means? If no, say so without the least hesitation, because I am anxious, and deeply interested, that you shall not be encumbered as you can be yourself.

Yours truly,
A. Lincoln[106]

Grant's response was:

Annapolis Junction Md.
Jan.y 21st 1865

A. Lincoln President,
Sir;

Your favor of this date in relation to your son serving in some Military capacity is received. I will be most happy to have him in my Military family in the manner you propose. The nominal rank given him is immaterial but I would suggest that of Capt. as I have three Staff officers now, of considerable service, of no higher grade. Indeed I have one officer with only the rank of Lieut. who has been in the service from the beginning of the war. This however will make no difference and I would still say give the rank of Capt.—Please excuse my writing on a half sheet. I had no resource but to take the blank half of your letter.

Very respectfully
your obt. svt,
U.S. Grant
Lt. Gen[107]

Grant assigned Robert Todd Lincoln to the safe task of escorting visitors to the Potomac army.[108]

Historian Brooks Simpson stated, "Perhaps the most important relationship that Abraham Lincoln formed during the American Civil War was the one

---

106. Letter from Abraham Lincoln to Ulysses S. Grant (Jan. 19, 1865), *in The Papers of Ulysses S. Grant: November 16, 1864–February 20, 1865*, at 281–82 (John Y. Simon ed., 1985).

107. Letter from Ulysses S. Grant to Abraham Lincoln (Jan. 21, 1865), *id.* at 281.

108. Donald, *supra* note 105, at 571.

with the man who would eventually lead the Union armies to victory—Ulysses S. Grant."[109] The relationship was important to the Union's success in the war, but Grant and Lincoln also grew to be close personal friends. The loyalty in both men was "a marked trait" and was "nowhere better exemplified than in their relationship toward one another."[110] They had a warm relationship built on trust and mutual respect. Simpson explains:

> They discovered that they often saw eye to eye on the important issues raised by the war. And they also came to understand that their fates and that of the Union were inextricably linked. When Grant left Lincoln to launch his last campaign against Lee, Lincoln cried out, "Remember, your success is my success." Side by side, the tall, lanky president and the short, cigar-smoking general must have seemed a comical pair to the observer. But they were indispensable to each other and to the survival of the nation through the transforming crucible of civil war.[111]

Lincoln and Grant's ability to write and speak to each other with clarity and brevity was an essential building-block to their relationship. That relationship, in turn, was critical to the entire country. Grant biographer Jean Edward Smith summed it up:

> Lincoln and Grant deserve the nation's credit for saving the United States, eradicating slavery, and striving to provide equality for the freedman. One could not have succeeded without the other. And while Lincoln set the course, it was Grant who sailed the ship.[112]

Lincoln's assassination hit Grant hard. The Lincolns had invited the Grants to attend the theatre with them on April 14, 1865, but the Grants declined because they wanted to visit their children in New Jersey,[113] although some suspect the Grants did not want to spend time with the erratic Mary Todd Lincoln.[114] Grant recalled, "It would be impossible for me to describe the feeling that overcame me at the news of ... the assassination of the President. I knew his goodness of heart, his generosity, his yielding disposition, his desire to have everybody happy, and above all his desire to see all the people of the United States enter

---

109. Simpson, *Lincoln and Grant, supra* note 47, at 109.

110. Eaton, *supra* note 78, at 314.

111. Simpson, *Lincoln and Grant, supra* note 47, at 120.

112. Jean Edward Smith, *Abraham Lincoln and Ulysses S. Grant, in Lincoln Revisited* 180 (John Y. Simon, Harold Holzer & Dawn Vogel eds., 2007).

113. *Personal Memoirs, supra* note 50, at 640.

114. Simpson, *Lincoln and Grant, supra* note 47, at 119–20.

again upon the full privileges of citizenship with equality among all."[115] Grant also knew that Andrew Johnson did not share Lincoln's views on reconstruction, but instead Johnson's "denunciations with great vehemence" towards the South "did engender bitterness of feeling."[116] With brevity and clarity, Grant concludes, "Mr. Lincoln's assassination was particularly unfortunate for the entire nation."[117]

Grant stood for hours at the head of Lincoln's casket, openly weeping. He later declared that it was the saddest day of his life.[118] Grant said of Lincoln, "He was incontestably the greatest man I have ever known."[119] It was the end of great man, but also the end of one of the most important friendships in American history.

Abraham Lincoln and Thomas Jefferson

Lincoln knew about Jefferson's reputation as a stellar writer and classically-trained intellectual. Lincoln did not aspire to the breadth of learning modeled by Jefferson, but "Lincoln's mind instead cut deeply, perhaps slowly or at least with concentrated attention, into a relatively few subjects."[120] One area of interest for Lincoln was persuasion, so he studied composition from the ancients to the moderns, including an examination of Jefferson's "eloquent simplicity."[121]

Lincoln began public speaking when he entered politics. His speeches were carefully written in advance because he did not like speaking spontaneously.[122] His habit was to write out his words before he spoke.[123] Lincoln recognized that the most effective writing and speaking was a "succinct expression in the

---

115. *Personal Memoirs, supra* note 50, at 641.

116. *Id.* at 641.

117. *Id.*

118. Jay Winik, *April 1865: The Month That Saved America* 356–57 (2001).

119. Joan Waugh, *U.S. Grant: American Hero, American Myth* 112 (2009) (quoting Bruce Catton, *Grant Takes Command* 479 (1968)).

120. William Lee Miller, *Lincoln's Virtues: An Ethical Biography* 13 (2002).

121. Fred Kaplan, *Lincoln: The Biography of a Writer* 103 (2008). There is some dispute about whether Lincoln admired Jefferson. *Compare* Garry Wills, *Lincoln at Gettysburg: The Words That Remade America* 85 (1992) (Lincoln "was unstinting in his admiration for Jefferson") *with* Richard Brookhiser, *Founder's Son: A Life of Abraham Lincoln* 157 (2014) (quoting Lincoln's law partner William Herndon as reporting that Lincoln "hated Thomas Jefferson as a man—rather, as a politician").

122. Kaplan, *supra* note 121, at 103. Lincoln also studied President Washington's "sensible succinctness." Kaplan points out that when Lincoln "spoke without a text, he usually spoke from memory, creating the illusion of spontaneity." *Id.*

123. *Id.*

service of truth."[124] His former law partner Joshua Speed noted that Lincoln's goal in studying composition was to "make short sentences & a compact style."[125] He knew he could learn from great writers and speakers, even if he did not agree with the underlying ideas of those role models.[126] Lincoln "read Jefferson's own works with care."[127]

Lincoln knew many of Jefferson's writings and speeches from his own reading, but others also reminded Lincoln of Jefferson's words. When Lincoln's future Secretary of State William Seward made his suggested changes to Lincoln's first inaugural, he compared Lincoln's situation to Jefferson's when he became president.[128] Seward reminded Lincoln that when Jefferson was inaugurated the Federalists were angry about losing the contentious election of 1800. Seward told Lincoln that Jefferson, "sank the partisan in the patriotic in his inaugural address, and propitiated his adversaries by declaring: 'We are all Federalists, all Republicans.'"[129] Seward added, "I could wish that you would think it wise to follow this example in this crisis."[130] In short, Seward wanted Lincoln to moderate his tone and soften some of his arguments.[131] Lincoln took some of Seward's advice, and in doing so showed his adeptness at effectively going "in different directions."[132] Douglas Wilson points out:

> [A]s a writer, [Lincoln] could do conciliation as convincingly as he could do confrontation.... [H]e had to sacrifice some things that had been important to his original conception [to partially accommodate Seward] ... But his talents as a writer were such that he could successfully cover his retreat, principally by means of a truly memorable conclusion whose warmth and conciliatory tone left a lasting impression.[133]

Thus Lincoln, inspired by Jefferson's famous statement, "We are all Federalists, all Republicans" wrote in his concluding paragraph, "We are not enemies,

---

124. *Id.*
125. *Id.*
126. *Id.*
127. Douglas L. Wilson, *Lincoln the Persuader*, Am. Scholar, Autumn 2006, at 31, 43 [hereinafter Wilson, *Lincoln the Persuader*].
128. Ronald C. White, Jr., *The Eloquent President: A Portrait of Lincoln Through His Words* 69 (2005) [hereinafter White, *The Eloquent President*].
129. *Id.* (quoting Seward's "General Remarks" at the beginning of his letter to Lincoln).
130. Douglas L. Wilson, *Lincoln's Sword: The Presidency and the Power of Words* 60 (2006) [hereinafter Wilson, *Lincoln's Sword*] (quoting Seward).
131. *Id.* at 61–62.
132. *Id.* at 69.
133. *Id.*

but friends. We must not be enemies. Though passion may have strained, it must not break our bonds of affection."[134]

Lincoln relied on Jefferson's words from the Declaration of Independence that "all men are created equal" as the foundation for our nation and as the fundamental principle for his presidential speeches. Even before he was president, Lincoln relied on Jefferson's words to support his argument for equality.[135] In April 1859, Lincoln, by letter, declined an invitation to speak at Jefferson's birthday commemoration in Boston. He ended his letter by referencing Jefferson's words:

> All honor to Jefferson—to the man who, in the concrete pressure of a struggle for national independence by a single people, had the coolness, forecast, and capacity to introduce into a merely revolutionary document, an abstract truth, applicable to all men and all times, and so to embalm it there, that to-day, and in all coming days, it shall be a rebuke and a stumbling-block to the very harbingers of re-appearing tyranny and oppression.[136]

Lincoln again turned to Jefferson's words when preparing his Gettysburg Address. As a lawyer, he was confident in relying on precedent, so he used Jefferson's words that "all men are created equal" as a binding precedent because representatives of all thirteen colonies signed the Declaration of Independence.[137] The Declaration of Independence was Jefferson's greatest accomplishment. "The high point of Jefferson's life became the lodestar of Lincoln's life."[138]

When Lincoln began the Gettysburg Address with "Four score and seven years ago our fathers...," he was referring to all the authors of the Declaration of Independence, but most especially to Jefferson.[139] And he quoted that same founding father, Jefferson, when he ended that sentence with the country's dedication to "the proposition that all men are created equal." Lincoln's Get-

---

134. White, *The Eloquent President, supra* note 128, at 91, 346 (2005).

135. Wills, *supra* note 121, at 84.

136. Letter from Abraham Lincoln to Henry L. Pierce and others (Apr. 6, 1859), *in Collected Works of Abraham Lincoln 1809–1865*, at 376 (Roy P. Basler ed., 1953). Ronald C. White noted that after 1854 Lincoln used the historical precedent of Jefferson and the Declaration of Independence "to ground his arguments for political equality for black Americans." Ronald C. White, *Lincoln's Greatest Speech: The Second Inaugural* 65 (2002).

137. Brookhiser, *supra* note 121, at 164.

138. *Id.*

139. Wills, *supra* note 121, at 84. Lincoln's opening subtly referred to the fathers and generations of the Bible. White, *The Eloquent President, supra* note 128, at 244.

tysburg Address was a turning point for the meaning of equality in America, even though he ended the sentence with an everlasting truth. "Jefferson's words had been timeless and universal, almost cosmic in scope. The challenge was to make them timely, and applicable to the struggle at hand."[140] Lincoln, with his ability to meld opposites, melded the past with the present, and gave Americans a way to understand, appreciate, and embrace human equality.[141]

Lincoln had looked to Jefferson as a writing role model, but in the end Lincoln's eloquence surpassed Jefferson's. As Fred Kaplan explained:

> What the nation could not have anticipated as Lincoln left Springfield ... was that his lifelong development as a writer had brought it a president with the capacity to express himself and the national concerns more effectively than any president ever had, with the exception of Thomas Jefferson, although nothing Jefferson wrote during his presidency, not even his dramatic first inaugural address, had a permanent place in the literary or political canon.[142]

The writing quality that Lincoln had, but Jefferson did not, was his "profoundly emotional apprehension of experience."[143] Lincoln's words captured the essence of the Civil War in a way that shaped how our nation could both view the war historically and move on from it. Douglas L. Wilson gives Lincoln the credit for shaping public opinion: "In fact, it is hard to imagine how we could engage the question of what that terrible war was about without Lincoln's words."[144]

Teddy Roosevelt

Teddy Roosevelt was not a contemporary of any of the other eloquent presidents, but he was influenced by Lincoln and, to a lesser degree, by Grant. Roosevelt, like many presidents, knew the power of Lincoln's words, so he used those words to his advantage. Ironically, Roosevelt was at the funeral processions of both Lincoln and Grant. As a six-year-old child, he peered out his

---

140. Wilson, *Lincoln's Sword*, *supra* note 130, at 232.

141. *See id.*

142. Kaplan, *supra* note 121, at 320. Kaplan later notes that Jefferson's pre-presidential Declaration of Independence does last in "the American national memory." *Id.* at 321.

143. Miller, *supra* note 120, at 146 (quoting Carl Lotus Becker, *The Declaration of Independence: A Story on the History of Political Ideas* (1922)).

144. Wilson, *Lincoln the Persuader*, *supra* note 127, at 36.

window in New York when Lincoln's coffin traveled through New York as part of its journey across the United States from Washington to Illinois.[145] As a 26-year-old adult, he marched in Grant's funeral procession as a captain in the National Guard.[146]

Roosevelt's admiration of Lincoln began very early in his life. At the age of three he heard his father Theodore Roosevelt Sr.'s accounts of his buggy rides with President and Mrs. Lincoln in Washington, D.C.[147] Although Theodore Sr. hired a substitute soldier to serve for him in the Civil War, he committed himself to drafting a bill to allow the soldiers to set aside voluntary pay deductions for their families; he spent months during 1861–1862 traveling though the Union camps to urge the soldiers to take advantage of the deduction.[148] The relationship Theodore Sr. formed with Lincoln's personal secretary John Hay proved invaluable to Roosevelt. Hay and Roosevelt shared an affection for each other that began when Theodore Sr. introduced thirty-one-year-old Hay to eleven-year-old Theodore Jr.[149] Hay was President McKinley's secretary of state, and stayed on as Roosevelt's secretary of state after McKinley was assassinated.[150]

No one can doubt the tremendous influence Lincoln had on Roosevelt. Roosevelt's office in the Executive Wing at the White House had an oil portrait of Lincoln over the mantel "where he could see it at all times."[151] He wore a lock of Lincoln's hair in a ring on his finger during his second inauguration.[152] Hay had given it to Roosevelt, and asked him to wear it when he was sworn in, saying, "You are one of the men who most thoroughly understand and appreciate Lincoln."[153]

Hay was right. Roosevelt did appreciate Lincoln. Roosevelt even considered writing a Lincoln biography late in his life, but the project fell through when

---

145. Michael Beschloss, *When TR Saw Lincoln*, N.Y. Times (May 21, 2014), http://www.nytimes.com/2014/05/22/upshot/when-tr-saw-lincoln.html?_r=0. Roosevelt's wife Edith Carow Roosevelt identified Roosevelt and his brother Elliott at the open window. She said that she was also there that day (Roosevelt and Edith had been childhood friends), but she started crying when she saw all the black drapings, so "[t]hey took me and locked me in a back room." *Id.*

146. Edmund Morris, *The Rise of Theodore Roosevelt* 298–99 (1979).

147. *Id.* at 12.

148. *Id.* at 9–10.

149. Edmund Morris, *Theodore Rex* 240 (2001).

150. *Id.* at 4, 109.

151. *Id.* at 184.

152. *Id.* at 376.

153. *Id.*

potential publishers wanted delivery in six months.[154] Roosevelt is also responsible for putting Lincoln on the penny.[155]

It was the influence of Lincoln's words that helped Roosevelt when he, too, was seeking to persuade. As a student at Harvard, Roosevelt quoted Lincoln's speeches; this contributed to his charm and helped him gain acceptance among the elite students.[156] Roosevelt talked about Lincoln beyond the academic setting of Harvard. During his 1883 hunting trip to the Badlands of North Dakota, he discussed Lincoln, along with multiple other topics including literature, politics, hunting, and conservation, with his host Gregor Lang.[157] Lincoln Lang, Gregor's 16-year-old son, listened to the conversations after supper for as long as he could, and was "awed by the verbosity of 'our forceful guest.'"[158]

Roosevelt called Lincoln "my great hero" several times during his life.[159] Roosevelt wrote in one letter, "I do not have to tell you that my great hero is Abraham Lincoln, and I have wanted while President to be the representative of the 'plain people' in the sense that he was—not, of course, with the genius and power that he was, but according to my lights along the same lines."[160] Roosevelt admired Lincoln's writing. Roosevelt believed Lincoln was a stronger writer than Demosthenes and Cicero.[161] He was dismayed that Lincoln's writing, at least during Roosevelt's lifetime, did not seem to get the credit it deserved.

Roosevelt mentioned both Lincoln and Grant in the 1900 Galena Address he gave in honor of Grant.[162] Roosevelt noted that as "we look back with keener wisdom into the nation's past, mightiest among the mighty dead loom the three great figures of Washington, Lincoln, and Grant."[163] He affirmed,

---

154. Edmund Morris, *Colonel Roosevelt* 141 (2010).

155. Courtney Waite, *The Origination of the Lincoln Penny*, Living Lincoln (April 16, 2015), http://livinglincoln.web.unc.edu/2015/04/16/the-origination-of-the-lincoln-penny/.

156. Morris, *The Rise of Theodore Roosevelt*, *supra* note 146, at 60.

157. *Id.* at 204.

158. *Id.*

159. Richard Striner, *Lincoln's Way: How Six Great Presidents Created American Power* 48 (2010).

160. Letter from Theodore Roosevelt, Pres. of the U.S., to William Sewall (June 13, 1906), http://www.shapell.org/manuscript/president-theodore-roosevelt-on-abraham-lincoln.

161. Adriana Maynard, *A Man of Strong Opinions*, Theodore Roosevelt Center blog (July 8, 2011), www.theodorerooseveltcenter.org/Blog/2011/July/08-A-Man-of-Strong-Opinions.aspx.

162. Theodore Roosevelt, *Grant Speech Delivered at Galena, Illinois* (April 27, 1900), *in* Theodore Roosevelt, *The Strenuous Life: Essays and Addresses* 205–25 (1902).

163. *Id.* at 206.

"[T]hese three greatest men have taken their place among the great men of all nations, the great men of all time."[164] Roosevelt recognized the intertwining importance of Lincoln and Grant:

> In the second and even greater struggle the deeds of Lincoln the states-
> man were made good by those of Grant the soldier, and later Grant
> himself took up the work that dropped from Lincoln's tired hands
> when the assassin's bullet went home, and the sad, patient, kindly eyes
> were closed forever.[165]

Roosevelt pointed out that Lincoln and Grant were both critical in the Civil War when he said that many men "were saving the Union," yet "the brightest among their names flame those of Lincoln and Grant, the steadfast, the unswerving, the enduring, the finally triumphant."[166] Roosevelt admired Grant's plain and direct approach, which was partly based on his plain and direct communication style:

> [Grant] was not in the least of the type which gets up mass-meetings,
> makes inflammatory speeches or passes inflammatory resolutions, and
> then permits over-forcible talk to be followed by over-feeble action.
> His promise squared with his performance. His deeds made good his
> words. He did not denounce an evil in strained and hyperbolic lan-
> guage; but when he did denounce it, he strove to make his denunci-
> ation effective by his action.[167]

Roosevelt emulated the direct, strong, and common-sense writings of Lincoln and Grant.

Roosevelt was not a fan of Jefferson. He acknowledged publicly that Jefferson, along with Benjamin Franklin, Alexander Hamilton, and Andrew Jackson, was a great man "in the second rank."[168] But in his private correspondence, such as in this October 15, 1915, letter to his son Kermit, Roosevelt revealed his true feelings about Jefferson:

> It is just as it was a century ago when Jefferson, another shifty phrase-
> maker who was "too proud to fight," was President. Jefferson dragged
> our honor in the dust, and was responsible for the ignoble conduct

---

164. *Id.* at 207–08.
165. *Id.* at 208.
166. *Id.* at 216.
167. *Id.* at 217–18.
168. *Id.* at 207.

of the war that followed; but he pandered to the worst side of the people, and they supported him with enthusiasm.[169]

Roosevelt was referring to the War of 1812, which he blamed on Jefferson's failure to build an adequate army and navy. Roosevelt had "contempt for Thomas Jefferson," partly because he thought Jefferson's democracy subverted the common man.[170] Roosevelt noted that the New York aldermen were almost all controlled by local ward or municipal bosses, so "the machine ... ultimately governed the city; and Roosevelt did not consider that democratic."[171] Roosevelt also thought Jefferson was scholarly and timid.[172]

Ironically, some have made comparisons between Jefferson's and Roosevelt's writing styles. One scholar noted, "[Jefferson's] style is easy and flowing, and frequently it concentrates in a 'curious felicity' of phrase that has made many of his sayings familiar in the mouths of men. In other words, he had a certain facility for phrasing commonplaces memorably and well that recalls the similar facility of Mr. [Theodore] Roosevelt."[173] In short, Roosevelt may not have admired Jefferson, but he shared Jefferson's ability to capture complex national values with memorable, short phrases.

The friendships between Jefferson and Madison and Lincoln and Grant benefitted them in many ways, not the least of which was a subtle improvement of their writing styles based on their letter writing and reading. Later presidents, such as Lincoln and Roosevelt, consciously studied the writings of earlier eloquent presidents. We, too, can be inspired by the words the presidents wrote to each other as friends and by the words in their other writings that inspired other eloquent presidents.

---

169. Letter from Theodore Roosevelt to Kermit Roosevelt (Oct. 15, 1915), http://www.theodorerooseveltcenter.org/Research/Digital-Library/Record.aspx?libID=o281206.

170. Morris, *The Rise of Theodore Roosevelt, supra* note 146, at 220.

171. *Id.*

172. *Id.* at 330.

173. Max J. Herzberg, *Thomas Jefferson as a Man of Letters*, 13 S. Atl. Q., Oct. 1914, at 310, 324.

Chapter 9

Final Thoughts: Character Traits and Writing Habits

Regrettably, there isn't a simple, easy formula that we can follow to guarantee that our writing will be more persuasive. Writing is too complicated. Writing to persuade is even more complicated.

Lawyers, like all writers, face the complications that accompany any writing. A single word can mean more than one thing. On the other hand, several single words can mean basically the same thing, but any one of those words might still fail to convey the idea in the writer's mind to the reader's mind. A combination of words can also mean more than one thing, and a reader might interpret the combination of words in a way the writer never intended. A written work stands on its own, so a writer cannot react to a reader's confusion or clarify the intended meaning if the writer is misunderstood.

In the particular business of writing to persuade, legal writers have several added obstacles. We write under both time and cost pressures. We write knowing that there is more than one way to solve a legal problem. Opposing counsel will try to persuade the judge to reach a different solution from the one we have proposed. The judge and law clerks may also suggest potential solutions. We write knowing that every new writing project will be unique. An organizational structure that provided clarity in our last brief may be useless for our new client. A policy argument that tilted the scale in our favor for one issue might be inapplicable in a new case. We realize that our writing is not separate from our thinking, but instead our writing helps solidify and clarify our thinking. Sometimes our thinking is muddled or our understanding is not complete, so it is no surprise that our writing is not clear. There are moments in every lawyer's life when writing seems overwhelming. We somehow make it through and gain a little more confidence. Committed persuasive writers must embrace this complexity, messiness, and uncertainty.

Our willingness to adopt an accepting, and perhaps even a positive, attitude about the writing process will take us a long way in our journey to becoming more persuasive. It won't be easy. We'll make mistakes. Sometimes we'll need to completely reorganize. Sometimes we'll have to cut sentences that took us hours to write. Sometimes we'll realize that we need to add another argument to strengthen our position. Sometimes a more experienced lawyer will read our motion brief and recommend a total overhaul by saying, "You need to start over completely. I'm on the same side as you, but even I'm not convinced by this brief."[1]

Actually writing—including making false starts, editing, failing, writing and editing again—is the single best way for us to improve. But we can help speed our development as persuasive writers in other ways, too. We can read books about persuasion, style, and the process of writing.[2] We can review the written work of successful lawyers. We can read judicial opinions written by judges known for their brilliant writing. We can talk about writing and the process of writing with other professional writers. We can develop relationships with colleagues who are willing to review and edit our work.

Our writing can also improve if we are willing to learn from great persuaders like Jefferson, Madison, Lincoln, Grant, and Roosevelt. These presidents all started with a natural ability to convince others about the rightness of their thoughts, views, interpretations, and visions. Then they found ways to hone those natural persuasive skills.

In considering all five presidents as a group, two things are particularly striking. First, the presidents shared several essential character traits which helped them develop into persuasive writers. Second, the presidents shared many common writing habits. A good place for us to start in our efforts to improve our persuasiveness is to emulate their character traits and writing habits.

---

1. As you might imagine, all of those scenarios have happened to me.
2. Two excellent books for lawyers to begin with are Joseph M. Williams, *Style: Toward Clarity and Grace* (Joseph Bizup, rev'd, 11th ed. 2014) and William Zinsser, *On Writing Well* (30th anniv. ed. 2006).

Character Traits

Writing is a personal act, so writing often reveals something about the author's character. This is especially true when the author is able to speak for himself like the presidents did in their speeches, letters, and books. Yet even when we lawyers are acting as agents or representatives of others, our writing will reveal something about us. The arguments we raise will show our focus and our belief about what is important. The counterarguments we anticipate will show our fearlessness. The language we choose will show our commitment and passion or, on the other hand, our uncertainty. The attention to details will show that we are devoted to making things easy for our readers.

It isn't hard to recognize that our written work product reveals something about our character, but it is less intuitive to see that the writing *process* also reveals character. This writing process is often unconscious; our eloquent presidents may not have made conscious decisions about their actual writing process. All of the presidents would likely react with surprise if anyone had asked them, "What is your process of writing?" They may not have thought consciously about their writing process or their writing habits, but all were doing most everything right to produce writing that was likely to persuade.

The presidents were successful persuaders, at least in part, because of their character. A recent study of the qualities lawyers need to be successful emphasized that, in addition to intelligence and interpersonal skills, lawyers need some level of "character quotient."[3] The study compiled 24,000 responses from lawyers in all 50 states, emphasizing, "[Lawyers beginning their careers] need to have a blend of legal skills and professional competencies, and, notably, they require character. In fact, 76% of characteristics (things like integrity, work ethic, common sense, and resilience) were identified by half or more of respondents as necessary right out of law school...."[4]

The writing process worked for Jefferson, Madison, Lincoln, Grant, and Roosevelt because all were hardworking, gritty, confident, realistic, and creative. These five character traits are the distinguishing qualities of the presidents' personalities that contributed to their persuasiveness. The presidents had these character traits because they practiced the virtues of diligence, per-

---

3. Alli Gerkman and Logan Cornett, *Foundations for Practice: The Whole Lawyer and the Character Quotient* (July 2016), http://iaals.du.edu/sites/default/files/reports/foundations_for_practice_whole_lawyer_character_quotient.pdf.

4. *Id.* at 5.

severance, tenacity, acceptance, courage, and resilience. William Lee Miller noted in *Lincoln's Virtues*:

> An ethical biography presupposes the freedom of the subject, within some limits, to choose different courses of action. It assumes that he can, by a sequence of choices, shape abiding patterns of conduct— virtues. It presupposes that out of his margin of freedom, with whatever the given conditions of his life may be, he can over time mold a structure of conduct, a certain character.[5]

We lawyers can make the conscious choice to further develop these five character traits as a way to improve our writing process. These five character traits helped our eloquent presidents succeed—and succeed in a spectacular way— in persuading through their writing.

1. Hardworking

As sports journalist Red Smith quipped, "Writing is easy. You just sit at a typewriter until blood appears on your forehead."[6] Because writing is difficult, the first essential character trait for success in persuasion is hard work. Bryan Garner advises law students and lawyers, "Start with the premise that writing well isn't easy.... [I]t takes hard work."[7] There can be no disagreement about it, except that anyone who has been a legal writer would add "very" before "hard work."

Our eloquent presidents were hardworking. Roosevelt proposed that two separate kinds of human ability resulted in success: genius or hard work.[8] He declared, "I need hardly say that all the successes I have ever won have been of the second type. I never won anything without hard labor and the exercise of my best judgment and careful planning and working long in advance."[9] Roosevelt provides a useful model for the components of hard work that are necessary to produce good writing—labor, careful planning, and working in advance.

Instead of being afraid of the labor of writing, the eloquent presidents embraced it. Madison was a notoriously hard worker; he could outwork anyone when he was researching, thinking about, and writing about a political prob-

---

5. William Lee Miller, *Lincoln's Virtues* xv (2003).
6. Ralph Keyes, *The Quote Verifier: Who Said What, Where, and When* 257 (2006).
7. Bryan A. Garner, *Legal Writing in Plain English* 1 (2d. ed. 2013).
8. Theodore Roosevelt, *An Autobiography* 51 (1920).
9. *Id.* at 52.

lem. Lincoln wrote—and rewrote—his speeches. It wasn't easy for him because he worked slowly and deliberately. William Herndon, Lincoln's law partner, recalled that Lincoln wrote with his long legs stretched on a chair with any needed books on his lap or on a table.[10] He wrote to clarify and organize his thoughts. Lincoln was "not in the least put off by what most people consider the onerous labor of writing."[11] Instead, he embraced the intellectual challenge of writing and "writing was often a form of refuge for Lincoln."[12]

Careful planning is another part of the hard work needed to write persuasively. Some suggest that writing may have been easy for Grant.[13] But that may have been because, even though Grant claimed that he did not always know what he was going to write before he wrote, he had anticipated how he would handle many situations. Writers know that writing takes a long time. Even with a perfect plan to attack a writing project, the writing process often takes much longer than anticipated. At least lawyers have the advantage of knowing exactly how long writing can take because court rules usually set the outside parameters for persuasive writing projects—the filing deadlines. Lawyers often see the deadlines as a negative, but those deadlines give shape and certainty to every project. Even procrastinators cannot ignore the court deadlines. The careful planning for a persuasive legal writing project starts at the filing deadline with the lawyer working backward to set interim deadlines for the completion of initial research, brainstorming, developing an outline or plan for the writing project, drafting, researching again as additional issues arise, revising, and finally editing and proofreading. A new lawyer may be surprised by the number of steps involved in this writing process, but meeting these interim deadlines will aid in timely work. A more experienced lawyer will develop a sense for her own individual writing process and thus be able to accurately predict how much time each of the steps will take. Significantly, all lawyers should spend a bit of time at the end of a writing project reflecting on their process. A review of whether the process worked, whether the lawyer predicted the correct steps in the process, how much time each step took, and what the lawyer might do differently next time will help advance the lawyer's goal of writing more persuasively.

Lawyers may lament the compressed deadlines, but our eloquent presidents were under even greater time pressures. For example, *The Federalist* was writ-

---

10. Ronald G. White, Jr., *The Eloquent President: A Portrait of Lincoln Through His Words* 109 (2005) [hereinafter White, *The Eloquent President*].
11. Douglas L. Wilson, *Lincoln's Sword* 5 (2007) [hereinafter Wilson, *Lincoln's Sword*].
12. *Id.*
13. William S. McFeely, *Grant* 504 (1981).

ten quickly. Madison recalled, "In the beginning it was the practice of the writ-ers, of A.H. & J.M. particularly to communicate each to the other, their re-spective papers before they were sent to the press. This was rendered so inconvenient, by the shortness of the time allowed, that it was dispensed with."[14] All the presidents were under similar short deadlines. While Lincoln was president, "almost everything he wrote, except for a stray poem or two, was produced under the pressure of an immediate political situation."[15]

Roosevelt's practice of working in advance as part of his hard work should also be emulated. All the eloquent presidents thought about and started writ-ing projects early. Madison was famous for his hard work and academic ap-proach to political issues. He thought about problems in advance, took copious notes, and meticulously worked through all possible arguments to the prob-lem. Lincoln started writing his great speeches long before he was scheduled to speak. Grant often had to react in the moment while preparing his military dispatches, but he had set his battle policies well in advance, so he wasn't forced to hurriedly draft his orders. Even at Appomattox, Grant said, "I only knew what was in my mind"[16] and, as a result, he was able to draft the terms of sur-render on the spot.

It may be that working hard came naturally to the presidents. Jefferson was dismayed when he learned that one of the young men he was counseling had not diligently started his studies. He wrote:

> I am much mortified to hear that you have lost so much time and that when you arrived in Williamsburg you were not at all advanced from what you were when you left Monticello. Time now begins to be pre-cious to you.... However the way to repair the loss is to improve the future time.[17]

Every lawyer has likely experienced some self-directed mortification for not working hard enough on a writing project. Jefferson's advice that we can "im-prove the future time" is inspiring as we build the hard-working component of our character.

---

14. James Madison, *Detached Memorandum*, in *James Madison, Writings* 769 (Jack N. Rakove ed., 1999).

15. Miller, *supra* note 5, at 273.

16. Ulysses S. Grant, *Personal Memoirs of Ulysses S. Grant* 631 (1992) [hereinafter *Per-sonal Memoirs*].

17. Letter from Thomas Jefferson to Peter Carr (August 19, 1785), *in Thomas Jefferson Writings*, 814 (Merrill D. Peterson ed., 1984).

We must work hard because writing is hard work. "Remember this in moments of despair. If you find that writing is hard, it's because it *is* hard."[18] A hardworking lawyer will know the case better than anyone else; for a lawyer, there is no substitute for preparation. That preparation means that a lawyer must spend time getting to know both the facts and the law. Like Roosevelt, we know the value of labor, careful planning, and working in advance.

2. Gritty

"Determination" might be a more refined word than "gritty" to describe this important character trait. But Roosevelt's "man in the arena" one-liner compels the choice of "gritty." We can visualize that struggling person, with grit and grime on his face, gritting his teeth as he strives to accomplish his worthy cause.

Besides, "grit" is a character trait making a comeback. Psychologists now posit that grit, instead of intelligence, is the best predictor of success in school and the workplace.[19] The word "grit" includes many different traits such as perseverance, focus, and passion. The presidents had this trait in abundance, and it served them well in all aspects of their lives, including in their lives as writers.

Grant is an ideal example of perseverance. He admitted that whenever he started to do something, he "would not turn back, or stop until the thing intended was accomplished."[20] Grant continued, "I have frequently started to go to places where I had never been and to which I did not know the way, depending upon making inquiries on the road, and if I got past the place without knowing it, instead of turning back, I would go on until a road was found turning in the right direction, take that, and come in by the other side."[21] James Longstreet, who knew Grant at West Point and served with him in Mexico, was one Confederate soldier who did not underestimate Grant, "I tell you that we cannot afford to underrate him and the army he now commands. We must make up our minds to get into line of battle and stay there; for that man will fight us every day and every hour till the end of this war."[22] Roosevelt described

---

18. Zinsser, *supra* note 2, at 9.

19. Angela Lee Duckworth, *Grit: The Power of Passion and Perseverance*, TED, https://www.ted.com/talks/angela_lee_duckworth_grit_the_power_of_passion_and_perseverance?language=en (last visited Sept. 2, 2016).

20. *Personal Memoirs*, *supra* note 16, at 35.

21. *Id.*

22. General Horace Porter, *Campaigning with Grant* 47 (1897).

this quality of Grant's as "doggedness."[23] Roosevelt was convinced that this doggedness was the secret to Grant's success. Roosevelt followed Grant's model and persevered when writing. Edmund Morris commented, "Like many voluble men, [Roosevelt] was a slow writer, painfully hammering out sentences which achieved force and clarity at the expense of polite style."[24] Grant's perseverance can be inspiring to lawyers because persuasive legal writing projects can sometimes feel like battles—and these are battles that can only be won if we, too, don't look back, but instead push ahead to complete our writing.

Focus is another part of grit. We have vivid and memorable images of our eloquent presidents focusing while they were writing. Madison was meticulous and thorough while taking notes at important events, including at the Constitutional Convention.[25] Lincoln could be interrupted while writing the middle of a sentence "and take up his pen and begin where he left off without reading the previous part of the sentence."[26] Grant was able to focus on writing his military orders even "when a shell burst immediately over him."[27] Grant's focus while writing his lengthy *Personal Memoirs* allowed him to write the book in less than one year.[28] Roosevelt had such an eclectic love of the world that he knew he had to remove anything from nature that might distract him while he was writing. He resorted to turning his desk towards a wall, so that he couldn't easily look out the window.[29]

Grit also requires passion. Roosevelt was a model of passion; it often seems that passion, not blood, must have run through his veins. He was able to persuade his audience because he completely and without a single doubt believed in the message that he was delivering.

Writing with grit means that we can't wait for inspiration to strike; we must instead just step into that arena and start writing. That grit may take the form of literally gritting our teeth as we work though a writing project that isn't going particularly well. We may have to persevere while we are writing a brief even after we learn about new weaknesses in our case. Obviously, we will need to focus. We may think that we, like Lincoln and Grant, can work effectively even with distractions. That may be true, but honesty is imperative here. I

---

23. Theodore Roosevelt, *Grant Speech Delivered at Galena, Illinois* (April 27, 1900) *in* Theodore Roosevelt, *The Strenuous Life: Essays and Address* 205, 216 (1902).

24. Morris, *The Rise of Theodore Roosevelt* 64 (1979).

25. Garrett Ward Sheldon, *The Political Philosophy of James Madison* 53–54 (2001).

26. Wilson, *Lincoln's Sword, supra* note 11, at 7 (quoting Lincoln's friend Joshua Speed).

27. Edmund Wilson, *Patriotic Gore: Studies in the Literature of the American Civil War* 134 (1962) (quoting Adam Badeau).

28. Jean Edward Smith, *Grant* 627 (2001).

29. Morris, *supra* note 24, at 378–79.

know far more people who think they work effectively with distractions than the handful of lawyers I have seen actually pulling it off. Face it—our world is filled with constant distractions and our profession is inherently filled with interruptions. We face not only the distractions of a beautiful view out the window, but the interruptions of phone calls, email, text messages, and the mental diversion of competing clients, cases, and responsibilities—all vying for our time and attention and throwing us off from our writing. We should give serious consideration to following Roosevelt's lead and finding a way to both literally and figuratively face our desks to the wall. We can start with a private physical space, but we will also have to turn off all ringing, buzzing, beeping, popping, and anything else that may tempt us to divert our focus from our writing. Passion for our client's cause, or at a minimum passion that we are representing our client to the best of our abilities, will be the final ingredient that helps us develop grit.

3. Confident

Not surprisingly, all of the presidents were confident because self-confidence is a required character trait for any president. That confidence was sometimes quiet, as when Madison combatted his natural shyness with certainty that he had prepared for every possible argument, or when Grant made his quiet appearances but believed always in his tactical plans. Jefferson and Lincoln, too, were confident that they knew what was best for America and could steer the country on its correct course. Roosevelt exuded confidence, believing that he was the best man for almost any job.

Confidence in one's own writing can be precarious, even for a confident president. If pressed, all the presidents would likely admit to some confidence in their writing ability. Still, they would also admit to at least some doubts. Lincoln did not consider himself a brilliant writer, even though he thought some of his speeches would "wear" well.[30] Grant thought that people who suggested he write his memoirs might be making fun of him. Intuitively, Grant knew that confidence in the message and a forthrightness in delivering it was critical, even if the writing was plain. Grant explained in detail how he saw the differences between the writing styles of General Scott and General Taylor:

> In their modes of expressing thought, these two generals contrasted quite as strongly as in their other characteristics. General Scott was

---

30. Ronald C. White, Jr., *Lincoln's Greatest Speech* 197 (2002) (Lincoln was referring to his Second Inaugural).

precise in language, cultivated a style peculiarly his own; was proud of his rhetoric; not averse to speaking of himself, often in the third person, and he could bestow praise upon the person he was talking about without the least embarrassment. Taylor was not a conversationalist, but on paper he could put his meaning so plainly that there could be no mistaking it. He knew how to express what he wanted to say in the fewest well-chosen words, but would not sacrifice meaning to the construction of high-sounding sentences.[31]

Unfortunately, when Grant was president he lost confidence in his writing because he was convinced that his writing should be more formal. As a result, his writing lost its typical clarity and strength. Even the supremely self-assured Roosevelt wondered, as a young man, if he would ever be a successful author.

This strange mix of some confidence flavored with some doubt is not uncommon among professional writers. One bestselling author described her writing process this way:

[P]anic would set in. I'd write a couple of dreadful sentences, xx them out, try again, xx everything out, and then feel despair and worry settle on my chest like an x-ray apron. It's over, I'd think, calmly. I'm not going to be able to get the magic to work this time. I'm ruined. I'm through. I'm toast.[32]

After giving more details about the tortuous process of writing, the author concludes, "Almost all writing begins with terrible first efforts."[33] Every lawyer can relate to those sentiments.

The presidents were also humble about their writing. Notably, all recognized that writing was about the readers, not about themselves as the writers. They tried to write with the reader in mind—making every effort to both make their message understandable and make things easy on the reader. Madison's modesty helped others see past him to his well-developed ideas. Lincoln used "plain speech—the direct sentence, the building of rhythm and emphasis through selective syntactical repetition, with climax as the moment of maximum sense rather than of the highest oratory"[34] to convince his readers. Grant also used a simple and direct style. Roosevelt knew that interesting writing would more likely appeal to the reader.

---

31. *Personal Memoirs*, *supra* note 16, at 85.
32. Anne Lamott, *Bird by Bird* 23, 25 (1994).
33. *Id.*
34. Fred Kaplan, *Lincoln: The Biography of a Writer* 103 (2008).

Seeking advice about writing also shows a humility. Jefferson and Lincoln consulted with trusted colleagues, asking for editing suggestions. They perhaps suspected that their written work could be improved, and they also wanted advice about how readers would interpret their messages. They wanted to be prepared, but they also did not want to offend readers. Madison often was his own editor. He considered the weaknesses of his position and anticipated the areas where his position might be subject to attack.

The presidents strike an admirable balance between confidence and humility. Each new persuasive legal writing project will likely give us the chance to experience moments of both confidence and humility. Lawyers should start with confidence in the positions they are taking on behalf of their clients. A lawyer confident about the underlying legal arguments will be able to write with more confidence. Asking a trusted colleague to review and critique our writing will help us see our written work through the eyes of a reader. Any editing suggestions—even those we ultimately do not adopt—give us the chance to take a deeper look at our writing. As for personal confidence in our writing ability, we can remember that even the best writers, including our eloquent presidents, suffer some moments of doubt. They model for us that the opposite of confidence is not doubt, but paralyzing fear. Even in their moments of doubt, they pressed forward. If we remain committed to a lifelong devotion to improving our writing and pressing forward, our confidence will also improve.

4. Realistic

The eloquent presidents were realistic. They were able to see life as it actually was, not as they wished it was. Their realism was rooted in their common sense and then bolstered by their resiliency in being able to adapt to reality. Part of what made Madison effective was that he never believed in an idealized notion of man's virtue, but instead he accepted the reality that people are flawed. Thus, his infamous statement, "If men were angels, no government would be necessary...."[35] Like Madison, Lincoln was realistic and knew that people could be self-interested.[36] Yet he understood "there are *two* principles at least, not just one—selfishness, but also love of justice."[37] It was Lincoln's

---

35. *Federalist*, No. 51 (James Madison) (reprinted *in* James Madison, *Writings* (Jack Rakove ed. 1999)).

36. Miller, *supra* note 5, at 263.

37. *Id.* (emphasis in original).

talent in appealing to a sense of justice that helped him persuade the American people that justice dictated equality for all men.

Grant's realism is perhaps the best example for lawyers because it was Grant's ability to accept the way things were that distinguished him from other Union military leaders and ultimately persuaded Lincoln to put Grant in command. Lincoln, in a conversation with his secretary William Stoddard, exclaimed with relief, "Grant is the first general I've had. He's a general."[38] Lincoln noted that Grant didn't "put the responsibility of success or failure on me.... I'm glad to find a man who can go ahead without me."[39] But it was Grant's critical quality of being able to accept reality that convinced Lincoln he had finally found his military leader:

> [All the previous commanders would] pick out some one thing they were short of and that they knew I couldn't give them and then tell me that they couldn't win unless they had it; and it was generally cavalry. When Grant took hold I was waiting to see what his pet impossibility would be, and I reckoned it would be cavalry, for we hadn't horses enough to mount even what men we had. There were fifteen thousand or thereabouts up near Harper's Ferry, and no horses to put them on. Well, the other day, just as I expected, Grant sent to me about those very men. But what he wanted to know was whether he should disband them or turn them into infantry.[40]

Grant may have been frustrated, but he was not daunted. He may have silently wished for a different reality, but instead he found a way to make the most of what was available to him.

Lawyers can easily relate to the difficulties of reality. As all lawyers know, there is no perfect case. Time spent wishing for a different fact or a different precedent will be time wasted. Instead, lawyers making an honest assessment of reality and then adapting to the way things are have a chance to persuade. Chief Justice John Roberts commented that lawyers in oral argument would benefit from a realist approach to difficult precedent cases. He noted the judges appreciate a lawyer helping them reach a correct decision by candidly acknowledging that the precedent case provides some difficulty instead of claiming the precedent does not hurt them at all.[41] A realistic approach to our clients

---

38. Smith, *supra* note 28, at 307.

39. *Id.*

40. *Id.*

41. *Chief Justice John Roberts on Oral Argument*, YouTube, (Oct. 6, 2009), https://www.youtube.com/watch?v=UJQ7Ds4nAmA.

and cases, coupled with common sense and resiliency, will bolster the persuasiveness of our legal writing.

5. Creative

The presidents, like lawyers, were writing about real events, but that doesn't mean they lacked creativity. They were creative in the way they saw the issues they faced and creative in the way they wrote about and explained those issues. This creativity allowed them to think of things in a new way, but also motivated them to lead based on their vision for America.

Jefferson chose the metaphor of "the wall of separation" to succinctly and artfully explain his views about the appropriate intersection between church and state. Madison made one small, but essential, change to The Virginia Declaration of Rights by removing the word "toleration" from the original draft.[42] His suggested replacement language ensuring the "free exercise of religion according to the dictates of conscience" guaranteed that belief or the lack of belief was a substantive right.[43] Jefferson and Madison knew that the full separation of church and state was essential for America's future.

Madison showed yet another flash of creativity when he studied the "literary cargo" of books Jefferson sent him about ancient and modern democracies. Lynne Cheney asserts that "[b]y the time of the Philadelphia convention, Madison was the political equivalent" of Mozart and Einstein.[44] Cheney concludes, "[Madison] was more knowledgeable and better practiced in the theories and realities of representative government than anyone in the country or even the world. And he was about to do what geniuses do: change forever the way people think."[45]

Lincoln, too, had a distinct vision for American. His Gettysburg Address created a new Constitution, based on its spirit of equality.[46] Significantly, Lincoln relied on the Declaration of Independence, instead of the Constitution, as the founding document of the nation.[47] He was thus able to use Jefferson's words in the Declaration of Independence to "reinforce the timeless American truth that ... *all men are created equal.*"[48] He was creative in looking backward, but

---

42. Ralph Ketcham, *James Madison* 73 (1990).
43. Garry Wills, *James Madison* 17–18 (2002).
44. Lynne Cheney, *James Madison: A Life Reconsidered* 7 (2014).
45. *Id.*
46. Garry Wills, *Lincoln at Gettysburg: The Words That Remade America* 38 (1992).
47. *Id.* at 130.
48. White, *The Eloquent President, supra* note 10, at 242.

also forward, as when he cast equality in a new way as forming the essential foundation of the United States. Lincoln further explained to Americans how the country could recover from the Civil War only through reconciliation and magnanimity.

Grant could see that the Civil War would only end if the Union was committed to striking hard at the Confederacy. But when that goal was finally accomplished, Grant showed incredible flexibility and creativity when he drafted the terms of surrender at Appomattox. He knew and supported Lincoln's view about reconciliation and magnanimity, so he found a way to include those themes in the terms of surrender. Famously, Grant paused before mounting his horse and saluted Robert E. Lee as he left Appomattox Courthouse. He also halted the firing of any celebration by the Union soldiers, including victory salutes, saying "The war is over. The rebels are our countrymen again."[49]

Roosevelt was ingenious in his ability to write short slogans that vividly described his thoughts and ideals. He looked ahead and emphasized that Americans should value personal character, particularly when that translated into a willingness to struggle toward a goal. Also, Roosevelt's appreciation for wildlife and nature inspired him to develop a "highly original theory about land management and wildlife protection."[50] Roosevelt's creativity was at work in his "crusade to save the American wilderness."[51]

Creativity is also critical in persuasive legal writing. This comes as a surprise to new legal writers who often feel constrained by what they see as overly rigid rules about organization, reliance on precedent, and formatting. These writers mistakenly assume that there is no room for creativity when they are writing about legal issues. One analogy is instructive. A sonnet has an extremely rigid formula of 14 lines, usually written in iambic pentameter.[52] But no one would question that every single sonnet requires creativity and imagination. Even within the confines of court requirements and long-accepted legal writing guidelines, there is much room for creativity in legal writing.

It is hard to write good persuasive legal writing without creativity, but it is almost impossible to write great persuasive legal writing without creativity. The law is organic. It is grounded in precedent, but lawyers and judges are constantly faced with new situations, requiring them to consider how to apply

---

49. Smith, *supra* note 28, at 406.

50. Douglas Brinkley, *The Wilderness Warrior: Theodore Roosevelt and the Crusade for America* 6 (2009).

51. *Id.* at 21.

52. *Webster's American Dictionary* 749 (2d College ed. 2000).

that precedent to new facts, new technology, new societal mores. The lawyers who are creative enough to see, and then write about, the nuances of the legal issue will more often persuade their readers.

Even a small dose of creativity helps. United States Supreme Court Chief Justice John Roberts was noted for his creativity when he was writing persuasive briefs. As just one example, he wrote in his brief for Alaska against the EPA, "Although Baker [a bush pilot] died before the significance of his observations [zinc and lead deposits] became known, his faithful traveling companion—an Irish Setter who often flew shotgun—was immortalized by a geologist who dubbed the creek Baker had spotted "Red Dog" creek."[53] This creative inclusion of the back story of how the mine was named helped him humanize the large mine and supported his theme that environmental compliance decisions should be made at the local level.[54] Justice Roberts frankly explained that he also included the Red Dog Mine detail because it was interesting and "gives a little texture to the brief," and would help readers feel invested in the case and "want to see how the story ends up."[55]

One final note about the eloquent presidents and their creativity. They focused on the clarity, strength, and persuasiveness of their writing, sometimes at the expense of things like spelling, capitalization, and punctuation. As readers of this book probably have noticed, many of the presidents misspelled words. For example, Jefferson spelled the word "knowledge" several different ways, but usually as "knoledge." He also began sentences without capitals and used periods and commas erratically.[56] Lincoln was also a careless speller; he often doubled consonants incorrectly.[57] Additionally, "throughout his life [Lincoln] made that error particularly calculated to set English teachers' teeth on edge, writing 'it's' for the possessive 'its.'"[58] The presidents can serve as an example even in their mistakes. A mistake in spelling pales in comparison to a mistake in clarity or brevity. Legal writers should follow usage rules, but also keep in mind that the primary goal is to communicate effectively, clearly, "even elegantly."[59]

---

53. Ross Guberman, *Point Made: How to Write like the Nation's Top Advocates* 59 (2d ed. 2014).

54. *See id.* at 52.

55. *Chief Justice John Roberts Jr. [Interview by Bryan A. Garner]*, 2010 Scribes J. Legal Writing 6, 18.

56. Roy J. Honeywell, *The Educational Work of Thomas Jefferson* xvi (1931).

57. Miller, *supra* note 5, at 5.

58. *Id.*

59. Williams, *supra* note 2, at 197.

Writing Habits to Adopt and Questions to Ask When Reviewing Our Own Writing

In addition to the five character traits, the presidents also shared several writing habits. Legal writers who want to persuade should use these same writing habits. Each writing habit is followed by questions to help writers see if they are following the writing habit. Also, some of the stories about how the presidents put the writing habit into practice are included as inspiration.

1. Start Writing Early

Questions:
- Have I started writing early?
- Have I been realistic about the amount of time needed to complete this writing project?
- Have I separated the complete writing process into interim steps—researching, outlining, organizing, drafting, researching again if needed, revising, and proofreading?
- Have I set deadlines for completion of each interim step?
- Have I been careful to avoid procrastination in writing by spending too much time on another step in the process (such as researching)?
- Have I used my writing to help clarify my thinking?
- Have I left enough time to edit?

Inspiration:
- Lincoln worked for days, and sometimes for months, on his speeches.
- Madison thought through political problems early on.

2. Remove Distractions

Questions:
- Have I removed all distractions?
- Have I turned off everything (like email or a cell phone) that might distract me while I am writing?
- Have I designated a physical place for my writing where I will not be interrupted?
- Have I chosen the time of day to write when I will not likely be distracted?
- If I have not removed all distractions, am I confident that I am immune from the distractions?

Inspiration:
- Lincoln could be interrupted in the middle of a sentence and then turn back to the sentence to complete it.
- Grant calmly wrote while bullets zoomed over his head.
- Roosevelt placed his desk right up to a wall, so that he would not be distracted by the beautiful view out the window.

3. Visualize Audience

Questions:
- Am I visualizing the audience before I start writing?
- Have I thought about the reading preferences of my audience?
- Am I visualizing the audience while I am writing?
- Am I thinking about the limited amount of time that my audience is willing to spend on my written product?
- Am I writing to the primary audience without being distracted by others who might read my work?
- Am I writing to make everything as easy as possible for my reader?

Inspiration:
- Jefferson wondered how the New England clergy and other Northerners would react to his views about religious liberty.
- Madison pictured his audience, knew which audience members were the important decisionmakers, and raised counterarguments even before the audience members could think of any objections.
- Lincoln wrote with his diverse audience members in mind and spoke to reach all of them—Southerners, Unionists, dignitaries, soldiers, African Americans, his supporters, and those who despised him.
- Grant wrote directly to his audiences—the Union and Confederate military leaders when he was writing his war dispatches, and his beloved soldiers, sailors, and all Americans when writing his *Personal Memoirs*.
- Roosevelt, too, imagined his audience when preparing speeches or writing his books; he had a need to share his stories and philosophies with as many people as he could reach.
- As the presidents visualized their audience, they wrote to make the reading and listening experience as easy as possible for that audience.

4. Be Brief

Questions:

- Am I getting to the point as quickly as possible?
- Am I writing compact sentences?
- Am I making every word count, so that Lincoln wouldn't say I am "compressing the most words into the smallest ideas"?[60]
- Am I choosing short words over long words?
- Am I using single-syllable words?
- Am I choosing Anglo-Saxon words over Latin words?
- Am I using words that are part of my spoken vocabulary?[61]
- Have I eliminated all redundant words?
- Have I kept only the words that will help me convince my reader?

Inspiration: Abraham Lincoln (Chapter 4)

5. Be Clear

Questions:

- Do I know exactly what ideas I want to convey?
- Have I developed the arguments that will help persuade my reader about the correctness of those ideas?
- Have I organized my arguments, so that my logic is easy to follow?
- Have I written, like Grant wrote, "so that there can be no mistaking it"?
- Will my reader understand what I am saying after one reading?
- Am I writing with precision and accuracy?
- Have I eliminated all ambiguity?
- Have I used a simple and direct style?
- Have I used a conversational tone whenever possible?

Inspiration: Ulysses S. Grant (Chapter 5)

6. Be Rigorous

Questions:

- Do I thoroughly understand the facts?
- Do I thoroughly understand the law?

---

60. *Lincoln's Own Stories* 36 (Anthony Gross ed., 1912).

61. Part of the appeal of Lincoln's speeches were that they were like his conversations. Kaplan, *supra* note 34, at 104.

- Have I thoroughly researched the legal issues?
- Have I fully developed my arguments?
- Am I, like Madison, the most prepared person in the room?
- Am I thinking like a lawyer?
- Am I thinking practically about all the implications of the legal issues?
- Am I thinking about the institutional effects of my arguments?
- Is my argument well-organized?
- Would a reader unfamiliar with the nuances of the legal problem be able to follow my argument?
- Have I considered all the likely counterarguments?
- Have I followed all the court rules?

Inspiration: James Madison (Chapter 3)

7. Be Zealous

Questions:
- Am I using vivid words?
- Am I using the power of story?
- Have I made my writing interesting?
- Am I using forceful and confident language?
- Am I bold in making my case on behalf of my client?
- Do I have conviction when stating my arguments?
- Am I enthusiastic when presenting the strengths of the case?
- Am I, like Roosevelt, the "man in the arena" who is willing to strive for my client's cause?
- Am I honest about both the strengths and weaknesses of the case?

Inspiration: Teddy Roosevelt (Chapter 6)

8. Use Metaphor Effectively

Questions:
- Did I use a metaphor to clarify a difficult legal concept?
- Have I, like Jefferson, chosen an effective and vivid metaphor?
- If I am using a decorative metaphor, does it add to the reader's understanding of the legal concept?
- Did I use a concrete metaphor, so that the reader can visualize the metaphor?
- Is my metaphor creative or is it a repeated use of an overused metaphor?
- Is my metaphor as concise as I can make it without sacrificing clarity?

- If I am using a metaphor to make an analogic point, will the reader will be able to understand the analogy?
- Is my metaphor understandable to people from different cultures and backgrounds?
- Have I considered how my metaphor can be attacked?
- If the metaphor is subject to attack, have I considered how to modify the metaphor, so that it more accurately reflects the legal idea?

Inspiration: Thomas Jefferson (Chapter 2)

9. Ruthlessly Edit

Questions:
- Am I visualizing my audience as I edit?
- Am I visualizing a reader with a limited attention span?
- Have I captured the reader with my first sentence, paragraph, and page?
- Have I provided point headings to help the reader process individual arguments?
- Have I provided transitions to help guide the reader?
- Have I been ruthless in my edits?
- Have I made this document as short as possible?
- Have I attempted to eliminate at least 25 percent of the length of my first draft?
- Have I tried to eliminate everything that does not further my purpose, even though it may be an elegantly framed sentence?
- Have I edited this document to make sure that I am choosing the shortest paragraph, the shortest sentence, and the shortest word?
- Am I editing to make everything as easy as possible for my reader?
- Have I proofread to catch grammar, spelling, and punctuation errors?
- Have I proofread to catch legal citation errors?

Inspiration:
- Lincoln edited the Gettysburg Address even while seated on the platform waiting to deliver his remarks.

10. Reflect on Your Writing

Questions:
- Have I thought about what worked in my last writing project?
- Have I recorded, in detail, what worked?
- Have I thought about the mistakes I made during my last writing project?

- Have I recorded, in detail, what mistakes I made?
- Have I reviewed the opposition's writing to identify what worked?
- Have I reviewed the opposition's writing to identify mistakes?
- Have I developed a plan for how I can continue to improve my writing?

Index